MOUNTAINS AND MOLEHILLS

OR RECOLLECTIONS OF A BURNT JOURNAL

WITH ILLUSTRATIONS BY THE AUTHOR

BY FRA...

Skyhorse Publishing

Skyhorse Publishing books may be purchased in bulk at special
discounts for sales promotion, corporate gifts, fund-raising, or
educational purposes. Special editions can also be created to
specifications. For details, contact the Special Sales Department,
Skyhorse Publishing, 307 West 36th Street, 11th Floor, New York,
NY 10018 or info@skyhorsepublishing.com.

Skyhorse® and Skyhorse Publishing® are registered trademarks of
Skyhorse Publishing, Inc.®, a Delaware corporation.

Visit our website at www.skyhorsepublishing.com.

10 9 8 7 6 5 4 3 2 1

Library of Congress Cataloging-in-Publication Data is available on file.
ISBN: 978-1-62873-735-6

Printed in the United States of America

PREFACE.

NOTHING that I can say here will blind the reader to the deficiency of these pages; they are in truth, as their title expresses, the recollections of a " Journal burnt," and I present here but an outline of what I have seen or heard during three years of my life; and if I am wanting in figures and statistics and anything of weight as regards the country written of, it is certainly because I recalled this Journal unexpectedly, and far from the scenes it once depicted.

I may have remembered too little, but that is preferable to remembering too much.

I have tried to confine myself to what is most pleasant, and it may be that a rambling truthful story is the best, if to make the work elaborate one must have recourse to fiction.

It is right that a man should submit anything he

does modestly, yet for all that a preface need not be an apology; for I look on a tale written as a tale told, with this advantage to the reader, that if the tale written please him not, he can close the book and have done with it. I am no button-holder, and would rather, sir, that you would desert me at my second chapter, than that you should wade wearily through this volume, and then, because we do not suit each other, say that I have bored you.

In these days, when new discoveries of Nature's gifts, and increased facilities of communication with them invite man to roam, any record of travel should possess some interest for the adventurous.

I have proved to myself, what these pages may not show, that a man with health may plant himself in any country in the world, and by the exercise of those reasonable faculties that are denied to few, may there live well and happily.

It is nothing, perhaps, to state this for a fact, but I would have each emigrant hug it to his breast as a warm hope that will uphold him in the hours of adversity and trial that will meet him in the path he pioneers for himself in a new country.

Reader, these pages are so much black and white, and will pass as nearly all such matter does, rapidly to oblivion ; but if they bring no smile to you, nor help momentarily to efface a care, I would ask that they should bring no frown, for they are written earnestly, and with a good intention, even though from first to last they stand against me as printed errors, to cause regret in later years.

.   FRANK MARRYAT.

December 1st, 1854.

Note.—As my sketches were destroyed by fire, I have been unable to illustrate the scenery of California, but in the accompanying drawings I have endeavoured to be faithful to the characteristics of the people.

WHERE THE GOLD COMES FROM.

CONTENTS.

ERRATUM.

Page 204, fifteenth line, *for* " Athletes," *read* " Athletæ."

LIST OF WOODCUTS.

DRAWN ON WOOD BY MR. L. C. MARTIN, FROM DESIGNS BY
FRANK MARRYAT.

MOUNTAINS AND MOLEHILLS;

OR,

RECOLLECTIONS OF A BURNT JOURNAL.

CHAPTER I.

CHAGRES RIVER—CURIOSITY—ISTHMUS OF PANAMA—WASHINGTON HOTEL—
ANTS—A NATIVE OF VIRGINIA—GOLD TRAIN—ROBBERY—PANAMA BELLS
—AN EMIGRANT SHIP—AN AFFECTING PREACHER—SAN FRANCISCO.

April, 1850.

AT eight, A.M., Chagres was reported in sight, and as we neared the land, it presented an appearance far from inviting.

The American steamer, "Cherokee," ran into the anchorage with us, and immediately disgorged five hundred American citizens in red and blue shirts.

I landed with as much expedition as possible, and commenced at once to bargain for a canoe to take me up the river. This I at last effected at an exorbitant price, and on the express condition that we should not start until sunset. A few months back

1

the native Indians of this place considered themselves amply repaid with a few dollars for a week's work, but since the Californian emigration has lined their pockets with American eagles, they have assumed American independence : and now the civilised traveller, instead of kicking the naked aborigine into his canoe, or out of it as his humour prompts, has to bargain with a "padrone," as he calls himself, dressed in a coloured muslin shirt and a Panama hat, with a large cigar in his still larger mouth ; and has not only to pay him his price, but has to wait his leisure and convenience.

The town of Chagres deserves notice, inasmuch as it is the birthplace of a malignant fever, that became excessively popular among the Californian emigrants, many of whom have acknowledged the superiority of this malady by giving up the ghost, a very few hours after landing. Most towns are famous for some particular manufacture, and it is the fashion for visitors to carry away a specimen of the handicraft ; so it is with Chagres. It is composed of about fifty huts, each of which raises its head from the midst of its own private malaria, occasioned by the heaps of filth and offal, which putrefying under the rays of a vertical sun, choke up the very doorway.

On the thresholds of the doors, in the huts them-

selves,—fish, bullock's heads, hides, and carrion, are
strewed all in a state of decomposition ; whilst in the
rear is the jungle, and a lake of stagnant water, with a
delicate bordering of greasy blue mud. As I had with
me my man Barnes and three large blood-hounds, I
hired a boat of extra size capable of containing us
all, together with the baggage, this being preferable
to making a swifter passage with two smaller canoes
and running the risk of separation. At about three
we started, the " Cherokees" in boats containing
from ten to a dozen each. All was noise and excitement,—cries for lost baggage, adieus, cheers, a parting
strain on a cornet-à-piston, a round dozen at least
of different tongues, each in its owner's own peculiar
fashion murdering Spanish, a few discharges from
rifles and revolvers, rendered the scene ludicrous,
and had the good effect of sending us on the first
step of a toilsome journey in a good humour. So up
the river we went, and as Chagres disappeared behind
us, we rejoiced in a purer air. There is an absence
of variety in the scenery of the Chagres river,
as throughout its whole length the banks are lined to
the water's edge with vegetation. But the rich
bright green at all times charms the beholder, and the
eye does not become wearied with the thick masses
of luxuriant foliage, for they are ever blended in

grace and harmony, now towering in the air in bold relief against the sky, now drooping in graceful festoons from the bank, kissing their own reflections in the stream beneath.

Every growing thing clings to and embraces its neighbour most lovingly; here is a bunch of tangled parasites that bind a palm tree by a thousand bands to a majestic teak, and having shown their power, as it were, the parasites ascend the topmost branch of the teak, and devote the rest of their existence to embellishing with rich festoons of their bright red flowers, the pair they have thus united.

The teak, which is here a very bald tree, is much improved by the addition of these parasites, which give him quite a juvenile appearance, and form, in fact, a kind of wig, to hide the infirmities of age. Here is a dead and well bleached sycamore tree, half thrown across the river, but still holding to the bank by its sinewy roots; and at its extremity is an ants' nest, about the size of a beehive, and along the trunk and branches green leaves are seen to move about at a prodigious rate, under which ants are discovered on inspection.

Immediately under the ants' nest are some glorious water-lilies, and close to these, by way of contrast, floats an alligator who has been dead some time, and hasn't kept well, and on the top of him sit two black cormorants, which having, evidently, over-eaten themselves, are shot on the spot and die lazily. So we ascend the river; a-head, astern, on every side are canoes; here, surmounting a pyramid of luggage, is a party of western men in red shirts and jack boots, questioning everybody with the curiosity peculiar to their race. Presently it is my turn.—

" Whar bound to, stranger ? "

" California."

" Come along ! Whar d'ye head from ? "

" England."

" Come along ! Whar did yer get them dogs ? "

" No whar," I had a mind to reply, but at this stage I relapsed into dogged silence, well knowing that there are some lanes which have no turning, and among these is a western man's curiosity. The padrone of my canoe, who steered the boat, had brought his wife with him, and she sat with us in the stern sheets, laughing, chattering, and smoking a cigar.

I could find no heart to object to this increase of our live freight, and indeed so far benefitted by her presence as to be able to practise Spanish, and before we arrived at the anchorage I had relieved her of the false impressions she laboured under, that my dogs were "tigers," and that some cherry brandy I produced was poison. At night, having reached a small village on the river, out jumped the lady, who scrambled up the bank followed by the boatmen, and I scrambled after them as fast as I could, to ascertain the meaning of this sudden desertion; but quick as I was, by the time I reached the huts that constituted the "pueblo," I found my padrone already seated as banker at a well-lighted monte table, surrounded by an anxious crowd of boatmen, natives, and American passengers, his pretty wife looking over his shoulder watching the game.

The short time he took to change his profession was very characteristic of the gambling habits of these Central Americans.

I slept in the canoe, and at daylight the boatmen returned, having made a night of it. The monte banker had been lucky, he informed me, and had left his wife behind, to which I was ungallantly indifferent. Another day on the river, and another night spent at a hut, and on the third morning we arrived at Gorgona, from whence we had to take mules to Panama.

The bargaining for mules at Gorgona was in every respect similar to the canoe transaction at Chagres; and after passing a day in the sun, and accomplishing in the evening what might, but for the vacillation of the natives, have been done at once, we started for Panama in company with the baggage, Barnes walking from choice with the dogs. With our mules in a string we plunged at once into a narrow rocky path in the forest, where palm trees and creepers shut the light out overhead ;—splashing through gurgling muddy streams, that concealed loose and treacherous stones—stumbling over fallen trees that lay across our road—burying ourselves to the mules' girths in filthy swamps, where on either side dead and putrid mules were lying—amidst lightning, thunder, and incessant rain, we went at a foot pace on the road to Panama. The thunder-storm changed the twilight of our covered path to darkness, and one of my mules missing his footing on the red greasy clay, falls down under his heavy load. When he gets up he has to be unpacked amidst the curses of the muleteer, and packed again, and thus losing half an hour in the pelting storm, file after file passes us, until, ready once more to start, we find ourselves the last upon the road. At Gorgona a flaming advertisement had informed us that half way on the road to Panama the "Washington Hotel" would accommodate travellers with "forty beds." Anxious to secure a resting-place for my own party, I left the

luggage train under the charge of Barnes, and
pressed forward on the bridle road.

At nightfall I reached the " Washington Hotel," a
log hut perched on the top of a partially cleared hill;
an immense amount of fluttering calico proclaimed that
meals could be procured, but a glance at the interior
was sufficient to destroy all appetite. Round it, and
stretching for yards, there were mules, drivers, and
passengers, clustered and clamorous as bees without
a hive. To my surprise the crowd consisted for the
most part of homeward bound Californians—emigrants from the land of promise, who had two days
before arrived at Panama in a steamer. Some were
returning rich in gold dust and scales, but the
greater part were far poorer than when first they
started to realise their golden dreams.

And these latter were as drunken and as reckless
a set of villains as one could see anywhere. Stamped
with vice and intemperance, without baggage or
money, they were fit for robbery and murder to any
extent; many of them I doubt not were used to it,
and had found it convenient to leave a country where
Judge Lynch strings up such fellows rather quicker
than they like sometimes. They foretold with a
savage joy the miseries and disappointment that
awaited all who landed there, forgetting that there

travelled on the same road with them those who had in a very short space of time secured to themselves a competency by the exercise of industry, patience, and temperance. The Yankee owner of the Washington was "realising some," judging from the prices he charged, and that every eatable had been consumed long before my arrival. The "forty beds" respecting which we had met so many advertisements on the road, consisted of frames of wood five feet long, over which were simply stretched pieces of much soiled canvas—they were in three tiers, and altogether occupied about the same space as would two fourposters—they were all occupied.

Wet with the thunderstorm, I took up my station on a dead tree near the door, and as night closed in and the moon rose, awaited the arrival of my man and dogs with impatience. Hours passed, and I felt convinced at last that fatigue had compelled Barnes to pass the night at a rancheria I had seen a few miles back. Rising to stretch my limbs, I became instantly aware of a succession of sharp stings in every part of my body; these became aggravated as I stamped and shook myself. In sitting on the dead tree I had invaded the territory of a nest of ants of enormous size—larger than earwigs; they bit hard, and had sufficiently punished my intrusion before I managed

to get rid of them.   During the night file upon file of
mules arrived from Panama.   These were unloaded
and turned adrift to seek their supper where they
could ; and travellers, muleteers, and luggage were
spread in every direction round a large fire that had
been lit in the early part of the evening.   Deserting my inhospitable tree, I found myself comfortable
enough among a heap of pack saddles, buried in
which I slept till morning.   With the first streak of
day everything was moving, luggage was replaced on
kicking mules ; the sallow, wayworn, unwashed tenants
of the "Washington," with what baggage they had
on their backs, started for Gorgona on foot.   The
morning oath came out fresh and racy from the
lips of these disappointed gentlemen ; nor could the
bright and glorious sun reflect any beauty from their
sunken bloodshot eyes ; when they disappeared in
the winding road leading to Gorgona, it was quite a
comfort to me to reflect that we were not about to
honour the same country with our presence.   In less
than an hour I found myself alone at the half-way
house ; the crowd had dispersed on either road, but
as yet my baggage had not arrived.   When it did
come up at last we were all very hungry, but as there
was nothing left eatable at the "Washington," we
started for Panama without breaking our fast.

Through a tortuous path, which had been burrowed through the forest, we stumbled on at the rate of a mile and a half an hour; at times the space between the rocks on either side is too narrow to allow the mules to pass; in these instances all our efforts are directed to the mule that is *jammed*; heaven knows how we get her clear—several shouts, some kicking, a plunge or two, a crash, and, the mule being free, proceeds on her path, whilst you stop to pick up the lid of your trunk, which has been ground off against the rock, as also the few trifles that tumble out from time to time in consequence. And shortly afterwards we meet more travellers homeward bound, some on foot, with a stout buckthorn stick and bundle, and others on mules, with shouldered rifles. Each one, as I passed, asked me what state I was from, and if I came in the " Cherokee " steamer. I had been questioned so much after this manner at the " Washington " that I began to think that to belong to a state and to arrive in the " Cherokee " would save me much trouble in answering questions, for my reply in the negative invariably led to the direct query of Where did I come from? So along the road I surrendered myself invariably as a " Cherokee " passenger and a native of Virginia, and was allowed to pass on in peace. At last the country becomes more open, huts appear occasionally, and the worst part of the journey is well over. Still the human tide flows on to Gorgona, for another California steamer has arrived at Panama ; and now we meet some California patients carried in hammocks slung upon men's shoulders, travelling painfully towards a home that some of them will not live to see. Trains of unladen mules are going down to meet the emigration, some with cargoes of provisions for the Washington Hotel perhaps.

Pass on filth, squalor, and poverty, and make way as you should for wealth, for here, with tinkling bells and gay caparisons, comes a train of mules laden with gold—pure gold from Peru ; as each mule bears his massive bars uncovered, glittering beneath the cordage which secures them to the saddle, you can touch the metal as they pass. Twenty of these file by as we draw on one side, and after them, guarding so much wealth, are half a dozen armed natives with rusty muskets slung lazily on their backs ; but behind them, on an ambling jennet, is a well " got up " Don, with muslin shirt and polished jack-boots, richly-mounted pistols in his holsters, and massive silver spurs on his heels, smoking his cigarette with as much pomposity as if the gold belonged to him, and he had plenty more at home. This gentleman, however, is in reality a clerk in

an English house at Panama, and when he returns to
that city, after shipping the gold on board the English
steamer, and getting a receipt, he will change this
picturesque costume for a plaid shooting-coat and
continuations, and be a Don no longer. As the gold
train passed, I thought, in contrast to its insecurity,
of the villains I had parted from in the morning, all
of whom were armed. Then followed a train much
larger than the first, and just as little guarded,
carrying silver. For years these specie trains have
travelled in this unguarded state unmolested, *not*
from the *primitive honesty* of the natives, for a
greater set of villains never existed, but from the
simple difficulty of turning a BAR of gold to any
account when once it has been taken into the jungle.
Since the time of which I am writing many
attempts have been made to rob the gold trains,
but, when pursuit has been active, the bars have
invariably been discovered in the jungle a short
distance from the scene of the robbery.

The country became more open as we approached
Panama, and when the town appeared in the distance,
we had no shelter from the sun, and the dogs, panting
and footsore, dragged on very slowly. Here I found
a man by the roadside attacked with fever, shivering
with ague, and helpless. He was going to Gorgona,

but as he had no mule, he wished to return to Panama. I hoisted him on to mine, and we proceeded ; he was very ill, wandered in his speech, and shook like a leaf; and before we got into Panama, he died from exhaustion. As I did not know what to do with him, I planted him by the road-side, and on my arrival at the town, I informed the authorities, and I presume they buried him. Weary and sunburnt, we arrived at the gates of the town, outside of which we found a large American encampment, in the midst of which we pitched our tent. Every bed in the town had long before been pre-engaged, and these cribs, after the fashion of the " Washington," were packed from fifty to a hundred in a room. We slept comfortably that night under one of Edgington's tents, the baggage inside, and the dogs picquetted round us.

Since Panama has become the half-way resting-place of Californian emigration, the old ruin has assumed quite a lively aspect. Never were modern improvements so suddenly and so effectually applied to a dilapidated relic of former grandeur as here. The streets present a vista of enormous sign-boards, and American flags droop from every house.

The main street is composed almost entirely of hotels, eating-houses, and "hells." The old ruined houses have been patched up with whitewash and paint, and nothing remains unaltered but the cathedral. This building is in what I believe is called the "early Spanish style," which in the Colonies is more remarkable for the tenacity with which mud bricks hold together, than for any architectural advantages. The principal features in connection with these ancient churches are the brass bells they contain, many of which are of handsome design; and these bells are forced on the notice of the visitor to Panama, inasmuch as being now all cracked, they emit a sound like that of a concert of tin-pots and saucepans. At the corner of every street is a little turretted tower, from the top of which a small boy commences at sunrise to batter one of these discordant instruments, whilst from the belfries of the cathedral there issues a peal, to which, comparatively speaking, the din of a boiler manufactory is a treat. If those bells fail to bring the people to church, at all events they allow them no peace out of it. The streets are crowded day and night, for there are several thousand emigrants, waiting a passage to California. Most of these people are of the lower class, and are not prepossessing under their present aspect; and many of them, having exhausted their means in the expenses of their detention, are leading a precarious life, which neither improves their manners or their personal appearance. Long gaunt fellows, armed to the teeth, line the streets on either side, or lounge about the drinking bars and gambling saloons ; and among these there is quarrelling and stabbing, and probably murder, before the night is out. The more peaceably disposed are encamped outside the town, and avoid these ruffians as they would the plague ; but the end of this, to the evil-disposed, is *delirium tremens*, fever, and a dog's burial. With a good tent and canteen, an abundant market close at hand, and plenty of books, the time passed pleasantly enough, until I had arranged for my conveyance to California, which I shortly succeeded in doing, in a small English barque.

It is nothing new to say that the Central Americans are an inert race, and that the inhabitants of New Grenada, of Spanish blood, seem to assimilate in habits with the famous military garrison of Port Mahon, the members of which were too lazy to eat ; —for these people are too indolent to make money when it can be done with great rapidity and very little trouble, consequently, the advantages of the Californian emigration are entirely reaped by foreigners. Not a *permanent* improvement has been added to the town, and if this route was abandoned altogether, the *city* would be little the richer for the millions of dollars that have been left there during the last few years. The sole exception, almost, is that of a native firm, which has amassed much wealth by contracting for mules for transportation. The projected railroad will be undoubtedly carried out, and will give a vast importance to the isthmus : but it is built with American money and for American purposes. The new town of Aspinwall, in Navy Bay, is American ; it is in its infancy at present, and likely always to remain rather " thin," for the reason that the marshes that surround it render it unhealthy. I cannot see what the New Grenadians are to gain by all this exercise of energy and capital ; some day or other, perhaps, the brass guns on the ramparts of Panama may be remounted, and the breaches in the walls will be repaired, but by the time these events occur, I think the flag that will float from the citadel will not be that of New Grenada.

* * * *

I must confess I felt great delight when we made the mountains at the entrance of San Francisco Bay ; I had been cooped up for forty-five days on board a small barque, in company with one hundred and seventy-five passengers, of whom one hundred and sixty were noisy, quarrelsome, discontented, and dirty in the extreme. I had secured, in company with two or three gentlemen, the after-cabin, and so far I was fortunate. We had also bargained for the poop as a promenade, but those fellows would not go off it ; so there would some of them sit all day, spitting tobacco juice, and picking their teeth with their knives. Occasionally they became mutinous, and complained of the provisions, or insisted upon having more water to drink ; but the captain knew his men, and on these occasions would hoist out of the hold a small cask of sugar, and knocking off the head, place it in the middle of the deck, and immediately the mutinous symptoms would subside, and the jack-knives would cease to pick teeth, and diving into the sugar cask would convey the sweetness thereof to their owners' mouths !

Quarrels were of daily occurrence ; there was a great deal of knife-drawing and threatening, but no *bloodshed*, and this was probably attributable to the fact that there was no spirit on board.

It requires a dram or two even for these ferocious gentry to conquer their natural repugnance to a contest with cold steel ; and I may remark here that on first finding himself amongst a swaggering set of bullies armed to the teeth, the traveller is apt to imagine that he is surrounded by those who acknow-ledge no law, have no fear of personal danger, and who will resent all interference ; but a closer acquaintance dispels this illusion, and the observing voyager soon finds that he can resent a man's treading on his toes none the less that the aggressor carries a jack-knife and revolver. One Sunday during our voyage we were addressed spiritually by a minister who dissented from every known doctrine, and whose discourses were of that nature that rob sacred subjects of their gravity.

He shed tears on these occasions with remarkable facility; but under ordinary circumstances, I should imagine him not to have been sensitive in this respect, as I overheard him during the voyage threaten to "rip up the ship's cook's guts," and he carried a knife with him in every way adapted for the contemplated operation. Under all circumstances I was very glad when the land about San Francisco Bay appeared in sight. The morning was lovely; and it needs, by the way, a little sunshine to give a cheerful look to the rugged cliffs and round gravelly grass-less hills that extend on either side of the bay;—in foggy weather their appearance is quite disheartening to the stranger, and causes him to sail up to the anchorage with misgivings in general respecting the country. Quarrels were now forgotten, and each heart beat high with expectation, for now was in sight that for which many had left wives and children, farms and homesteads, in hopes of course of something better in a land so favoured as undoubtedly was this before us. But hope as we will our best, fear and doubt will creep in ; and who knows what blanches the cheek of yonder man! Is it the exhilaration consequent on reaching a goal where certain reward awaits him ? or is it a lurking fear that all may *prove illusion?*

It is a more intense feeling, perhaps, than that of the man who sees before him the card which carries on its downward side his ruin or his fortune ; for the gambler cannot if he would find any stake against which to risk the happiness of wife and children, the affections of a well-loved home, and the *chance* of misery and speedy death in an unknown land. Such the emigrant knows to have been the lot of thousands who have gone before him ; but he has also heard of rich "pockets" and "great strikes," of fortunes made in a month—a week—a day : who shall then say which of these emotions blanches his cheek, as we now fly rapidly past the "Golden Gate" rocks that guard the harbour's mouth?

As we open the bay, we observe dense masses of smoke rolling to leeward ; the town and shipping are almost undistinguishable, for we have arrived at the moment of the great June Fire of 1850, and San Francisco is again in ashes !

CHAPTER II.

———

June, 1850.

THE fire was fast subsiding; and as the embers died away, and the heavy smoke rolled off to leeward, the site of the conflagration was plainly marked out to the spectator like a great black chart. There is nothing particularly impressive in the scene, for although four hundred houses have been destroyed, they were but of wood, or thin sheet iron, and the " devouring element " has made a clean sweep of everything, except a few brick chimneys and iron pots. Everybody seems in good humour, and there is no reason why the stranger, who has lost nothing by the calamity, should allow himself to be plunged into melancholy reflections ! Planks and lumber are already being carted in all directions, and so soon as the embers cool, the work of rebuilding will commence.

21

I found it amusing next day to walk over the ground and observe the effects of the intense heat on the articles which were strewed around. Gun-barrels were twisted and knotted like snakes; there were tons of nails welded together by the heat, standing in the shape of the kegs which had contained them; small lakes of molten glass of all the colours of the rainbow; tools of all descriptions, from which the wood-work had disappeared, and pitch-pots filled with melted lead and glass. Here was an iron house that had collapsed with the heat, and an iron fire-proof safe that had burst under the same influence; spoons, knives, forks, and crockery were melted up together in heaps; crucibles even had cracked; preserved meats had been unable to stand this second cooking, and had exploded in every direction. The loss was very great by this fire, as the houses destroyed had been for the most part filled with merchandise; but there was little time wasted in lamentation, the energy of the people showed itself at once in action, and in forty-eight hours after the fire the whole district resounded to the din of busy workmen.

On the "lot" where I had observed the remains of gun-barrels and nails, stands its late proprietor, Mr. Jones, who is giving directions to a master carpenter, or "boss," for the rebuilding of a new store, the materials for which are already on the spot. The carpenter promises to get everything " fixed right off," and have the store ready in two days. At this juncture passes Mr. Smith, also in company with a cargo of building materials ; he was the owner of the iron house ; he says to Jones interrogatively,—

" *Burnt* out ? "

JONES.—" Yes, and *burst up.*"

SMITH.—" Flat ? "

JONES.—" Flat as a d—d pancake ! "

SMITH.—" It's a great country."

JONES.—" It's nothing shorter."

And in a couple of days both Smith and Jones are on their legs again, and with a little help from their friends live to grow rich perhaps, and build brick buildings that withstand the flames.

This fire was attributed to incendiarism, but when the general carelessness that existed is considered, it is quite as probable that it resulted from accident. It is much to be regretted that these fires did not sweep off the gambling houses ; but these buildings were now constructed of brick, and were tolerably well secured against all risk. When the burnt portion of the city was again covered with buildings, I had an opportunity of judging of the enormous strides the place had made since two years back, when it was,

by all accounts, a settlement of tents. Three fires
had checked its growth in this short space; but a
daring confidence had laughed as it were at these
obstacles, and any one who knew human nature might
see, that so long as that spirit of energy animated
every breast, the city would increase in size and
wealth, in spite even of conflagrations so calamitous.
For though many individually are ruined by the
flames, and are forced to retire from the field, yet in a
small community where all are armed with strong
determination, the vacant ranks are soon filled up
again, and shoulder to shoulder all march on in unity
of purpose, and gain the victory at last, though at
ever so great a sacrifice. Twelve months back there
was little else but canvass tents here, and a small,
shifting, restless, gambling, population: who was it
then, when all looked *uncertain in the future*, that sent
away so many thousand miles for steam excavators,
and tramways, and railway trucks? who were those,
again, who sent from this hamlet of shanties for all
the material for large foundries of iron and brass,
for blocks of granite, bricks and mortar, for pile-
drivers and steam-boats? I don't know,—but these
things all arrived; and now, in eighteen hundred and
fifty, the sand-hills tumble down as if by magic, and
are carried to the water's edge on a railroad where

the pile-drivers are at work, and confine them to the new position assigned them on a water lot. The clang of foundries is heard on all sides, as machinery is manufactured for the mines,—brick buildings are springing up in the principal thoroughfares, steamers crowd the rivers, and thousands of men are blasting out huge masses of rock to make space for the rapid strides of this ambitious young city. The better portion of the population of San Francisco in eighteen hundred and fifty, may be said to have consisted of adventurers; these were of all nations, the Americans being in the proportion of about one-third. Many people object to the term adventurer, as one that has been generally associated with a class who travel with scanty purses and easy consciences. But Johnson defines an adventurer as " one who hazards a chance;" and when we consider that the population here have to a man almost made sacrifices elsewhere, in hopes of the speedier reward held out by the vicinity of these vast gold-fields, the term is not misapplied. Neither is it one that should ever carry opprobrium; while fresh countries remain to be explored, and facilities of communication are daily increasing, I have no objection to call myself an adventurer, and wish that I had been one of those fortunate ones who conferred a vast benefit upon mankind (and secured *moderate advantages for them-selves*) by the discovery of the gold-fields of California and Australia. The most successful merchants of San Francisco were needy men, who by chance were on the spot when first the gold was discovered. The colossal fortunes that a few of these have reaped, sprung only from the chances that were open to all. Sam Brannan is probably the wealthiest of these speculators, and he commenced, they say, by levying a tax on the profits of a party of Mormons whom he piloted to the diggings. When the Mormons declined to pay the tax any longer, he called them a parcel of fools for having paid it so long, and then speculated in building-lots and real estate in San Francisco and other cities. The rapid rise in the value of this property elevated Sam to the top round of the ladder of fortune, where he will probably hold on as long as he can.

The stranger in San Francisco at this time is at once impressed with the feverish state of excitement that pervades the whole population ; there is no attention paid to dress, and everyone is hurried and incoherent in manner. Clubs, reading-rooms, and the society of women are unknown ; and from the harassing duties of the day's business, there is nothing to turn to for recreation but the drinking-saloons and gambling-houses, and here nightly all the population meet. Where the commerce engaged in fluctuates with every hour, and profit and loss are not matters of calculation, but chance—where all have hung their fortunes on a die, and few are of that class who bring strong principles to bear upon conduct that society does not condemn—the gambling-tables are well supported, and the merchant and his clerk, and perhaps his cook, jostle in the crowd together, and stake their ounces at the same table.

Drinking is carried on to an incredible extent here; not that there is much drunkenness, but a vast quantity of liquor is daily consumed.

From the time the habitual drinker in San Francisco takes his morning gin-cocktail to stimulate an appetite for breakfast, he supplies himself at intervals throughout the day with an indefinite number of racy little spirituous compounds that have the effect of keeping him always more or less primed. And where saloons line the streets, and you cannot meet a friend, or make a new acquaintance, or strike a bargain, without an invitation to drink, which amounts to a command; and when the days are hot, and you see men issuing from the saloons licking their lips after their iced mint juleps ; and where Brown, who has a party with him, meets you as he enters the saloon, and says,

" Join us ! " and where it is the fashion to accept such
invitations, and rude to refuse them ;—what can a
thirsty man do ?   The better description of drinking-
bars are fitted up with great taste, and at enormous
expense.   Order and quiet are preserved within them
during the day; they are generally supplied with
periodicals and newspapers, and business assignations
are made and held in them at all hours.   Everybody
in the place is generous and lavish of money; and
perhaps one reason for so many drinks being consumed
is in the fact that there is ever some liberal soul who
is not content until he has ranged some twenty of his
acquaintances at the bar, and when each one is
supplied with a " drink," he says, " My respects
gentlemen ! " and the twenty heads being simulta-
neously thrown back, down go " straight brandies,"
" Queen-Charlottes," " stone-fences," " Champagne-
cocktails," and " sulky sangarees," whilst the liberal
entertainer discharges the score, and each one hurries
off to his business.   There is no one in such a hurry
as a Californian, but he has always time to take a
drink.   There is generally a sprinkling of idlers
hanging about these saloons, waiting for any chance
that may turn up to their benefit, and particularly
that of being included in the general invitation of
" drinks for the crowd," which is from time to time

extended by some elated gentleman during the day. These hangers-on are called " loafers." There is a story told of an old judge in the southern part of the country, who was an habitual frequenter of the bar-room, and who with his rich mellow voice would exclaim, " Come, let's all take a drink ! " Gladly the loafers would surround the bar, and each would call for his favourite beverage ; but when all was finished, the judge would observe, " *And now let's all pay for it !* " which the loafers would sorrowfully do, and then retire wiser men.

* * * *

Perhaps in no other community so limited could one find so many well-informed and clever men—men of all nations, who have added the advantages of travelling to natural abilities and a liberal education. Most of these are young, and are among the most reckless, perhaps, just now ; but by-and-by, when this fever of dissipation has given way to better impulses, these men will gladly abjure a life which has been entailed more upon them by circumstance than choice, and will be the first to help to elevate society to a standard adapted to their real qualities—and tastes.

The banks of San Francisco are naturally important, as being the depositories of the wealth that thousands are hourly accumulating on the rich " placer " fields.

These buildings are of brick, and have fire-proof
cellars ; and although at the time they were erected
the outlay was enormous, both for material and
labour, it was a mere trifle in comparison with the
profits of their owners. The banks line one side of
Montgomery Street, the principal thoroughfare of
the city ; and as the space on all sides has been
entirely cleared for some distance by the fire, this
row of buildings stands alone just now and solitary,
like the speculative " Terrace " with " extensive marine
view " that fronts an unpopular watering-place in
England. At the corner of a street is Burgoyne's
Bank ; you enter and find it very crowded and full of
tobacco-smoke ; instead of the chinking of money,
you hear a succession of thumps on the counter, as
the large leathern bags of gold-dust come down on
it. Some of the clerks are weighing dust, some are
extracting the black sand with a magnet, and others
are packing it in bags and boxes. The depositors are,
generally speaking, miners who have come down from
the diggings, fellows with long beards and jack-boots,
and of an unwashed appearance for the most part.
However, many of these are not by any means what
they seem ; they have just arrived, perhaps, from a
toilsome dusty journey, and deposit their gold as a
first precaution ; and before the evening they will

have been metamorphosed into very respectable-looking members of society, and will remain so until they return again to the diggings. Large blocks of quartz lie about the room, in all of which are rich veins of gold. These have been sent down from the mountains to be assayed; and the rich yield that these solitary specimens afforded led some time afterwards to a great deal of very ruinous speculation, for it had been represented that these specimens were average samples of great veins, and it was only when money had been expended in large sums that it was discovered that these rich morsels were merely accidental deposits of gold, and by no means indicated the value of the veins. A few rich lumps were brought to England, and, by a little judicious handling and a few public dinners, were turned to good account; and nothing but the bungling stupidity of some of those who were sent here to *pull the wires* prevented the consummation of some of the greatest swindles that ever were imposed upon the English public. I feel sore upon this point, for the dishonesty thus practised produced an ill feeling against the country which was undeserved, and the stigma of fraud and dishonesty was unjustly cast upon the whole population.

There are no public lamps in the town at this time,

so that the greater part of it is admirably adapted for that portion of the population who gain their livelihood by robbery, and *murder* in those cases where people object to being robbed. But Commercial Street, which is composed entirely of saloons, is a blaze of light, and resounds with music from one end to the other. No expense is spared to attract custom, the bar-keepers are " artists " in their profession ; rich soft velvet sofas and rocking-chairs invite the lounger ; but popular feeling runs strongest in favour of the saloon that contains a pretty woman to attend the bar. Women are rarities here ; and the population flock in crowds and receive drinks from the fair hands of the female dispenser, whilst the fortunate proprietor of the saloon realises a fortune in a week—and only has that time to do it in, for at the end of that period the charmer is married ! A French ship arrived during my stay, and brought as passengers a large number of very respectable girls, most of whom were tolerably well looking ; they were soon caught up by the saloon proprietors as waiting-women at salaries of about 50*l.* each per month, and after this influx the public became gradually inured to female attendance, and looked upon it as a matter of no moment.

Near the centre of the town is a square, which, in

common with many other things in the country, retains its Spanish appellation, and is called the " Plaza ; " two sides of this are occupied by brick buildings, devoted solely to gambling. We have the " Verandah," " Eldorado," " Parker House," " Empire," " Rendez-vous," and "Bella Union," in one row. Most of these establishments belong to companies, for the amount of capital required is very large. One or two of the houses are under French superintendence ; companies having been formed in Paris, who openly avowed their object in the prospectus they issued. On entering one of these saloons the eye is dazzled almost by the brilliancy of chandeliers and mirrors. The roof, rich with gilt-work, is supported by pillars of glass ; and the walls are hung with French paintings of great merit, but of which female nudity forms alone the subject. The crowd of Mexicans, Miners, Niggers, and Irish bricklayers, through which with difficulty you force a way, look dirtier (although there is no need of this) from contrast with the brilliant decorations. Green tables are scattered over the room, at each of which sit two " monte " dealers surrounded by a betting crowd. The centres of the tables are covered with gold ounces and rich specimens from the diggings, and these heaps accumulate very rapidly in the course of the evening, for "monte," as played by these dexterous dealers, leaves little chance for the staker to win. The thin Spanish cards alone are used, and although the dealer is intently watched by a hundred eyes, whose owners, in revenge for having lost, would gladly detect a cheat, and fall upon him and tear him to pieces, yet are these eyes no match for his dexterous fingers, and the savage scrutiny with which he is assailed as his partner rakes in the stakes produces no emotion on his pale unimpassioned face. The duty of a "monte" dealer is one of great difficulty; although surrounded by a clamorous crowd, and the clang of music, his head is occupied by intricate calculations, his eyes are watchfully (though apparently carelessly) scanning the faces that surround his table, yet they appear to be rivetted to his cards; he has, in the presence of vigilant observers, to execute feats, the detection of which would cost him his life;—nightly almost he draws his revolver in self-defence;—and through all this he must never change a muscle of his face, and must be ready at all times to exercise a determined courage in resenting the mere suspicion of dishonesty on his part, if such is expressed incautiously by those about him.

There is no limit to the introductions one is subjected to in a Californian crowd;—if the "monte"

dealer rises from his chair, you will probably be introduced to him, and I had the honour of shaking hands
with a murderer quite fresh from his work, who had
been acquitted a day or two previously by bribing the
judge, jury, and the witnesses against him. I should
have declined the honour had I learnt his profession
with his name, but custom insists on your shaking
hands on being introduced to a fellow-mortal; and to
refuse to do so is tacitly to deny one of the great
principles of the model republic, which holds that
" one man is as good as another ; " and, as I heard a
democratic Irishman observe, " *a d—d sight better !* "

Amidst all the din and turmoil of the crowd, and
the noisy music that issues from every corner, two or
three reports of a pistol will occasionally startle the
stranger, particularly if they should happen to be in
his immediate vicinity, and a bullet should (as
is not uncommon) whistle past his head and crack
the mirror on the other side of him. There is a
general row for a few moments, spectators secure
themselves behind pillars and under the bar ; there is
a general exclamation of " don't shoot, " which means
of course " don't shoot till we get out of the way ; "
but after the first discharges the excitement settles
down, and the suspended games are resumed. A
wounded man is carried out, but whether it is a

"monte" dealer who has shot a player, or one gentleman who has drawn on another gentleman, in the heat of altercation, one does not learn that night, but it will appear in the morning paper; if the former it will be headed "*Murderous affray*," if the latter, "Unfortunate *difficulty*." There are different names for the same thing, even in a democratic colony! The climate of California is very healthy;—there is a tendency in it to intermittent fever and ague in some parts of the mountains; but in the mines, sickness has generally resulted from imprudent exposure, and the drinking of the worst possible description of ardent spirits. On the sea coast and at San Francisco, the weather is very changeable during the summer months. When the sun rises and clears away the fog that hangs over the Bay, the air is as pure and transparent as that of Naples; by noon the glass is at 90°, and then the sea breeze sets in, and would be welcome, but that it does not fan one gently like other sea breezes, but bursts on you with the force of a hurricane, blows off a bit of the roof of your house, and sends the fine dust in whirling clouds along the street, in such a way that the people would profit by lying down flat on their stomachs, as they do in a regular Simoom! As the sun goes down the "doctor" subsides, after having done a great deal of good in airing the town, which as yet is unprovided with sewers. Then there creeps in steadily a heavy, fat fog, which takes up its quarters in the Bay every night, and disappears as before mentioned when the sun rises—under whose influence it does'nt melt like other fogs, but goes out to sea, and watches the town gloomily, until it is time to come in again.

These varieties of temperature during some months are methodically regular, but are not productive of sickness of any kind. The front of the city is extending rapidly into the sea, as water-lots are filled up with the sand-hills which the steam excavators remove. This has left many of the old ships, that a year ago were beached as storehouses, in a curious position; for the filled-up space that surrounds them has been built on for some distance, and new streets run between them and the sea, so that a stranger puzzles himself for some time to ascertain how the "Apollo" and "Niantic" became perched in the middle of a street, for although he has heard of ships being thrown up "high and dry," he has probably sufficient nautical experience to observe that the degree of "height" and "dryness" enjoyed by the "Apollo" and "Niantic" resulted from some other cause than the "fury of the gale." Leaving San Francisco for the present to return to it again by-and-

by and watch its growth and improvement, I got all
ready for a start for Benicia, a little town on the
Bay, from whence I intended to travel leisurely to
Russian River.   I had chosen this district as it
abounded in game; and was in quite an opposite
direction to the diggings—a visit to which I post-
poned until the ensuing summer, my object for the
present being to encamp myself in some snug place
in the mountains, and there live upon my gun, in
all the enjoyment of a free life and the pleasures of
the chase.

CHAPTER III.

July, 1850.

GREAT labour and capital have been expended on
the wharves of San Francisco; there is little space
left between these, and ships ride at their sides, and
discharge their cargoes with as much rapidity and
comfort as if they were in dock. The central wharf
is nearly a mile in length, and from the end of this
the river steamboats take their departure every day
at four o'clock. At these times the wharf is always
densely crowded, and it has always seemed strange
to me that this every-day occurrence attracts a
crowd without fail, although directly the boats are
off, every man runs back to the city as if he had
forgotten something. Perhaps they come down on
the chance of an explosion, in which they are occasionally gratified; whether or no, there must be some

39

great attraction, for these curious people have to walk a mile to get there, and run a mile to get back! The "Senator" was our boat, and with one leg on board of her and the other buried in this observing crowd, I had to work briskly to get my provender on board—sacks of potatoes and flour, dogs, rifles, shovels, and pickaxes, were handed in with astonishing celerity, considering that I was not born a porter, and as the ship's bell ceased tolling we cast off from the wharf and threading the shipping at full speed, were soon steaming up the Bay. The "Senator" is a fine boat, but no description of her is requisite, as much finer have been described by travellers who have sailed up the Mississippi River. She came round the Horn, and being the first boat to arrive in the Bay, she realised most incredible sums of money for her owners.

In two hours we arrived at Benicia, and the steamer ran alongside of an old hulk connected by a gang-way with the shore. Through the unusual degree of Yankee nautical smartness shown on this occasion, I lost some bags of potatoes, for the boat had scarcely touched the hulk, than we were driven out of it carrying all we could, and the word was given to "go a-head" again, the gang-board was hauled in, our potatoes were still on board, there was no time for expostulation, and away steamed the

" Senator," whilst we gazed dreamily at her receding hull, wrapt in admiration at the general smartness that evidently surrounded us. Benicia is a city in embryo, there is ample room for building, for in every direction extend undulating hills, covered with wild oats, but unobstructed by timber, of which none can be found within many miles. But the natural advantages of this spot have not been embraced by the public, for one reason, that the opposite town of Martinez is more fortunately planted among groves of trees, and for another, that no one requires a town in this particular part of the world. So Benicia is a failure just now ; and instead of raising an imposing front, in evidence of man's progress, it hides its diminished little head, among the few huts that stand in commemoration of its failure. I pitched my tent at a short distance from the beach, and as I afterwards discovered on reference to the "plan of Benicia," on the exact spot that had been selected as the site of the "Public Botanical Gardens"of that flourishing city. Our party consisted of three men and three dogs. Besides Barnes, I had with me Mr. Alexander Thomas, the son of an old friend of my father, who had come out to join the staff of a colossal mercantile house, but the house had unfortunately exploded, staff and all, before his arrival in the country.

Barnes had been a desperate poacher, but for years past had distinguished himself equally as a keeper on my father's estate. He was a good-natured, willing fellow, possessed of enormous physical strength, and could throw a stone with such force and precision, that he had been equally avoided by the keepers when he was a poacher, and by the poachers when he deserted their ranks, which he did as many others would, the moment the chance was offered him of making his bread honestly. My dogs consisted of two blood-hounds of the breed of Mr. Hammond of Norfolk— Prince and Birkham—the latter was of great beauty, but of very uncertain temper. A large half-bred Scotch slot-hound, called Cromer, completed the list—this latter had an unfailing nose and great intelligence, and was a perfect retriever in or out of water. An introductory note to an American gentleman who resided in one of the wooden houses that straggled over the hills, ensured me much civility, and enabled me to procure the mules I required for carrying the tent and baggage. During the interval that elapsed we had time to try the range of the rifles at a target, and get our " hands in " ready for the mountains. A distressing incident occurred very shortly after arriving at Benicia. We had been practising at a target, and were returning to our camp with our rifles unloaded—the heat was intense—the dogs were with us, and I was suddenly struck by the conduct of Birkham the bloodhound. For some time he hung back in the rear as if afraid of us, and as I advanced to caress him he retreated. There being evidently something wrong, I conjectured that he was about to have an epileptic fit, with one of which he had been attacked at San Francisco, but suddenly he lifted up his massive head in the air, and delivered that deep prolonged howl that only a blood- hound has at command, and which is so distressing to hear ; he then started at full speed away from us towards the hills, howling and leaping in the air as if in pursuit of something, and I had no doubt then that he was mad. Barnes and Thomas now loaded their rifles to be prepared for his return, I had expended my bullets in target firing. We had lost sight of him in the long wild oats which here grow to a great height, and scarcely expected him back, at least for some time; I was coupling Prince and Cromer together as a precaution, when suddenly Barnes ex- claimed " Here he is, sir," and I had just time to seize my rifle and swing it round, bringing the butt down on his head, as he passed within a foot of me.

I never witnessed any sight so dreadful as this dog when he turned now and deliberately attacked us,

his whole appearance was changed, and the saliva
frothed in his mouth.   He might have done much
mischief, now that he was in the humour for it, had
he made a rapid dash at us ; but as he stopped short
to give a howl, Barnes shot him in the shoulder, and
Thomas's ball entered his head.   It required two more
shots to finish him, and painful as it was to have to
kill the poor beast, even in self-defence, we could not
but congratulate ourselves on having experienced a
fortunate escape.   Birkham was a dog of enormous
power, and one grip of his jaw on a man's throat
would probably be quite sufficient to cause death ; he
had shown symptoms of uncertain temper immediately upon arriving in a warm latitude, and had twice
bitten me in the arm during the passage out.   Barnes
was a famous man for savage dogs, being both severe
yet temperate, but he always had his " doubts," as he
said, respecting Birkham, whose great crime consisted
in showing his teeth to his master, a misdemeanour
that required, and always received punishment.   This
consisted of one blow with a short dog-whip, and
only one, but that was remembered, particularly by
Birkham, who would lie down and place his great
head on the ground, wrinkle his forehead, and sulk
all day, refusing his dinner and taking no notice of
anything that passed around him.   Such a dog is

never safe, and had these qualities been developed
during the time he was in my possession in England,
I never should have brought him away from that
country.

Immense quantities of grasshoppers are to be found
in the vicinity of Benicia at this season; as you walk
through the wild oats and disturb them, they hop up
to an immense height, in every direction, and like
other insects they aim at your eyes, which they hit
with unerring certainty and great force, and as they
are as hard as little pebbles, they get the best of it
altogether.   The dogs are much puzzled with them,
and as they get knocked about the head, they give
short snaps in the air with their eyes shut.

I had great difficulty in procuring the mules I
required for my journey, and these I could only hire,
as a report of the discovery of a " Gold Lake " somewhere in the mining districts had taken deep root,
and all the Benicia mules had been called into requi-
sition.   A fine dashing-looking Spaniard rode up to
my tent one day in company with the gentleman who
had interested himself to get me mules; * he was
introduced as Don Raymond Carrillo, a native of
California, and owner of a ranche, or farm, at Santa
Rosa Valley, about forty miles in the interior.

* Captain J. B. Frisbie.

Many of the native Californians whose ancestors emigrated from Mexico, have good Spanish blood in their veins, they are a robust and well-favoured race, and probably in this respect have much improved the original breed, which is all blood and bone. Don Raymond was a striking-looking fellow, well built and muscular, with regular features, half concealed by his long black hair and beard. The loose Spanish dress, the heavy iron spurs, the lasso hanging from the saddle, and the gaunt but fiery colt on which he was mounted, were all for work and little for show; probably the whole turn-out, including the horse, was not worth twenty dollars; but he was more picturesque in his mountain costume, than the best Andalusian that ever got himself up in gold lace and silver buttons for " bolero " or " bull-fight." Don Raymond not only offered to send mules to convey ourselves and baggage to Santa Rosa, but most hospitably invited us to remain at his " ranche " until we could with his assistance purchase the animals we required. Whilst we were at Benicia the fourth of July, the anniversary of American Independence, came round; had Benicia been the city it was intended to be, what an opportunity would there not have been for the celebration of this day. Looking at the plan now before me, I can imagine the

Botanical Gardens thronged with holiday people, whilst the mayor and corporation having reviewed the troops in front of the *City Hall*, are now inspecting the *Infirmary for the Blind*, which (in the plan) occupies a position to the extreme right; fireworks echo in the " plaza," whilst the theatre opens its doors to an eager crowd, and the town pump is surrounded by little boys: but unfortunately Benicia is not far enough advanced to enable us to realise this scene. " The gardens " produce as yet but wild oats; the theatre is one unchanging scene of parched-up desolation; the town pump *is* not, and of the " plaza " no one knows the limits, for some of the oldest inhabitants, in happy ignorance of the fate of those who "remove their neighbour's landmarks," have pulled up the surveyor's pegs, and basely used them for firewood; but they say that Benicia will do better by-and-by. The *plan* is named after the wife of General Vallejo, and signifies " Blessed," and rather appropriately, as under present circumstances the proprietors are incorporated among those who are spoken of as being blessed if they expect nothing. Shortly afterwards, there arrived from Don Raymond eight mules, in charge of a young Californian " Vaccaro " * or cattle-driver; the mules were

* From Vacca or Vaca—cow.

accompanied by an old white mare with a bell hung on to her neck. It is usual to accustom the mules to follow a leader of this kind, and without the old lady leads the way they become very intractable.

Don Raymond had stated frankly that he had no pack mules that had not been turned out for a time with the wild horses, and those he had sent us, though fine strong beasts, were undoubtedly very little tamer than fresh-caught zebras. The first mule having been brought forward with some difficulty, a cloth was tied round his eyes, and he remained perfectly still whilst the loading was performed with great dexterity and expedition by the " vaccaro " and one or two assistants. When all were packed, the blinds were taken from the mules' eyes, and without any hesitation, and perfectly regardless of the white mare, who walked quietly towards home, away they scampered through the long grass, kicking and screaming ; here goes a tin kettle, there a ham, now a bag of flour falls out and bursts, and the place is strewed with the relics of our commissariat stores. Two mules, followed by the " vaccaro," have disappeared behind the hills, where the sun is dis-appearing also. Number three is motionless, for, not having succeeded in kicking the tent off his back, he has lain down with it in a small pond ;

whilst number four, having divested himself of every thing with which he was entrusted, including the pack-saddle, is making his supper off wild oats, under the full impression that he has performed his day's work meritoriously and deserves repose. We employed the daylight that remained in collecting our traps; and as our " vaccaro " soon returned with the missing mules and assistance, after a few more refractory attempts we got off shortly after dark, and took the trail that led towards a village called Napa.

When about twelve miles from Benicia we halted to encamp for the night at a clump of trees, the first we had seen since landing. We had " carte blanche " to shoot a calf whenever our necessities required, from among the droves of tame cattle with which the plains on our route were well stocked. Our first object on halting was to avail ourselves of this permission, and it being too dark to kill with the rifle, our " vaccaro " brought in a calf with his lasso, as soon as the mules had been unpacked and turned off to feed. We had no occasion for the tent, the night air was so pure and mild, so we sat half buried in the tall soft grass, a bed of down from which nothing could have roused us but the grateful smell of the calf's ribs as they roasted by our bright camp fire. As long as it lasted, our sleep was delicious, but it was interrupted most unseasonably, about the middle of the night, by the yells of a pack of "coyotes," (a kind of jackal,) that had collected round the remains of the calf.

These beasts had the audacity to approach us within a few yards. We killed some, wounded many, and the dogs drove them away in every direction, still they always congregated somewhere and sent forth their hideous yell in chorus, first from one side of us, then from another, and not until dawn appeared would these brutes allow us to rest; then they disappeared, and I congratulated myself on being able to resume my slumbers; but almost immediately after the "coyotes" had gone, the sun appeared, and there was an end of the luxuries of an oat-straw bed al-fresco, for that night at least. The mules submitted more readily to be loaded this morning, and followed quietly in the steps of the white mare.

On approaching Napa, which is distant from Benicia about twenty miles, we entered a very beautiful valley about three miles in breadth, studded with oak trees, and bounded on either side by mountains that rose abruptly from the plain, and whose summits were crested with heavy masses of the red-wood tree and white pine. As yet there was no sign of cultivation or enclosure, nor did we see a dwelling-house until the village of Napa appeared in sight; but the whole of this rich and fertile valley was shortly to be made productive, and it was to supply the wants of the many settlers, who were now on the eve of improving this wild tract, that the little bunch of houses called " Napa City " had sprung into existence.

We had to cross a small stream in a ferry-boat to enter Napa, and we found the little place in a very lively state. Music was playing, the stars and stripes were waving from each house, whilst the street was thronged with people. The outside settlers had come in to celebrate their fourth of July, it was now the fifth, and they were in the thick of it, and there was to be a " ball " in the evening. At twelve o'clock they prepared to fire a salute from three old honey-combed cannons that had probably been fished up out of the river; whether or no, a serious accident imme-diately occurred—the first gun fired exploded like a shell, blowing off the arm of one man and destroying the sight of another, besides peppering the spectators more or less seriously. This damped temporarily the pleasure of the afternoon, but the public dinner, which took place under an enormous booth, seemed to restore cheerfulness. The settlers were nearly all " Western people," small farmers from Missouri, and other Western states, who emigrated with a wife and half-a-dozen children to California in search of good land ; on this they *squat* until the land-claims are decided, and with their thrifty habits make money, not only more surely and comfortably, but faster than the miners, whose wants they supply.

The soil here is admirably adapted for the growth of wheat, barley, and potatoes ; and although the price of labour is so great that these immigratory agriculturists, having little or no capital, can only till a patch of land at first, yet so rare a luxury as yet is a vegetable, that large profits attend their earliest efforts, and the settler of these valleys, if prudent, is a rising man from the moment his spade first raises the virgin sod.

During the day a Mexican tight-rope dancer performed to the crowd : I considered him rather a bungler at his work, but my opinion was not shared by the spectators, one of whom, an old farmer, " kinder, reckoned it was *supernatural*," in which he was supported by an old back-woodsman, who said " It warn't nothing else."   I left these good folks in the height of enjoyment, and should not perhaps have said so much about them, but that having all very lately come from the United States across the plains, they had brought with them, and as yet retained, the simple manners and wants of a rural population. These people form the most valuable portion of the emigration, for they come as permanent settlers, and they continue permanent improvers. Under their hands forests are cleared, and valleys enclosed, grain is raised and mills are erected, the country no longer relies on foreign ventures for its chief wants, and monopolising flour companies cease to fatten at the expense of a hard-working population.

I did not wait for the " ball," as I wished to reach Sonoma that night, the luggage having gone on. On our first arrival at the Creek, the ferryman, who was an American, had refused all toll on the strength of the " Anniversary." We could not but admire such a striking instance of real charity, as it enabled many of the surrounding farmers to cross over with their numerous families, which at the rate of one dollar for each person they could not have afforded to do. But there was nothing said about going back for nothing, and our Yankee friend having succeeded in filling the village gratis, had now the satisfaction of emptying it at a dollar a-head. So there they were like the nephew of " Gil Perez," caught like a rat in a trap. The scenery still improves in beauty as we approach Sonoma, the valleys are here sprinkled with oak trees, and it seems ever as if we were about to enter a forest which we never reach, for in the distance the oaks, though really far apart, appear to grow in dark and heavy masses. Sonoma was one of the points selected by the early Spanish priests for a mission; the remains of the mud church and other buildings used by the priests still exist. It has been chosen as a military station, and about a couple of dozen United States dragoons are quartered here.

General Vallejo, a native Californian, who is owner of a large portion of the surrounding valley, resides at Sonoma; he took part in some skirmishing which occurred, previous to the cession of California to the United States, between the natives and a handful of adventurers, who hoisted a flag with a Grizzly Bear on it, and took the field under that standard. The General was also on one occasion taken prisoner, and perhaps it was during his term of incarceration that he designed a tall square building, which he afterwards erected here, of mud bricks, and which is now the principal feature of the place; as the General informs his friends that this was intended for a fortress, they take his word for it, though it has neither guns or embrasures. Overlooked by the fortress is a quadrangle of mud huts, these are now converted into stores intended to supply the farmers who are fast settling on the surrounding plains.

But there are too many stores in Sonoma; there are so many people in California who can only live by keeping small retail shops, that directly a good opening for making money in this way appears, there is a regular rush of small speculators in soap and candles, who all arrive at the desired spot about the same time, each one undoubtedly congratulating himself that *he alone* has been struck with the bright idea. A man who came to the country in 1848, told me that he managed with great toil and at great expense to get a large cask of whiskey to some rich diggings on the banks of the Yuba, where he commenced retailing it at immense profits; but on the second day his customers fell off, and he found that another Yankee had also rolled up a cask and was underselling him higher up the river. So he moved higher up again by a circuitous route, until again supplanted; and these two continued " cutting each other out," and living a life of uncertainty until they formed a junction, with the intention of jointly reaping the profits that attend a monopoly of the article in demand. But almost as soon as the new concern was started, up went a canvass house by the side of them, and out went a board on which was written, " Liquor Store." So with every opening where the chances of large profits are held out, where there are so many calculating speculative people, competition steps in and monopoly is destroyed. This is partly the reason why the San Francisco markets are so uneven and fluctuating.

Brown is a clever fellow, and says to himself, Coals will be very scarce next fall, I'll write for coals; every one else, being as clever as Brown, writes for coals from the same motives, and the spring sees coals tumbling in on all sides : or Brown says, everybody will be writing for coals for the spring, I shall advise my correspondents not to ship ; every one else thinks as Brown thinks, no one writes for coals, and next spring coals can't be had at any price.

We pitched our tents outside the fortress, and the only event that occurred worthy of notice was in the fact of an enormous bull making a clean bolt at it, about the middle of the night. The moon was up, and I presume its reflection on the white canvass annoyed him ; he annoyed us excessively, for he not only tore down the tent, but we narrowly escaped being trodden upon. As he stood in the bright moonlight pawing the ground at a short distance, meditating another charge at us, I shot him in the head, and he fell, never again to rouse honest gentlemen from their sleep in the dead of night, or wantonly to destroy private property for the gratification of a senseless animosity.

CHAPTER IV.

——◆——

August, 1850.

LEAVING Sonoma at daylight, we passed through
the Sonoma Valley, which in many places, but a few
hundred yards in width and studded with groups of
oaks and flowering evergreens, has all the appearance of a private park bounded by mountains—the
herds of deer, of which now and then we catch a
glimpse, strengthening this resemblance. After following the trail for fifteen miles, we ascended a rise
from which we had a view of Santa Rosa Valley. It
was a continuation of that we had traversed, and was
divided from it only by a small stream, which marked
the boundary of either. From our elevation, the twenty
miles of well timbered land, of which Don Raymond
was owner, lay stretched before us : large herds of
cattle were grazing on the plain, and near the moun-

57

tains which bounded the ranche, "mañadas" of wild horses could be perceived, with here and there a drove of elk or antelopes.

Previous to the occupation of this country by the Americans, its fertile plains had been granted away by the Mexican government, to such as chose to settle here and stock the land. The terms on which these grants were to be held, easy as they were, were for the most part evaded, and after a new settler had portioned out for himself so many square leagues of a fat valley, and had sent the record of his property to head quarters, he built himself a house, bought a few head of cattle and horses, which were turned off to breed, and he became from that time a "ranchero." Cattle increased and multiplied, and at last were killed for their hides, which were sent down occasionally to San Francisco, and there placed on board ship.

By the treaty formed between the United States and Mexico previous to the occupation of California, the original Spanish grants of land were guaranteed to the native settlers in all cases where the claim could be properly established. A commission to enquire into these land claims was appointed by the United States government, and its labours still continue. The Americans therefore on their arrival in the country had the mortification to discover that nearly every foot of arable land was private property, and that there remained nothing but barren hills and swamps to settle on and improve, under the pre-emption laws of the United States. They therefore *squatted* where they pleased on the Spanish ranches, under the plea that the land commissioners *might* decide the grant on which they were to be illegal ; but in reality because each man wanted a piece of land and was determined to have it, the Spanish owners being powerless to dispossess them of the part they chose to select. The consequence is, that even now in " eighteen hundred and fifty-four," when most of the land-claims have been confirmed by the commissioners, the Spanish owner of a ranche may cast his eye over the property that was but the other day a waving tract of wild grass, and behold, it is parcelled out and enclosed, and cultivated from end to end, and from squatters' huts curls the smoke on every side. Armed with the law, the Spanish owner says " Vamos usted," (be off) ; armed with his rifle the squatter says something much ruder, but to the purpose, and remains. Already have there been serious squatter fights ; the papers daily record " Squatter difficulties," in which men fight, and shed each other's blood savagely, over a patch of soil, which in many instances belongs to neither of them.

So that one of the wisest and most beneficent laws of the United States, is here productive of evil to society.

The squatters in the vicinity of Sacramento city organised themselves into a banditti, and fought "en masse" in defence of their stolen property; but they had made the great mistake of squatting on land that belonged to Americans; these latter sallied from the city with the mayor at their head, and the squatters were defeated and retired with loss, leaving some dead on the field—not however without riddling the mayor, who behaved with great courage, and who must have been much damaged, as the cost of repairing him, when sent in to government by his medical attendant, amounted to about two thousand pounds sterling. But as there are reasonable men among all classes, so among the squatters are to be found many who are willing to purchase their claims, conditionally on the owner's grant being eventually found to be valid; still taken altogether the subject will be one of endless strife, if not bloodshed.

Hundreds have settled down quietly on land from which the present owners are unwilling or unable to dislodge them. These men will raise around them permanent improvements, and will look to the few acres of land they have enclosed for a livelihood for themselves and families; a year or two hence, perhaps, the land they have appropriated will change hands, and the new purchaser will ask his belligerent friends down, as I have witnessed more than once, to stay at his house and help him to "*turn off the squatters.*" Down go the friends and take their fire-arms, as coolly as if they were accepting an invitation to a week's partridge shooting. Occasionally when the proprietor and his friends, armed to the teeth, present themselves at the door of a squatter's log-hut, they find the owner surrounded by *his* friends, prepared to resist intrusion. Sometimes the rival parties exchange shots, but I have always found that in these cases, the owner of the property has walked quietly back again, and the squatter has remained.

*   *   *   *

We dismounted at the door of a long low "adobe" * house, where we were met and hospitably greeted by Don Raymond. Having much refreshed ourselves by bathing in the rivulet which ran past the house, we were rejoiced to find that our host had prepared a dinner, for of this we were in need; and whilst we eat, a couple of Indian girls tickled our ears and noses with long green boughs, with the intention of keeping off the flies. We cheerfully acknowledged the merit not only of the

* Sun-dried brick.

Mexican cookery, but of the native wine of the south, which our host brought out for the occasion. We were then introduced to his wife and two sisters ; these latter were young, with handsome sunburnt faces. My knowledge of Spanish was very limited, but I always prefaced my remarks by a statement of this fact, thus I relieved myself from the necessity of paying those unmeaning compliments which, particularly when delivered in bad Spanish, must be highly amusing to Mexican ladies. As there was an absence of ceremony, and an evident wish on the part of the family to set us at our ease, before night we were on excellent terms, and whilst one of the " vaccaros " played the guitar we waltzed. Don Raymond produced more wine of the south and " cigarittas " in abundance ; and when the ladies retired and Don Raymond showed me to my quarters, I determined on not hurrying myself respecting the purchase of mules so long as the hours could be made to pass so agreeably ; as for Thomas, into whose head the wine of the south had mounted, it was with the greatest difficulty he could be prevented from embracing Don Raymond in the warmth of his satisfaction. Our host then left us, and we were immediately attacked by the fleas with a vigour that was perfectly astonishing.

In the course of my experience I have been tortured by sand-flies in the Eastern Archipelago, and have made acquaintance with every kind of mosquito, from Malta to Acapulco, including of course the famous " tiger " breed, against which there is no resource but flight. I remember that, when sick at Hong Kong, I was crammed into the cabin of an old store-ship so full of cockroaches, and these so ravenous, that they kept my toe-nails quite close every night, and would even try the flavour of the top of my head, and, when they found that to be all bone, they eat my hair and whiskers, the last circumstance being very annoying, from the fact that whiskers were scarce with me in those days ; but I would have preferred any of these annoyances to the attack of those Santa Rosa fleas. On lighting a candle we found the place alive with them ; unlike, both in appearance and manner, the modest flea of ordinary life, that seeks concealment as soon as by accident it is unearthed, these insects, reared in the rough school of a wild bullock's hide, boldly faced as they attacked us. We discovered the next day that the room, the floor and walls of which were of earth, had contained hides, and had been cleared out for the purpose of our accommodation.

But, as a general rule, the Californian houses are alive with fleas, they thrive in the cracks of the mud-brick walls and in the hides with which these places are always strewed. No pains are taken to eject them, and Don Raymond remarked, on our mentioning the fact, that we should get used to them; he and his family never gave the little " malditos " a thought.

After an early breakfast of "tortillas" and fresh milk we commenced at once to look up our shooting gear. Close to us, on one side, was a marsh full of wild fowl, and, stretching for miles round, was the wooded plain, covered with grass, in some places as tall as ourselves. This plain, our host assured us, abounded with deer, elk, and antelope. For a reason, which afterwards appeared, Don Raymond was very anxious that Thomas and I should mount two of his horses, and, in company with some of his Spanish friends, ride over the ranche; we were to take our rifles and shoot all that came in our way. I should of course have preferred to have been allowed to go out on foot and seek my venison in a more sportsman-like manner, than in the company of a dozen clattering, jingling " Caballeros ; " but I could not do otherwise than accept the invitation, particularly as it suggested itself to me that Don Raymond's main object in mounting us was that we should at once appreciate the beauty and extent of the Santa Rosa Ranche.

So that even among these most primitive of agriculturists vanity of possession stands uppermost in all its vulgarity ; what has this man, I thought, to show me but a tract of land, rich certainly in nature's gifts, but in which his only pride consists that *he owns* it ? I could have seen it much better by myself when walking over it, but to please his egotism I must admire it *his way* and sacrifice my own pleasure ; but how I hugged myself when I considered that here at least were no fat pigs, no model styes, with which to bore one ; no oatcake-fed bullocks to be measured with a cambric pocket-handkerchief and praised, whilst you held your nose ; not even a heap of " compo-manure " to sit and gloat over. At the worst it was but a pleasant gallop over the wild oats, in a pure air, and through a lovely country.

In front of the house was a court-yard of considerable extent, and part of this was sheltered by a porch. Here, when the " vaccaros " have nothing to call them to the field, they pass the day, looking like retainers of a rude court. A dozen wild, vicious little horses, with rough wooden saddles on their backs, stand ever ready for work ; whilst lounging about, the " vaccaros " smoke, play the guitar, or twist up a new " riatta " * of hide or horse-hair. When the sun gets warm they go to sleep in the shade, whilst the little

* Lasso.

horses, who remain in the sunshine, do the same apparently, for they shut their eyes and never stir. Presently a "vaccaro," judging the time by the sun, gets up and yawns, and staggering lazily towards his horse, gathers up his "riatta" and twists it round the animal's neck ; the others, awakened, rise and do the same, all yawning with their eyes half open, looking as lazy a set as ever were seen, as indeed they are when on foot. Huppa!—Anda!—away they all go in a cloud of dust, splashing through the river, waving their lassos round their heads with a wild shout, and disappearing from the sight almost as soon as mounted. The "vaccaro" wants at all times to ride furiously, and the little horses' eyes are opened wide enough before they receive the second dig of their rider's iron spurs.

We found great bustle and preparation going on in the court-yard when we rose; it was full of horses and " vaccaros," and some neighbouring ranche owners having arrived, their horses, which were handsome and of large size, were standing near the house, champing their bits. The saddles and bridles of these were ornamented with silver, and the stirrup-leathers were covered with bear skins in such a way as to form a very secure armour for the legs against the attacks of wild cattle.

Breakfast over, the Spanish guests were introduced; they were all fine dashing looking fellows, with the exception of one, a short stout man; from the first moment of our meeting war was tacitly declared between us and this gentleman; we found that he was a suitor for the hand of the eldest sister, who, by the way, owned a part of the ranche, and I suppose he imagined it was our intention to contest this prize with him; for he commenced at once to show his disapprobation of our presence; we called this fellow Quilp. Each of the party had his horse waiting in readiness—ours had yet to be selected from a drove of about a hundred, which were enclosed in a " corral," or circular enclosure, that was close by the house.

The wild horses of the country generally are small, of these I shall speak by and and bye; but Don Raymond, who took the lead among the *fast* Californians, prided himself on the possession of a "mañada" of horses of a superior breed; these he had pointed out to me the day before, and among them I had observed, all rough as they were, some fine beasts. A few steps brought us to the "corral;" Quilp in the foreground, muttering something which we took for granted was insidious advice to Raymond to pick us out "wild ones."

"You English ride?" asked Raymond. I replied modestly, that we rode a little sometimes, as I knew that the slightest approach to assurance on my part would be the signal for a wild stallion being selected for my accommodation. However, Raymond picked us out two high-spirited, but broken-in beasts, that seemed about as well behaved as any that were there. When they were brought into the court, and blinded as usual, Thomas and I produced, and girthed up, our English saddles, on which we had ridden up from Benicia; we were immediately surrounded by the whole crowd of guests and "vaccaros;" bah! those were not saddles—there was no horn to which to fasten the lasso—the stirrups did not protect the foot and leg when the horse fell down and rolled over you! I did not know Spanish enough to answer them, and perhaps it was as well, for I should most certainly have addressed myself to Quilp most strongly on the subject, as the instant he saw my " pigskin " he made a point of turning up what nose Providence had endowed him with, and that was not much. But I observed with pleasure that their observations were directed principally to the fact of the flat smooth surface of our saddles as compared with their " demi-peaks," from which the body receives support on every side. Thomas had a fine seat on a horse, and both of us had had some practice in rough riding both at home and abroad, or otherwise I should have remonstrated with Raymond respecting the wish so evidently expressed by his friends of amusing themselves at our expense.

I had but one rifle I could carry on horseback, so slinging that on my back, away we went, and as the horses warmed under their exercise, and we shook ourselves into our seats, I observed with pleasure that Thomas was both sitting and handling his horse well, and took the fallen timber that came in our way in capital style. However, to shorten this part of the story, the Spaniards soon became less bumptious on the subject, and we flew over the plain at great speed.

Before long we saw a herd of antelope grazing at

some distance, and the Spaniards pulled up and prepared their lassos.   The antelope at this time of the
year are very fat, and comparatively speaking do not
run, or bound rather, fast through the long grass, so
that if headed there is a *chance* for an expert horseman
to catch one with the " riatta," and it was with the
intention of showing me if possible this feat, that our
host had made up the party.   I had no sooner un-
slung my rifle than I was satisfied that there was no
possibility of shooting from the saddle, for my beast,
who would have been quiet as a lamb had I whirled
a lasso round his head, became unmanageable at the
presence of the rifle.   We were to ride round and
head the antelope whilst the " vaccaros " drove them
towards us.   As we galloped through the long grass
towards the position chosen, I told Thomas to keep
close to me and prepare to hold my horse, for I felt it
would be excessively annoying if such a fellow as
Quilp for instance should catch an antelope with his
bit of rope, and I be debarred from even a shot at
the herd.

When we were well ahead of them, the drove
started at the sight of the " vaccaros," and a few
strides of our horses brought some of us right in the
line they were taking; my foot had scarcely left the
stirrup when they flew past with rapid bounds.   Don

Raymond spurred at the headmost bucks, but his lasso fell short; three does brought up the rear; at one of these I fired and wounded it, but it plunged into the thicket with the rest. Seeing that nothing had fallen to the report of the rifle, the Spaniards now went slowly homewards; whilst I searched the thicket and found my doe dying within a few hundred yards. Raymond returned for us, and leaving the venison in charge of the " vaccaros," we rode home. On the way I succeeded in explaining to Raymond that we preferred hunting the deer on foot not only for the advantages of exercise, but of the cover which was afforded by the long grass.

Raymond now, for the first time, pointed out to me that the rattlesnakes were very abundant in the valley, and this we afterwards discovered to be true. It destroyed in a great measure the pleasure of our sport, for we lost many a good shot from looking on the ground—which men are apt to do occasionally when once satisfied of the existence of a venomous reptile, the bite of which is by all accounts mortal. The rattlesnake is seldom seen, it glides away through the long grass on the approach of man or beast, and for this reason cattle are seldom bitten by it. But it allows you to approach very closely before it moves, and the rattle of its tail even in retreat is very unpleasant to hear. Higher up the country we afterwards killed one or two young ones ; but we soon exercised such precautions as insured our not being brought too frequently in contact with them. I have heard of many remedies for rattlesnake bites, and of many fatal cases ; but had any of my party been unfortunate enough to have been bitten very seriously it was agreed between us that the unbitten ones should immediately apply a red-hot iron to the part affected, and then give the victim a powerful dose of castor oil, and leave him to repose ; but I doubt if the complete c̆autery would have been carried out!

Before we arrived at the house Quilp had got scent of the antelope, and had departed.

From this time we found ample employment for our guns, and soon succeeded in bringing in some black-tailed deer. Hares were in abundance close to the house, whilst in the marshes wild fowl were plentiful, so that we kept our host's larder well stored, and Quilp (who returned and made himself quite at home) became quite sleek from good living.

As we were always tired with our day's work, and had moreover our guns to clean, we left Quilp to do all the waltzing ; and when he had enjoyed this pastime until he panted like an over-driven prize ox, he would sit down on a stool in the porch, and

QUILP

throwing one leg over the other, would twang the old guitar and accompany it with a Spanish hymn to the Virgin, which, being delivered in a dismal falsetto, bore much resemblance to the noise of a wheelbarrow that requires greasing, and was about as musical.

The small native horses of the country are re- markable for sureness of foot and great powers of endurance; half-starved, unshod, and overweighted, these ponies will perform long journies at great speed, with great courage; but, alas! for them, in a country where horseflesh is so cheap and riders are so merciless, the noble qualities of this animal meet no reward; and the long day's journey bravely accomplished, the "vaccaro" takes his saddle off the panting beast, and turns him off to die or not, according to his constitution.

The Californian saddle is very rough in appearance, being formed simply of wood and hide, but great care is bestowed both on the material and form, and for the duties required of them they are admirable. The "vaccaro" is in his saddle all day, and it forms his pillow by night; when once he gets a good "saddle-tree" nothing can induce him to part with it, and you may see a dozen of these "vaccaros" standing round a rusty-looking saddle, listening to its owner's praises as he points out its beauties. These saddles are also well adapted for long journies, affording, as they do, so much support to the body.

When the tame horses attached to a ranche begin to be "used up" with hard work, and the stud requires replenishing, the "vaccaros" start for the mountains, and return shortly driving before them a band of wild colts, which, with some difficulty, they force into the corral, where they are enclosed.

The " vaccaros " now enter to select the likely colts, the mad herd fly round the corral, but the unerring lasso arrests the career of the selected victim, who is dragged, with his fore feet firmly planted in the ground, half-strangled, to the court yard, where a strong leather blind is at once placed over his eyes; at this he hangs his head, and remains quite still, his fore feet still planted in the ground ready to resist any forward movement. Then the " vaccaro," always keeping his eye on the horse's heels and mouth, places a folded blanket on his back, and on that the saddle, divested of all incumbrances, this he girths up with all his power; the bridle is on in an instant, so simple is its construction; how free from ornament is the bit, how plain and unpretending is that rusty iron prong, which, at the least pressure on the rein, will enter the *roof of the horse's mouth*. Now the " vaccaro " is seated, and nothing remains but to remove the blind; this is done by an assisting " vaccaro," who gets bit on the shoulder for his trouble, and the work begins. Single jumps, buck jumps, stiff-legged jumps; double kicks; amalgamated jumps and kicks, aided by a twist of the back bone; plunges and rears; these constitute his first efforts to dislodge the " vaccaro," who meets each movement with a dig of his long iron spurs: then the horse stands still and tries to shake his burden off, finally he gives a few mad plunges in the air, and then falls down on his side.

It is now that the formation of the Californian saddle and the large wooden stirrups protect the rider : a small bar lashed crossways to the peak of the saddle prevents the horse from rolling over, and when he rises his tormentor rises with him unhurt ; finding all efforts useless, he bounds into the plain, to return in a few hours sobbing, panting, but mastered. The blind is again put on, the saddle and bridle removed, several buckets of cold water are thrown over his reeking sides, and he is turned into the "corral," an astonished horse, to await the morrow, when his lesson will proceed, and receive less opposition from him! In three days he is considered broken, and is called a "manzo," or tame horse, but admirably as docility has been inculcated in this short period, he is not yet by any means the sort of horse that would suit those elderly gentlemen who advertise in the "Times" for a "quiet cob," nor indeed is he fit for any one but a Californian "vaccaro."

CHAPTER V.

———◆———

August, 1850.

The capabilities of Santa Rosa Valley had not been
overlooked by the early missionaries, and the house
now occupied by Don Raymond had been built by
them. The object of these priests had been, first, to
encourage the wild Indians of the country to settle
near their mission-houses, and then gradually to
domesticate them and employ them in bringing the
land under cultivation ; but in the northern portion of
the country, their efforts seem on all sides to have
been unattended with success, for with the exception
of the existence here and there of a few bands of
" Manzos," or tame Indians, nothing remains in
evidence of the exertions of these early colonists.
In the southern portion of the country, where the
climate is better adapted for the growth of fruit-trees

77

and vines, signs of improvement everywhere mark the presence of the land-loving Jesuit. The missions there consist of several houses, part of the surrounding country is producing grain; a breed of small sheep has been introduced; and the Indians having been made available for agricultural purposes, large quantities of vines are reared, from which an excellent wine, to which I have already alluded, is produced. For this more genial clime the northern valleys had been abandoned, but a band of domesticated Indians remained attached, like cats, to the mud building, where first they made acquaintance with the white man. The Indians of the country are called Diggers, from the fact of their subsisting on roots and acorns. Filthy and degraded in their habits, not one ennobling trait is to be found in them; whether domesticated, or in a primitive state, they are ever the most debased of tribes, morally and physically. It might have been from this that the process of civilising these beings was abandoned by the priests, for so thankless a task might damp the energy even of a Jesuit.

The tribe in question occupied a few huts not far from the house, and Raymond had, with a spirit a little in advance of his fellow colonists, employed these Indians in enclosing a few acres of land, which were now sown with barley and peas. Every week a bullock was killed for the Indians, the whole of which, including entrails, they devoured on the instant. Of an evening they made a great disturbance, by indulging in what they intended for a dance; this consisted in crowding together in uncouth attitudes, and stamping on the ground to the accompaniment of primitive whistles, of which each man had one in his mouth, whilst the women howled and shrieked in chorus.

Business required Raymond's presence at Sacramento for a few days, and from that time Quilp's influence worked strongly to our disadvantage. We were no longer summoned to the early breakfast of fresh milk and " tortillas," and those meals that were prepared for us consisted for the most part of stewed beans. We reminded the ladies, whom now we seldom met, that we had deposited game in the kitchen but the day before ; " Possibly," they replied, " the gatos (cats) had destroyed it." The idea of palming this dreadful story on an Englishman was rather too good. We were now therefore often compelled to shift for ourselves, and although it was no great trouble to light a fire whilst out shooting, and roast a hare or wild duck, we felt our position to be very awkward, having promised Raymond not to depart before his return, an event we awaited with impatience. Not far from the house lived a "squatter" of the name of Elliot, he had been settled for some time in the country and had planted a small garden of vegetables ; we found that he was always supplied with venison, and on this discovery we soon made an arrangement with him that relieved the people of the ranche from all trouble respecting our meals. When we returned at night, Quilp would be found as usual twanging his guitar, but on one occasion, emboldened by our silent contempt, which he mistook perhaps for fear, he ventured on a liberty which, but for my inter- ference, might have been very summarily punished. Returned one evening from shooting, my dog, Cromer, went up inquisitively to Quilp as he sat in the porch, and this gentleman, perhaps to please the group of vaccaros who shared his dislike of us, undertook to kick the animal with his heavy spurred heel. Barnes' powerful grip was on his shoulder in an instant, and so long as it remained there, Quilp was held to his chair as if in a vice. I ordered Barnes at once to desist, and once released, Quilp drew a knife from his boot and swore, "Madre de Dios!" that all the English that ever lived should die under the application of that piece of cutlery ; but as his eye wandered down the barrel of the rifle that Barnes now brought in close proximity with his head, he evidently deferred his sanguinary intentions for the time being, and retired pale and trembling into the house. It was some time before the excitement died away, and I was not sorry when I had reduced Barnes to a calm state of mind, for he was by no means the right sort of person to "muddle," to use his own expression.

Whilst out on the ensuing day we came across a beautiful little animal of the size of a racoon, striped black and white. This was a species of skunk, that emitted an odour so overpowering, that the animal's instinct did not even induce it to attempt to run from the dogs, who flew at first to worry it, but surrendered at once to the poisonous smell, and refused to approach. We left the skunk in full possession of the field, and returned to find Quilp and a newly arrived party of Spaniards, enjoying themselves in-doors, drinking the "wine of the south" and cracking jokes, probably at our expense. I had paid little attention to the fact of Barnes having lagged behind us as we came home, and I was in the porch awaiting his return, when he suddenly appeared on the threshold of the door from which the merriment proceeded, and with the laconic remark of " D——n you, take that," before I was aware of his purpose he chucked the skunk into the middle of the party of Spaniards, where it alighted amidst the screams of the ladies and the oaths of the men. In a few moments the room was cleared, and the men soon afterwards, amidst many vows of vengeance, mounted their horses and rode swearing away. Quilp went with them, and we never saw him again.

Raymond returned, next day, and having explained to him as much as was necessary to account for the estranged terms on which he found us with his family, and apologised for my servant's inexcusable rudeness, I insisted upon being at once permitted to terminate my visit ; and the same day I erected my tent on the plain.

Raymond, who entertained much good feeling towards us, felt very sore to find on inquiry that we had been inhospitably treated during his absence ; but unable to persuade me to remain longer as his guest, he requested that we would wait and witness his annual " cattle-branding," then about to take place, and he would then procure us mules to pursue our journey.

No life is so thoroughly lazy as that of a Californian family, who, totally uneducated, can neither read or write ; and whilst there are no domestic duties on which to employ the women, the men leave to their vaccaros the little superintendence the cattle on a ranche require. Nor, as far as the women are

concerned, does the care of their children seem by
any means to engross their leisure ; for the rising
off-shoots are allowed, like the young cattle, to grow
unassisted and unembellished to maturity, though undoubtedly the naked little urchins benefit physically
by the freedom their young limbs enjoy. Raymond
had but one child, of about four years of age,
and this little fellow, with no covering but a scanty
shirt, strutted about the yard all day, practising
with a miniature lasso at the cocks and hens.

The Californian idea of religion is rather sketchy
and undefined. It is well known that the Spanish
Roman Catholic missionaries were never prone to
waste much time in expounding the tenets of their
faith ; the great principle was, in all instances, to
convert, and to increase the " army of the Faithful."
I remember that in the islands of Batan in the China
Sea, the process was excessively simple. So soon as
a nigger was caught—and in a small island he had
not much chance of escape from a Jesuit—a tin cross
was hung round his neck, and he was turned off
again, like one of Raymond's branded steers, one
being as wise as the other as to whom the new
allegiance was owing. The Californians have, however, learnt enough to know that every one not of
their faith, is a heretic, and the Carrillo family asked

us point-blank if we belonged to that unhappy class, and received gravely our modest reply, that we believed we had that misfortune. The Spaniards and their priests, are not only inveterate card-players, but practised cheats. One of these sleight-of-hand Padres, I was told, displayed great fervour in attempting to convert a heretic who lived near him, and who happened to be an English master of a merchant vessel, who had settled in the country ; as the story goes, the old Salt defended himself from the theological attacks of Father Bartoleméo on the score that he never could understand the principal articles of his new creed. " How so ? " exclaims the Padre, " with faith, and the help of the Virgin, all obstacles will melt like snow before the sun." " Then," observed the captain, as he produced a pack of Spanish monté cards, " how do you turn up the Jack when the seven and Jack are laid out and an open bet is made on the seven ? " " Toe-nails of St. Ignatius ! what has this to do with the tenets of the true faith?" roars the father. " This," says the other, in reply, " is the first tenet of *your faith*, teach me this and I embrace the rest." It is easy to imagine the wrath and indignation of the holy father when he thus heard his religion insulted, and, sympathising with him in his warmth, we are the less· prepared to hear that he not only controlled his feelings, but sat down and inducted the master into the art of turning up the Jack, too happy at so small a sacrifice to gain ANOTHER convert to his faith.

Where so much ignorance exists, a proportionate amount of superstition will of course be found, and in horse-racing, which is their passion, the Californians are regulated by a code of rules affecting the colours of horses and the hours at which they must start to ensure victory. Sailors used to dislike a Friday, but there is no day of the week that is not unlucky for something in California.

At Santa Cruz (in the south) some time ago, the " Virgin " was intreated for rain, and the hat being sent round, a sufficient amount was collected to back the request in the substantial manner that the priests point out as being acceptable. An old heretical American settler, who had a farm on the high land above the valley, declined either to contribute or to pray ; but, from his elevated position, his crops soon throve under genial showers, whilst the valley below as yet received no relief ; this unequal distribution of favour on the part of the saint astonished the occupants of the valley : and we will presume that fresh appeals brought down retribution on the heretic, for, in a very short time, his crops were set on fire, and he saved his house from destruction with some difficulty.

The dress of the vaccaro consists of a broad-brimmed hat, always secured under the chin, a loose shirt and jacket, and buckskin breeches ; round the leg is wound a square piece of leather, this is secured at the knee, and is a protection against falls or the attacks of cattle ; in one of these leggings he carries his knife ; his spurs, serapa, and lasso, complete his costume ; under his saddle he has a blanket, and thus lightly equipped is independent of everything.   The lasso is generally constructed of twisted hide, and is made with great care.   In the hands of a good vaccaro the noose is thrown carelessly, but with unerring precision ; it is a formidable weapon of attack, and in the guerilla warfare, which preceded the occupation of the country, it was not only used successfully, but horrible cruelties were practised by the Spaniards on those whom by chance they cut off in this manner.

The Californians are perfect riders—graceful, active, and courageous ; they ride with a straight leg when in the saddle, and this latter, when properly made, gives great support to the body and legs ; how otherwise could they endure, for hours together, the shock of bringing up *all standing* wild cattle running at full speed ?

When I first seated myself in a Californian saddle

belonging to Raymond, and found the lower part of
my body deeply imbedded in the soft skins which
covered it, I was led into an error which I dare say
has been shared by many others; I thought at the
time that riders accustomed to so much assistance
were less dependent on the muscles of the body; and
I have no doubt in those valuable papers, since lost,
I recorded a hasty opinion that their crack riders
would make a poor show on an English saddle over a
steeple-chase country; but this is only another proof
of the danger of trusting to first impressions. The
Californian will ride a bare-backed horse at speed and
bring him on his haunches with a seat undisturbed :
but what more particularly arrests the critical eye of
an Englishman is their beautiful handling of the
horse's mouth; with a bit, the slightest pressure on
which arrests the horse, they ride, in all the excitement of the cattle chase, with a lightness of hand that
is truly admirable. In the hunting counties, where
by chance some black-coated stranger takes and keeps
a forward position throughout the day, it is a matter
of duty after dinner for all legitimate red-coats to
depreciate the arrogant unknown; but when no fault
can be found either with his seat or his style of riding,
there is always some one who clinches the matter by
remarking sagely—" The fellow rides well enough,

but he has got no ' hands ! ' "   Now the Californians
have both seats and " hands," and may defy the
criticism even of the ill-natured.

Once a year it was customary to drive up all the
cattle on a ranche to brand the young steers.   On
these occasions the vaccaros are in their glory, crack
riders volunteer their assistance, and ranche owners
congregate from far and wide to point out and take
away such of their own beasts as have strayed
and become mixed with those on the ranche.   For a
week previously, the vaccaros scour the mountains
and plains, and collect the wild herds, and these
are at once enclosed in the " corrals."

The proprietor of the ranche keeps open house,
whilst the vaccaros adorn themselves in all the finery
they can muster, which is not much, and they are
specially mounted for the occasion.   Fires are lighted
near the corral, and in these the branding-irons are
kept heated.   The work is commenced leisurely, a few
vaccaros enter the corral, the gate of which is formed
of a bar of wood, easily withdrawn, to allow egress to
the cattle.   The first lasso is thrown over the horns of
a steer, and as the bar is withdrawn he rushes out with
the vaccaro at his side ; on the instant a second lasso
catches the hind leg and he falls on his side, as if shot.
The two lassos are then kept tight by the horses to

which they are attached, who are admirably trained to throw their whole weight on the rope; the brand is then applied. A shake of the lasso disengages it, and the steer after a wild look at the assembled company, rushes smarting with pain to the mountains, where he is soon joined by his fellows in a similar unfortunate predicament.

The corral becomes gradually thinned, and more vaccaros enter the lists, and as the large beasts are kept until the last, and become maddened by being driven round in the heat, and noise, and dust, every opportunity is afforded for a display of good riding. Savage-looking cows show fight from every quarter, and make fierce charges at the horsemen, who experience much more danger, and have more work to do, than the armed " torredores " of a bull-fight. The dust and excitement increase rapidly now, and the cattle thump the ground with their ribs on every side, as their legs fly from under them. A groan, a hiss, and a smell of roast meat, as the hot brand touches them, and away they go, tail on end.

But occasionally the scene is diversified by some cantankerous young bull, who having received the impression of his master's initials, makes a rush at the crowd that surround the corral, with the intention of revenging an insult never intended. This wayward conduct subjects him to increased punishment, for he is now brought down on his side again, until at last he thinks better of it, and makes the best of his way to some lonely spot on the plain, where he revenges himself by praiseworthy but unsuccessful attempts to gore the largest oak-tree he can find.

The work is now carried on with great rapidity, the vaccaros have renewed their horses many times, and under the influence of brandy, which is freely served to them, they begin to get as mad as the cattle. All ends at dusk, and the evening is devoted to a "fandango;" but the men are all so drunk and tired, that this amusement always terminates early, and generally seriously; for among so many boasting and quarrelsome riders, knives are soon produced, and the dispute, which always has reference to the *capacity* of some horse, is terminated for the time being by the letting of a little blood.

It is the nature of man to boast of his horse in all countries, and how unfortunate it is that these Spaniards are not sufficiently civilised to settle their disputes with a bet; then the only blood drawn would be from the horse's flanks, when he was called upon by his master to perform the feat in question, and the whole would be decided in a *gentlemanly manner!*

Shortly after the " cattle-branding," Raymond provided me with four handsome mules and a horse. I have already mentioned that the management of wild mules was a matter of great difficulty; to us it was an impossibility, and we found it requisite to hire the services of a vaccaro. We started for Russian River after bidding adieu to Raymond, who had behaved to us throughout with great hospitality and kindness. Our road led through another plain, oak-timbered like the valleys, and that there may be at least one good remark in my book, I shall borrow a description from Sterne, who says, " There is nothing more pleasing to a traveller or more terrible to travel-writers, than a large rich plain, especially if it is without great rivers or bridges, and presents to the eye but one unvaried picture of plenty; for, after they have once told you that it is delicious or delightful (as the case happens), that the soil was grateful, and that nature pours out all her abundance, &c., they have then a large plain upon their hands, which they know not what to do with."—*Tristram Shandy*, vol. ii., p. 123. The reader will then please to consider that my party has reached in safety the banks of the Russian River.

This is a broad stream, and in the summer months when the water becomes low, it runs sluggishly; but

high among the branches of the alder-trees that line
the banks, are accumulations of sticks and rubbish
that mark the height to which the river rises when the
mountain snow begins to melt, and it changes its
present lazy rippling pace for the turbulent roar of a
cataract, and overflows the adjacent plains.

Being nightfall, we encamped without crossing, and
at daylight we were dismayed at discovering that our
beasts had been stolen ; we had no reason to suspect
the vaccaro, who at all events acted surprise to
perfection, if guilty of connivance; but mules and
horses were gone, and the riattas with them.   Some
expert thieves had tracked us, and as we were in
ignorance as to who they were, we laid the whole
matter at Quilp's door.   I have since discovered by
experience, that if a band of Mexicans are determined
to have your horses, they generally manage it by
some means, in spite of the utmost vigilance; with
our inexperience and the possible connivance of
the vaccaro (of which, however, there was not a
shadow of proof) the task was easy.   I discharged
the vaccaro, and we crossed the river on foot,
taking off our clothes and carrying them in a bundle
on our heads.   The water was so refreshing, that the
task of taking over our baggage piecemeal, was one of
pleasure, and helped wonderfully to counterbalance

the annoyance I felt at the loss of my mules—a loss which entirely precluded my further advance into the country. Leaving Barnes with the baggage and dogs, Thomas and I proceeded in search of a back-woodsman's hut, which we had been informed existed in this direction; after following the river for some time, we ascended a steep hill, from the summit of which was presented the most lovely panorama— beneath us the thickly wooded plain extended for miles—on one side bounded by mountains, on the other, melting away in a blue hazy distance;—the windings of the Russian River were marked distinctly in contrast with the dark rocks and foliage that lined its banks, whilst immediately beneath us was a forest of firs and red-wood trees, over which the vultures wheeled incessantly, and not even the sound of an insect disturbed the silence of the scene.

From this hill we discovered the hut of which we were in search, situated near a running stream and surrounded by towering red-wood trees. We found the occupant at home; he was a tall sinewy man, a Missourian of the name of March, and he at once cheerfully assisted us. He lent us his mule to bring up our baggage, and by nightfall we were encamped within a few yards of his hut. There were two other backwoodsmen living with March, and these three

had just completed unaided a saw-mill, to which they had applied the power of the stream, by means of an over-shot wheel. The heavy beams that formed the mill-frame, the dam and race, had all been constructed from the adjacent forest trees, and now that the work was completed, wanting only the saw, for which they intended to go to San Francisco, it seemed incredible that so large a frame could be put together by so small a number of men. This saw-mill erected in the forest and of the forest, raising its long beams from the midst of the romantic scenery that surrounded it, was a glorious instance of what energy will accomplish, and of the rapidity with which each man in an American colony contributes towards the development of the new country's resources.

And it contrasts strangely with the languid inertness of those communities, who with equal brains and hands *ponder* and *dream* over the means of supplying wants, even when they have long been felt; to see that here even the uneducated backwoodsman devotes his time and energy to preparing for the wants *to come*; buoyed up by an admirable confidence in the rapid growth and prosperity of his country, which confidence is part of his education, and one great secret of his success. If the Americans go a-head, it is principally because they "look a-head." March when he planned his mill and felled his first tree in this solitary forest, ranked with those who wrote from the tents of San Francisco for steam-engines and foundries. Now as I write, these latter are performing their daily work in the city, and have become essential to its wants, whilst March's mill, seemingly so out of place where I first saw it, can now barely supply the wants of the numerous agricultural population that is settling round about it. March and his companions lived entirely on game, which he assured me abounded; and as for the present at all events I could not proceed, I

determined at his advice to walk over the hills and
look at a valley on which he strongly recommended
me to " squat ; " we therefore started the next morning in search of it, following the directions that
March had given us for our guidance to the spot.

CHAPTER VI.

—◇—

September, 1850.

THE country which we now traversed consisted of
a series of small round-topped hills, uniform in size
but varying in feature. The whole had been long
since subjected to violent volcanic action, so whilst
one hill was crowned with a grotesque mass of rock
and cinder, round which the tall wild oats waved
desolately, the next enchanted the eye with a profusion of evergreen oaks and flowering arbutus.
These hills altered in character as they had been
subjected to, or had escaped from the volcanic
shower; thus whilst on one side was a huge mound
of lava destitute of all vegetation, on the other was
a dense mass of rich underwood, from which rose
groups of the stately red-wood tree.

97

We saw several old craters, and the cindery desolation that encirled them for some distance yielded
suddenly to the encroachment of vegetation; a strife
for mastery between these two had existed, and you
may believe, if you please, as I do, the volcanic
agency to have been under the management of an
evil gnome, the wild vines and arbutus to have been
protected by a good fay, and that after numerous
fierce engagements, a lasting peace had been concluded and the territory equally divided.

We put up several hares and covies of partridges,
whose parents had never been shot at, and we fully
satisfied ourselves as to the existence in abundance of
both bears and deer.

Arrived at the summit of a hill, the little valley
we were in search of lay at our feet. It was scarcely
twenty acres in extent, level as a table, bounded on
one side by masses of red-wood trees, and on the
other by a fine stream, whose banks were shaded
with alders and wild vines. The valley itself was free
from shrub or tree, excepting that from the centre
there rose a clump of seven gigantic red-woods,
which growing in a circle, and meeting at the roots,
formed a natural chamber to which there was but
one inlet.

As the land we were on belonged to the United

States government, I determined to take March's advice, and *squat* on this valley, for I became at once enchanted with it, as indeed were my companions: I therefore affixed to the red-wood trees a paper I had long prepared and kept in my knapsack for immediate use, and which ordered all men to take notice that F. M. claimed, under the laws of preemption, one hundred and fifty acres of land measuring from that spot, and that he intended to defend his right by force of arms, &c. &c.

Considering that, saving the wild Indians, human foot had probably never crossed the spot, the notice scarcely seemed necessary, and the Indians did not respect it, as I shall have occasion to show hereafter.

By the time we had walked thoroughly over the property and discovered fresh advantages, and had drunk of the stream and found the water excellent, it was dusk, and not being sufficiently satisfied with our landmarks, to try our way back to our camp that night, we determined on passing it in the red-wood clump; the fire was soon stacked and lighted—that jolly camp-fire that on the instant suffuses everything around it with its cheerful ruddy glow, and sends its sharp crackle merrily up through the air, throwing a charm over the most inhospitable desert, and giving a zest to the hunter's meal be it ever so homely.

How naturally as we sit around it we recall the memory of wet seasons, when benighted, damp, chilly, and tired, we selected amidst the falling mist, the driest and most sheltered spot in the wet brushwood; how we laugh now at the vain attempt to kindle damp leaves and undergrowth; the partial success that engendered hope, only to render the failure of the last match more intolerable; the dark long night, dreary, drizzling, with one of us on guard for danger, and all unable to sleep, watching impatiently for the morning, with the first dull streak of which we stretch our half stiffened limbs, and shouldering the dead game, that no camp-fire over night converted into a well-earned and needful supper, seek some sheltered spot elsewhere, and make a breakfast of it. The recollection of nights like these— and they fall to the lot of every hunter—causes one to contemplate the blazing embers with a simple gratitude, that is not always engendered elsewhere by the possession of the comforts of this world.

We had a leash of hares, which being skinned and cleaned were impaled on withers and placed at the fire to roast, where they looked like three martyrs flayed alive, and staked. Whilst they were cooking we filled the red-wood clump with several armfuls of long oat-straw from the adjacent hill.

After worrying the three hares, we lighted our pipes, and picquetting the dogs round us, we gave ourselves up to the pleasures of a comparison of the happiness of our position as compared with that of other men, and then I sunk into a gentle slumber (of course), while my companions snored in unison with the dogs.

We rose with the sun; and properly speaking, I should take advantage of that fact to inform the reader what part of the surrounding scenery was first bathed in yellow light, and what remained in obscurity; what the deep blue of the distant mountains contrasted with, and what completed the picture in the foreground: but these things are to be found better described in any book of travels of the day; and moreover, at the time of which I am writing, I was not gazing at the landscape, but was proceeding rather unpoetically to bathe in the river, munching on my way the leg of a cold martyr.

In the course of the day we moved our baggage from March's Mill to our new possession, where I determined on passing the winter.

I decided upon enclosing the valley and rendering it fit for agricultural purposes, but as the winter was approaching, I saw that the first thing requisite was to send for a quantity of useful articles that I had stored in readiness at Sonoma, and which consisted of carpenter's tools, blankets, powder and shot, books, and a small quantity of groceries. For these I despatched Thomas, and the red-wood clump having been perfected in its internal accommodations, by the addition of a boarded floor, a brushwood roof, with a convenient rack for the rifles, and a secure magazine for the powder, Barnes commenced laying his axe to the red-wood trees on the other side of the stream, whilst I shouldered my rifle and supplied the larder.

There is but one species of deer here— the black-tailed—and the venison, though generally fat, is insipid, owing perhaps to the fact that the dry season parches up every blade of green stuff, and the deer live on the long self-made hay, which in some parts is very

plentiful, but not nutritious. The deer are generally found in herds of from five to seven, and it requires great caution to " bag them."

As the wind at this season of the year blows with little variation from the same point, my ground was almost always of the same nature, the river being in my rear, and the mountains before me. Stalking was out of the question, for from the peculiar formation of the country, which consisted of a series of undulations, no extended view could be procured of a herd, and the long grass which afforded them cover abounded with rattle-snakes. The only plan in such a country is to keep your eyes about you, not forgetting the ground, and walk the deer up, against the wind of course, taking advantage of any cover that may be in your path, in the shape of a rock, and using great caution in showing yourself over the rising ground. The herd will probably then start up with a bound from the long oat-straw at your feet, but seldom afford a fine shot, as they plunge away half concealed by it ; now you throw yourself down, and see, the herd has stopped within a hundred yards of you ; and here a buck advances chivalrously in defence of his harem—five paces—ten—now he is troubled ; for although there is pride in his nostrils, and anger in his stamping hoof, there is indecision in those working ears, and by his eye you may read that if anything very ugly appears, he will run away. But a doe advances ; this nerves her lord to a few paces more ;—now you may fire ;—full at the shoulder ;—crash—poor buck ! Now load again, and then rush up and cut his throat, he is stone dead ; rattle, tattle, tattle, tattle,—mind the snake ! Now flay him, if you want the skin, or quarter him if you don't : this done you can carry home a haunch, the skin, the antlers, the tongue and the brains, and these, with your accoutrements and the hot sun, will probably tire you before you get home. In the evening the poor does, with their soft hearts still palpitating, from the nasty noise your rifle made, and the very ugly appearance of yourself generally, will stand in a group, and turn their wistful eyes in the direction where last they saw their master, and wonder—poor innocents—why he is not there as usual to lead them proudly down to the stream, and take his station on the bank to ward off any danger whilst they drink. Night comes, but he does not appear ; then they wander about, and cry and pass a miserable night, whilst you are making a good supper off the buck, and are speaking jocularly of him as a " fat old rascal."

The deer is very inquisitive, and if when you have walked up a herd, and have thrown yourself down, in the long grass, you extend your loading rod above your head, with a piece of rag attached to it, the bucks will, even though they wind you, generally approach within killing distance, which, when shooting as I was, for subsistence, should not be more than *seventy yards* if possible. It is always better to make this rule when shooting for the " larder." Where game is thin, fire at nothing that you don't think certain, until the day wanes, and necessity and an empty stomach oblige you to shoot at everything you see. Where game is wild and difficult to approach, and you are living on your gun, too much precaution cannot be taken to insure, if possible, the bagging of everything you hit ; for if anything makes sporting cruel, it is the habit that some have of trying long shots, and sending poor brutes away to die a lingering death in the brush. Moreover, I was much in the position of a man with a preserve, and that not over-stocked. I could not afford to drive my game, by careless shooting, out of my own beat, and the nature of my country was such that the want of cover in the undulating hills rendered the deer very alert whilst feeding there, and when they took to the mountains in alarm they were lost to the hunter, if alone, so far as this, that they invariably managed to keep a large sized hill between him and themselves ; for the Russian River deer are actually *cunning*, and never did I see one take to a ravine, or lay himself open in any way when once he ascended the steep. I have often killed before I have left the house twenty minutes, but far more frequently have walked the whole day without seeing a deer.

We recovered some wounded deer with the assist-ance of the blood-hound, Prince ; but just as he became useful, he was attacked by a distemper peculiar to the country, which affects the hind-quarters with paralysis, and generally kills. I think I saved Prince's life by administering a tremendous dose of castor-oil on the first appearance of his symptoms, but he was a very sick dog for a long time, and staggered like a three days' old calf. Having mentioned castor-oil, I wish to do justice to its invaluable qualities, which would not perhaps have been so thoroughly tested by us were it not that our sole stock of medicine consisted of two quart bottles of it. It was successfully applied to both man and beast in every complaint, and acted with a little tobacco-leaf, as a balm for all outward wounds.

Barnes, who was a famous axe-man and was possessed of unusual physical strength and endurance, soon felled a large number of the giant red-woods in the rear of our valley, in order to split them and convert them into rails for enclosing the farm. If we should speak well of the bridge that carries us over, we should also speak well of the tree that roofs us in for the winter, but the red-wood tree (Arbor Vitæ) deserves especial notice on its own merits, which I shall proceed to detail. The size and height attained by the red-wood in California are very wonderful, and faithful accounts of these trees have been received with incredulity. The average size of the full-grown trees may be quoted at from five to six feet in diameter, and about 150 feet in height. This tree maintains in some instances so perfect a perpendicular, that in felling it on a calm day, if one is cut towards the centre, a very small portion of the heart will sustain the immense trunk. The largest tree we discovered at Russian River was not far from the house. Measuring it six feet above the ground, its circumference was 40 feet, and its height about 200 feet. But in Calaveras county, a group of trees exists which measure respectively, 27 feet, 20 feet, 23 feet, 18 feet, and 16 feet in diameter, and from 200 feet to 250 feet in height. The largest of these was felled and the bark removed to San Francisco, where it was erected in its original position, and formed a capacious room.

The timber of the red-wood is very durable, and is so easily worked that a man needs but an axe, a betel and a few wedges, to convert the largest of them, provided they are free from knots, into planks, rails or clap-boards, and I have seen Barnes fell a huge fellow, and in less than a fortnight he has carried it all away but the boughs and the bark. It is a fine sight to watch one of these trees fall to the axe; leaving the perpendicular at first so leisurely; then gathering impetus as it nears the ground, crushing all it meets, making the earth vibrate with its shock, and sending forth a booming echo, that startles the game far and wide. The bark of the red-wood is perforated in every direction, and with great regularity, by a kind of starling, called, from this peculiarity, *carpentaro*, or carpenter.   These birds form cells in the tree with great assiduity, and deposit therein acorns, which fit very tightly.   They are very quaint and noisy, and employ themselves continually, when not fighting, in depositing acorns in the red-woods.   You may see a dozen of them clinging to the bark of one tree in the most uncomfortable positions, pecking away, each at a hole.   But the carpentaros work for the more lazy portion of creation, and one of their enemies is the beautiful grey squirrel which abounds here.   I have often watched a grey squirrel ascend a red-wood; for the birds work in the upper part of the tree.   He is immediately surrounded by carpentaros, who, knowing him of old, are at no loss to divine his object, but the open day robber, nothing daunted, at once extracts an acorn, and popping it in his mouth, he turns his head from side to side in the quaintest manner possible, as if to say to the birds that chatter around him, " Pray go on, don't mind my feelings. "   Then down he comes whisking his beautiful silvery tail. Then the carpentaros assemble round the pillaged hole, and scream over the matter so much that you may imagine them to be abusing the squirrel in their choicest slang; and presently up comes grey squirrel again for another acorn, having found the first so good; and then, fresh carpentaros having arrived, the noise becomes so intolerable, that the most enthusiastic of naturalists would walk off with his fingers in his ears. The grizzly bear also takes advantage of the exposed condition of the carpentaro's winter provision, and climbs the red-wood in much the same fashion as the grey squirrel, though less gracefully; so they say: I never saw a bear in this position, and if unarmed I should not wait to study his habits, if I did; for although naturalists tell us that the bear is graminivorous, there is no doubt that the grizzly would sacrifice all the acorns that grow for a juicy piece of the calf of one's leg.

The carpentaro has a more destructive enemy than even the squirrel or the bear, and a greater beast than either—the Digger Indian. These miserable specimens of humanity will light a fire at the root of a well-stocked red-wood tree until it falls; they then extract the carpentaro's acorns and fill many baskets full, which they carry away.

"Eat as much as you like, but pocket none," the justly indignant carpentaros might say.

The red-wood tree is the main-stay of California. The supply is inexhaustible, but nature has been sufficiently capricious to make them most abundant in very inaccessible spots, whilst the level plains are covered with a short-grained dwarf oak, serviceable only for firewood. But, however steep the mountains, the Californian red-wood has to fall and to be fashioned to the use of man, and when a steam saw-mill gets perched upon a mountain-top the romance of the forest is gone; its silent grandeur no longer awes the mind; and the trees, whose size and beauty caused such deep impressions and such grave reflections, fall into insignificance as you see them torn into planks and packed on waggons, whilst the once still forest resounds to the sound of the axe and the shrill whistle of the steam-engine. I have been very disappointed at finding these sudden changes in revisiting some of my old hunting-grounds.

Thomas now arrived with our stores, which we unpacked with great pleasure, as they had not seen the light since we had boxed them up ourselves in England, and every article was associated with home. We set to work, and in a fortnight had completed a two-roomed house, close to the red-wood clump: we then converted that apartment into a larder and storehouse.

It is not my intention to dwell very much upon the subject of deer-shooting, as, even could I say what has not been said before by mightier hunters than I, the subject has interest for sporting men alone.

I have mentioned in the early part of this chapter, that bears were said to be plentiful in the country I had chosen for my sojourn. The Californian hunter holds the grizzly bear in great respect; and not without reason, when we consider that this animal is difficult to kill, that he is a relentless pursuer when wounded, and that he can run and climb under ordinary circumstances, with more agility than his assailant. On this account, and from the fact that you must, from the nature of his haunts, attack him on foot, a wounded grizzly bear is a worse enemy to encounter than a tiger. March had promised to make up a bear hunt for us, and in a day or two he came over to the farm with two hunters of the name of Sheldon and Carter; both hard-looking fellows, carrying nothing but their rifles, a knife, and a Colt's revolver, which latter is invaluable in all kinds of hunting.

The Americans carried rifles of their own make; capital make too, though too weak in the lock on account of the cheap price at which they are supplied. The bore of their rifles seemed small for bear-shooting, carrying a half-ounce ball, but they seemed to consider that their skill in shooting counter-balanced this deficiency. I carried the only rifle that I ever used of those I took out, one of German make, carrying a ball of an ounce and a half. I should say here that our rifles were often the subject of discussion with these honest fellows. I had two Rigby's with an accumulation of sights, which were perfectly useless for my work, although they were beautifully finished weapons; and Barnes's friendly disputes concerning the relative merits of the American barrel, with its enormous weight of metal and long point-blank range, and the English lock, with its wholesome click, and the American stock, with its carved butt, that gives so much steadiness to the muscles of the body when you aim, resulted in a combination that was highly approved of by all parties; for all these good qualities were amalgamated by the construction of a new stock, and thus a rifle was produced that amongst ourselves enjoyed great celebrity, and this rifle March has probably in his possession to this day.

The German rifle, to which I have alluded, was rather too short, but very true within a hundred yards, and its qualities were expressed by its name, " shoulder-breaker," engraved on the stock. It is a rare thing to get a good rifle carrying a heavy ball.

We started at once in search of our bear—six in number—and accompanied by a small dog belonging to Sheldon. It was not until the afternoon that we struck upon a fresh bear sign, of which March had had previous knowledge. The sign led into thick underwood in which the bear seeks shade, but which is the worst of all places for killing him. March disposed us in couples; we then spread and entered the thicket at a partially cleared part. Almost immediately I heard a crash, and an angry roar, and then a shot was fired to the left. It was necessary for us to retrace our steps, on account of intervening jungle, to rejoin our party, which done, the bear was in view. I was astonished at his size; standing on his hind-legs with his mouth open like a thirsty dog, and working himself up and down, he indicated that he felt the inconvenience of the pellet that March had intended for his heart, but which had lodged in his alimentary canal. However, in an instant, and as if by a sudden impulse, he again assumed the position of a quadruped and bounded towards March and Sheldon, clearing as much ground at each stride—for he was as big as an ox—as would have done credit to the winner of the Liverpool steeplechase. A shot from the right altered his course again in that direction, for the grizzly bear will turn to the last assailant, and this enforces the necessity of bear-hunters supporting each other.

A momentary uncertainty on his part gave me an opportunity of troubling him with one of my $1\frac{1}{2}$ oz. balls, but this only elicited a grunt and a rush in my direction. I confess that, as soon as my rifle was discharged, I felt great inclination to disregard March's directions, which were, not to use my revolver, but if possible to *reload my rifle directly I had fired*, under *all circumstances*. Whilst in a curious state of uncertainty on this point, though loading, the bear swerved suddenly on one side in chase of the little high-couraged dog that belonged to Sheldon.

This dog had been in other bear-hunts and was generally very useful, for the grizzly has a great suspicion of anything behind him, and if a dog can be trained to worry his hams, the bear will turn round and round and afford much facility to the hunters.

I fancy the dog must have got hurt or lost his pluck, for he now rushed straight to his master, and the bear followed; Sheldon fired as the grizzly approached, but without effect, and the next moment poor Sheldon was down bathed in blood, one blow had carried away the flesh entirely from one side of his face, fracturing his jaw-bone in the most frightful manner.

The bear disappeared, and probably retired to die, whilst we carried Sheldon home, with what feelings of grief I need not say.   We sent him on to Sonoma as soon as possible, and he afterwards recovered, though dreadfully disfigured, and with the loss of an eye.   It was perhaps on account of this accident that we made up no more parties for the express purpose of bear-hunting, but left it to chance to meet them, and as it happened, accident threw very few in our way.

The chief difficulty in killing the grizzly bear arises from the formation of his head, which is convex. The ball generally glances off sufficiently to avoid the brain ; you have in fact but three vital parts, the back of the ear, the spine, and the heart ; and it is said that the grizzly bear will live long enough after being shot in the latter part to do much mischief.   He is always in motion, and I think the steadiest of hunters will allow that his conduct when wounded is not calculated to improve one's aim.   The very fact of finding that you hit him so often without effect, destroys confidence, and the sudden rushes that the bear makes at his assailant is a great trial to the hunter's nerve. There are many accidents of the description I witnessed on record, although I know one or two instances of bears being killed at the first shot.

It appears to me that a recorder of travels has a difficulty to surmount, which falls to the lot of no other writer, for whilst duty admonishes him to give a strictly veracious account of everything that comes before his notice (and of a great deal that does not), inclination and the publisher prompt him to avoid prosiness, for this very good reason, that if he enters into details he bores his readers ; but then, on the other hand, if he is not sufficiently specific, he is pronounced a " superficial observer."

This observation is induced by the necessity of my introducing, at all costs, further accounts respecting the grizzly bear.

When we consider the weight of the grizzly, which often reaches fifteen hundred pounds, the enormous strength of which he is possessed, as evidenced by the limbs of trees which he will wrench from the trunk, and his extraordinary speed and activity, we have reason (speaking as one who lives in his vicinity) for congratulation that the animal is of inoffensive habits, and avoids the presence of man. The sole instance to the contrary is that in which you are unfortunate enough to invade the domestic circle of the she-bear when accompanied by her cubs : she invariably gives chase the instant she sees the in- truder, who, if he is wise, will " draw a bee-line " in an opposite direction.   In running * from a bear, the best plan is to turn round the side of a hill, for the bear having then as it were two short legs and two long ones, can't, under such circumstances, run very fast.   There is but one sized tree that you can climb in safety in escaping from a bear, and you may run a long way before you find it.   It must be just too small for your pursuer to climb up after you, and just too large for it to pull down, a nice point to hit. The she-bear is invariably irascible when nursing, and perhaps this accounts for the fact that the male- bear is seldom found in her company; to her he leaves the education and support of their progeny, whilst he seeks amusement elsewhere—I might say at his club, for it is the habit of bears to congregate in threes or fours under a tree for hours, and dance on their hams in a very ludicrous manner, with no apparent ostensible object but that of passing the time away and getting away from their wives.

I have heard many anecdotes related of grizzly bears.   I choose the following as characteristic of a well-established fact that the bear, even when

---

* I am supposing the case of an unarmed person suddenly meeting a she-bear, a not unusual occurrence in California.

infuriated, not only acts from the instinct of self-preservation, but seems loth to kill and mangle what it attacks.

In the hills round San José, an unarmed negro came suddenly on a she grizzly with cubs. She pursued him, and fortunately for him struck him on the head, which knocked him down, but did not of course (he being a nigger) inflict any serious damage on the part assailed. The man wisely remained perfectly still, whilst the bear, who knowing nothing about " darkies' " heads, supposed she had gained the day by a *coup de main*, retired for a short distance. After remaining quiet, as he supposed, sufficiently long, the negro thought of getting up, but his first movement was arrested by a crack on the other side of his head, and down he went again, and the bear retired to watch over his interests. It was a long time before the negro again attempted to rise (for more reasons than one), and this was not until the bear had quitted the spot, apparently satisfied ; but no sooner was Quashy up to look about him, than the bear darted out from another quarter, and this time she did poor Darky great injury : she tore his back and knocked him senseless, and then half covered him up with leaves. After this she was quite satisfied, and the negro was shortly afterwards discovered and resuscitated, and felt quite unwell all the next day ; but told this story long afterwards to me with great satisfaction, and, I need not add, with unimpeachable veracity.

I have mentioned the dexterity with which the Spaniard throws the lasso, and the weapon has been successfully employed in entrapping the bear. The noose is thrown over him when he is near a tree, and by riding in a circle he is secured by a dozen thongs. This is one of the feats which the Spaniards assure you they *can* do.

Although the grizzly's natural food consists probably of roots and acorns, I suppose he must be ranked as omnivorous, for he certainly crunches a bone with great gusto. The bears cleared off any bones that were lying round our hut; and, in one instance, we shot at a couple that came close to our door at night and stole the bones from under the noses of the dogs. One bear walked away with a large piece of meat and the iron hook on which it hung, but whether he swallowed the hook with the bait, or pulled it out with his fingers, we never ascertained; he never brought it back again, so we indulge in the hope that it sticks in his jaws to this day, and that he has found out " qu'il n'y a point de roses sans des épines."

Bear meat is eatable, but very devoid of flavour, and I think the grizzly indulges in too much gymnastic exercise to qualify him for the table of the epicure.   He figures in the bill-of-fare at all Californian Restaurants, and, as a great number of the common black bears are caught alive in traps, the San Francisco hairdresser has no difficulty in " sacrificing, on any occasion, a real animal for the benefit of his customers."

CHAPTER VII.

Christmas, 1850.

To render agreeable a life where men are thrown
entirely on their own resources, the chief point is to
ensure contentment, and nothing conduces more to
this end than to apportion to each one of the party an
equal and strictly-defined share of work. Forest life,
in my case, never altered the relations that existed
between myself and those in my employment, nor
will real respect ever vanish under the familiar contact
which such a life imposes.

I gave Barnes the woods and forests, which was not
such a sinecure as it is here, as he had full employment for the winter in felling the redwoods, and
splitting them into rails for enclosing the farm.
Thomas undertook the "hewing and drawing," the
cooking, and the internal cleanliness of the house;

122

and this latter is very essential in mountain life. Take everything out of your hut daily and hang it in the sun ; then, water well the floor ; this drives away the vermin, which abound in the deer and hare skins ; it also ensures you against scorpions and centipedes, which are apt to introduce themselves into the fire-wood. It devolved on me to supply the larder, and the amount of exertion required for this duty varied considerably. One day an easy walk would bring me to a marsh, and a few shots from my double-barreled gun would secure as many wild-ducks as we required, but on another I might be doomed, after a long journey, to extend myself over the carcase of a buck, and then, exposed to a glaring sun, unaided, flay my quarry and disembowel him, quarter him, and carry him home piece by piece, over four or five miles of successive cindery hills. I had no stout little pony with a shaggy mane and tail, such as one sees carrying home the deer in Landseer's splendid pictures. I had to take as much meat as I could " pick-a-back," or else leave it to the coyotes, who would appear in sight whilst I was yet at work on the carcase. If this part of a hunter's duty was entailed upon our fashionable deer-stalkers, many of the deer would reap the benefit, not so much by being flayed and carried home by members of the aristocracy, as in being left alone.

The monotony of this life was varied by excursions into the adjacent country, and these would last two or three days; during which time we left the hut to take care of itself; and, carrying each a rifle and a blanket, with a few other necessaries, we passed our nights by the camp fire, and in the day discovered wonders of nature that amply repaid us for our journey. The first object that attracted our attention was an immense hill of sulphur, and we discovered hot springs strongly impregnated with this mineral in its immediate vicinity. Round one of the springs was an apparently hard crust of sulphur, but this was treacherous, as Thomas found out, for it was the cause of his tumbling in and getting a medicated bath; and, although he soon dried, he smelt so strongly of lucifer matches for some days afterwards as to be almost unbearable. We brought some of the sulphur, which was very pure, away with us. We also discovered large craters, and igneous rocks, piled in such vast confusion as indicated the blind fury with which the earth had torn and rent itself on some former great occasion. The whole of California has been subjected to more than ordinary violent disturbances, but the vegetation of thousands of years has decomposed since then, and the huge rocks that were once hurled, red-hot, I dare say, into the air, are now deeply-embedded in the surrounding soil.

These excursions opened a new field for our rifles, for, whilst taking a bird's-eye view one morning from the elevation on which we had encamped, our attention was arrested by the appearance of a herd of wild cattle. Having observed the direction in which they were grazing, and finding that, unfortunately, the direction of the wind prevented our heading them, I adopted a plan which proved successful. Carefully keeping them in sight from the rear, as I knew that water was not immediately ahead of them, I foresaw that towards sunset they would alter their course, and, guided by their instinct, graze towards the nearest spring. This they did in the afternoon; and having now a side wind, we hastened to look for cover in their line of march, glad to exchange the slip-shod pace at which for hours we had followed their movements, for a brisk double in the other direction. As soon as we had hit our line, I sent Barnes out to reconnoitre, and he immediately returned, having discovered the spring and a good cover a little in advance of it. We soon took up our positions, and before long the herd appeared in view : five black bulls, one a young one. They were most beautiful beasts, with sleek and glossy coats ; thin in the flank, broad in the chest, and rather short of horn. They evinced uneasiness at once when within shot, and stared in our direction, snuffing the air and pawing the ground. As the young one presented his broad-side, he fell on his knees to "shoulder-breaker," and, tail on end, went the rest of the herd at a long trot over the hills. We walked up to our friend to give the "coup de grâce," but, through a want of caution, not usual with him, Barnes got a bad bruise, for the bull, by a sudden exertion, rose and plunged at him, catching him full in the chest, and knocking him down, then fell down himself, never to rise again. Barnes felt some pain for a day or two, which we allayed with the infallible castor oil ; but I rather suspect his chief annoyance was caused by having been floored by a young bull, for whom, under ordinary circumstances, I think he was a match in physical strength.

Although wild cattle are not described as being indigenous to the country, I have no doubt, from their appearance, that these were so, and that their cows were not many miles away. It is vexatious to be obliged to leave a fine carcase to the wolves and vultures ; but as a bullock is too much for three men, and we were far from home, we cut out the best part of it and returned to camp; and the coyotes made a fine noise, during the night, over what remained.

The wild fowl now came over in heavy flights and settled in our vicinity. The geese were in incredible numbers; white and grey geese and brant. Of ducks we had several varieties, many of them quite unknown to me, and I regret that I failed, from want of materials, in my endeavours to preserve specimens of them. The geese are very easily shot when first they arrive, but soon become very wary. The easiest and best plan is to construct little huts of green stuff near the marshes they frequent, and you are sure of good flight shooting at daylight. I had a large duck-gun that I had used in punt-shooting in Norfolk, but it was very rebellious, and kicked so, when used from the shoulder without a rest, that I placed it under Barnes's especial charge; and whenever he felt in particularly good health, he went out with it, and you might see him returning with geese and ducks suspended from every part of his body; his face wreathed in smiles at his good fortune; but the next morning would disclose a bruise on his right shoulder of about the size and colour of a certain popular green dessert plate. Herons and curlew were plentiful, and very tender, jack-snipe in great abundance, but I never disturbed them, for I am a bad snipe shot, and the first rule in the mountains is to spare your powder. Hares and partridges were in abundance, yet were also spared, as we wished them about the place; but rabbits were rather scarce and very small. If the love of sport, therefore, was sufficient to chain one to this spot, the above enumeration will show that we had not only ample occupation, but variety; yet I determined on adding farming to my other amusements, and although it recurred to me that when I gave up " gentleman farming " in England, I registered a vow to leave such things to those who better understood them, I thought there could be no danger in trying " an acre of maiden soil."

It was our custom of an evening, after our supper was over, the fire piled up with blazing oak logs, and each man had lighted his pipe and received a noggin of schnappes, after the fatigues of the day, to congregate in one room and there, after lighting a candle, one of us would read a book aloud. I had a good stock of books, though they travelled in a small compass, and as they were, for the most, by Fielding, Smollett, De Foe, Le Sage, Goldsmith, and that class of writers, they all bore reading twice, and more than twice; so that our evenings were passed very sociably. Barnes, too, who was an uneducated man, was taking instructions in writing from Thomas, and began to learn in this wild spot what they never tried to teach him in the Christian village where he first saw the light. One evening these amusements were set aside for the discussion of the subject of the cultivation of a piece of the farm. Onions were at this time commanding fabulous prices in San Francisco; and a very simple calculation proved, as distinctly as possible, *on paper*, that one acre planted with onions would realise an enormous profit, provided the onions came up. To ensure this last important point, I engineered a ditch, which was to convey water for their irrigation from our stream; and leaving the others to carry out these works, I started on foot for San Luis, where I arrived, after two days, very footsore. I procured a plough, a waggon, a yoke of strong American oxen, and a fresh supply of groceries, and I then paid a flying visit to San Francisco in a small fishing-boat, and returned to Sonoma with seeds of all kinds, a box of horse-radish roots, which came in very well afterwards with wild bull, and about 500 fine young fruit-trees. The difficulty now was to get my ox-team up to Russian River, for I knew nothing of driving oxen. However, I took lessons from an American teamster; and, as there are but two words of command, and each one, when delivered, is accompanied by a crack on the head of the ox nearest to you, I found the beasts soon recognised my voice and style of hitting. But I had several rather impetuous streams to pass, some of which were scarcely fordable, for the rain had set in; I was doubtful, therefore, as to the method to be adopted in forcing my team through these. This, my instructor informed me, could only be accomplished by " talking freely to the oxen; " and, to my demand for a specimen, he jumped on the waggon, and working himself into a state of apparent phrenzy, he stamped and swore, and beat them, and cracked his whip, and execrated them until they both broke into a round trot. I profited by his advice, and got through my gulches in safety, and I can only hope that the " freedom of speech " I indulged in was justified by the circumstances of the case.

I started alone, and as oxen travel very slowly, I was three days and a half getting to the farm. On my way I met a good-looking fellow with black beard and moustaches, who asked me in French the way to the nearest log hut. I entered into conversation with him, and found that he was a Normandy man of the name of Lebret. He had a gun, and a game bag, and gaiters on; in fact, he was a " Frenchman out shooting " all over, with nothing in his game-bag. I found that he was hard up and wanted employment, so I told him where I was going, offered him a berth, and with an " Eh bien ! " up he jumped, and after crossing Russian River, for which we were just in time, as it was much swollen, I landed my cargo and Frenchman safe and sound at the farm, which, after my temporary absence, seemed home in every sense. And it was so. The very dogs knew it for a happy place as they bounded out to bid me welcome back. Home speaks in the grip of Barnes's bony hand; in the studied polish that my rifle bears as it hangs above my bed; and home speaks in the eager faces that group around the fire and listen to my brief recital of what befel me since we parted.

*   *   *   *

I had a favourite little spot on my hunting ground that I always selected for my halt; it was a little clump of sheltered rocks, and, after poking about with my loading-rod, to turn out any rattlesnake that might be there, I would sit down and enjoy the luxury of the cool shade and a pipe. All good sportsmen agree, and with great truth, in the impropriety of smoking whilst working up to game; but, after walking a few hours in the hot sun, a pipe is a great luxury, and I was always glad to reach this cover where I could indulge my propensity without fear of tainting the surrounding atmosphere.

I have often mused, as I have sat in this little den, on the life I was leading, and reflected with regret that its charms must some day succumb to use, and that, in time, even deer hunting would pall on the taste, and the excitement of a wild life become monotonous. With health beating in every pulse, with God's best gifts strewed round him in profusion, and intellect to fashion them to use, a man acknowledges instinctively the infinite wisdom of the Creator, and feels a proportionate gratitude for His gifts.

It is easy to be grateful when one has health, strength, and freedom, and easy to flatter oneself into the belief that a life so primitive is more natural than one more civilised; but it is but the lazy gratitude of one who has nothing else to live for but himself, and who is freed, not alone from the conventionalities which a more civilised state imposes, but from all claim upon his self-denial. Freed in fact from the presence of all evils which beset man elsewhere, and tax his fortitude, his courage, and his virtue; living but for himself, with himself alone to study, he indulges in selfishness, and is happy. And this is the great foundation-stone of the charms we hear associated with a wild free life.

One night a herd of deer jumped our railings, and passing close to the hut, crossed the river at great speed, evidently under the influence of fear. We listened, and shortly afterwards heard a pack of wolves, giving tongue in the distance. The next morning the ground, which was soft, gave evidence that there had been an *estampede* the night before. Herds of deer had crossed and recrossed in every direction until they had forded the stream, when they made a clean bolt for the mountains. Not a hare was to be seen ; and for several days we had an empty larder,—living during that time on wheat cakes, for, unfortunately, we had expended all our small shot. I imagine that wolves are very uncommon in the country, from the facts of the game becoming so much excited at their presence, and that we never heard their bark again. We did not see a wolf, but their " sign " was unmistakeable. One day we observed the trail of a panther near the brook, and searched for him without success ; but Barnes bagged him next day to his own gun. He was up a tree when Barnes saw him, and came down with great rapidity on being shot through the skull. He was a heavy beast, a male, and of a tawny colour. This animal is called in the country the Californian lion.

The tiger cat is a beautiful animal, and very

ferocious for its size ; we saw two or three of these, about the size of a wild cat, and beautifully marked in the coat. I shot but one, and it was with the greatest difficulty that I could induce him to resign his life without having his skin spoilt. I was agreeably surprised, on my return one day to the hut, to find a horse, saddled and bridled, attached to our railing, and I ascertained that its owner was a country-man of mine who had been "prospecting" the surrounding country, and had been directed by March to our camp. They say we are a stiff and formal people : perhaps so ; but in the mountains, an Englishman needs no further introduction than to know a man for a countryman to place the best he has at the stranger's service. You show him the river and give him a towel : you supply him with a tin plate and spoon, and he helps himself from your smoking pot : you produce a bottle of whiskey in his honour, and after placing the tobacco cannister at his elbow, and pointing out the bundle of blankets that will form his bed, you enter into social conversation. When you part from the man the next morning, you feel quite sorry, and hope to see him again, although there is little probability of that, for these are chance meetings. It is my belief that there is an honest purpose in the hearty wring of the hand that such a stray visitor gives you as he mounts his horse to depart. Whether or no, he can't go away and say your rooms are *damp*, and your claret is *sour*, that your wife is a *fright*, and your pictures are *trash*, as people *sometimes* do in more civilised countries, after enjoying the hospitality of their friends. Our guest produced from his pocket, a number of Punch, and one of the Illustrated News—about five months old. I had had opportunities of reading these publications in a great many out-of-the-way parts of the globe, but I never expected that they would reach my log hut. But English periodicals creep in everywhere; and I remember that the first indication I received of some family news of importance was when, at a pic-nic at Mount Lebanon, I picked up a scrap of newspaper which had contained the mustard of some party who had preceded us, and casually glanced at its contents.

The rainy season was now approaching, and the heat became occasionally intense. At times the Indians would fire the surrounding plains, the long oat-straw of which would ignite for miles. The flames would advance with great rapidity, leaving everything behind them black and charred. At these times a dense smoke would hang over the atmosphere for two or three days, increasing the heat until it became insupportable. I had a thermometer with me during the whole of my stay in California, and could produce an elaborate* meteorological table; but as people say you should write as you talk, I shall dismiss the subject of the temperature of Russian River by remarking that in summer it was sometimes as warm as Hong Kong, and in the rainy season it was as cold as an average English winter. We have an officer of scientific renown in our naval service, who is selected by the Admiralty to explore the least known portions of the globe; of which parts, when he returns, he publishes an account, which would be interesting in the extreme, but, that, alas! his scientific knowledge oozes out in every line, and the reader, after hopelessly following him through a maze of figures, which are particularly addressed to, and understood only by, the Geographical Society, shuts the book in despair, and remains for life in ignorance of the habits of the Chow-chow Islanders.

The Digger Indians burn the grass to enable them to get at roots and wasps' nests; young wasps being a luxury with them. These fires have the good effect of destroying immense quantities of snakes and vermin; and one can scarcely imagine the extent to which these might multiply were they not occasionally

* Query :—(Printer's Devil.)

"burnt out." The wasps are so numerous here in summer, as to destroy with rapidity everything they attack. Fleas not only abound in the skins of every beast you kill, but even live on the ground, like little herds of wild cattle; and ants are of all shapes and sizes, and stand up savagely on their hind legs and open their mouths, if you only look at them. The wasps attack any meat that may be hanging up, and commence at once cutting out small pieces, which they carry home, and it is astonishing the quantity they will carry away with them. What they do with it when they get home, I never ascertained; but I presumed that they "jerked" it for winter use, as the Spaniards do.

It was hard work at dinner-time, to know who the meat belonged to, for these wasps used to sting on the slightest provocation; and it was the worst part of Thomas's duty to take a hare down from a peg and cut it up.

But neither ants nor fleas ever troubled our persons; the skins were always sent down to the river whilst yet warm, and the common precautions I adopted indoors insured us against all annoyance.

It now commenced to rain very heavily, but not before I had, fortunately, completed a shed, and laid in a stock of fire-wood, and had also erected an additional room for drying wet clothes, &c., and for sheltering the dogs. The first rain lasted for four days without cessation; and here again I am unable to state, scientifically, the quantity of water that fell in inches, but on the fourth day the water laid on our valley of such a depth that it just plummed the top of a pair of Cording's fishing-boots, which came up to about my knees. All the fruit trees and garden seeds were in the ground; and as we had no immediate use for our oxen, and they were up to their bellies in water, we let them run over the hills. Shortly after this the weather cleared up, and we were much distressed at missing my slot-hound. Many days elapsed before we gained any clue to his fate, until, beating up some new ground one day, I came upon what remained of the poor old fellow,—his skin and bones. He had broken away and indulged in a midnight ramble, and had evidently been attacked and overpowered by coyotes, of which two carcasses lay near him. We all felt much regret for the old fellow, for he was a good staunch dog, and had been a great favourite of my late father. We buried his remains and erected a mark to his memory; but, although I experienced the same feeling of regret that most men do when they lose a favourite and faithful hound, I shall refrain from inflicting upon the reader the doleful stanzas which are generally addressed " To my Dog," on these occasions.

January 1. For two months we had alternate rain and sunshine, and nothing of moment occurred. The farm was by this time entirely enclosed, and the *onions* with which Barnes had planted an acre, began to appear above the ground. We had also large patches of vegetables for home consumption.

When returning one day from an excursion, we found that the Indians had paid our valley a visit, and rifled our house of everything they thought valuable ; cooking utensils, blankets, clothes, and tools had disappeared,—but we had taken the precaution of depositing our powder in a secret place which they did not discover. Our rifles, and one blanket each, we had with us on our excursion. The two principal annoyances that resulted from this were, firstly, that the nights being very cold indeed now, and our house very thin, our blankets were a serious loss ; secondly, they had stolen *all our candles*. They also stole our skins ; not that I ever intended to bring these trophies away for the benefit of the public, for with the exception of the puma-skin, and some of wild cats, they were of that mild description which are only exhibited in tailors' shop-fronts, where they assume the form of gentlemen's hunting inexpressibles. The Indians, it afterwards appeared, were in the habit of annually following the course of our stream to gather the wild grapes which grew on its banks. These people will eat anything, but how they manage the wild grapes is a mystery, for these grapes never ripen, and green gooseberries give no conception of their acidity. In pursuit of these luxuries, however, they came upon our camp, and took away whatever they thought they understood the use of, but evidently departed in a great hurry. I never saw an Indian during the whole of my stay in that part of the country; but, after this robbery, had any ever come within rifle range either of my hut or March's, he would have been shot like a coyote; for once let an Indian think he can steal with impunity, he will soon attempt to murder you for the clothes on your back.

Although I had determined, after Sheldon's casualty, upon following no more bears into the bush, which is here too thick for the use of the rifle, I still hoped to kill a bear during the winter, trusting to a chance meeting under favourable circumstances; and in this respect I was gratified, inasmuch as I killed a bear to my own gun. Now, in writing from memory, one might almost be excused for a little inaccuracy in point of size and weight; and I must confess that I have an almost irresistible temptation to forget the real dimensions of the animal that surrendered life on this occasion, and, calling it simply a *bear*, leave its weight and ferocity to be conjectured from my general description of the species. In fact, it was a cub, that I once found playing by itself among some rocks. I should have liked to have taken him home alive, but although his movements were excessively infantine and playful to behold, I have no doubt that had I attempted to capture him, he would not only have bitten me until I had let him go, but would have hallooed for his parents, and brought those amiable persons to the rescue. So I shot him; and I had quite enough to do to carry him home dead, for he was very fat. I must mention here, that although we walked this country for nearly nine months, and continually alighted on the fresh "sign" of bear, with the exception of those that visited our hut at night, and the others above mentioned, our party saw but three bears, two of which were wounded, but escaped; and this is probably attributable to the fact that the bear's sense of hearing enables him to follow up his natural impulse of avoiding the hunter.

A Colt's revolver is invaluable to the deer-hunter, both for self-defence and killing wounded game. Perhaps the best praise I can award to this weapon is in saying that I have had mine for four years, during which time it has been much used and *more abused*, but at this moment it is perfect in every respect, and has never required repair.

We searched, or "prospected" the adjacent hills on many occasions, to discover if gold existed in the surface soil, but without success. It is worthy of remark, that this district of country is similar in every respect to that of the mining regions. Here, as there, is a succession of red gravelly hills, interspersed with veins of quartz, all of which have been subjected to volcanic agency that would long ago have ejected the gold from the quartz had there been any in it. But the mountain in labour here brought forth a mouse; whilst a few miles further south it has produced results of a much more satisfactory description. We, however, did discover a peculiar blue quartz, which, upon assay by fusion, was found to contain a large quantity of gold. The presence of silver in small quantities was also evident in another rock we discovered. But, with these exceptions, we found no trace of any description of metal but iron.

It was now spring, and I started alone, on foot, for San Francisco, where business required my presence. On arriving at Russian River I found the stream much swollen, but I struck a part of the river where I knew one of the hunters had a log-hut and a dug-out, or canoe. I reached the hut and found no one at home, but the dug-out was hauled up and the paddle was in it.

It was easy to launch the dug-out, which was very long and thin; so, seating myself in the stern, I was at once in the current. I need not say that I should never have dreamt of paddling myself over a swollen river in a canoe, had I not accustomed myself to them when in the Borneo rivers; but when I reached the middle of the stream I found the eddies made the dug-out so unmanageable, and the current was so much stronger than I imagined, and the water hissed and bubbled about me to such an extent that I had to keep the dug-out's head nearly straight up stream, and I began to get quite giddy and bewildered, and wished I was safe on shore. I did effect a landing, an hour afterwards, about a mile lower down the river; I had just strength enough to land, and just sense enough to feel excessively grateful for not having been carried out to sea, or, what is more probable, capsized in the eddies of the stream.

CHAPTER VIII.

———◆———

April, 1851.

It was long after dark when I arrived at Santa Rosa Valley, perfectly "knocked up." Englishmen are generally good pedestrians; but there is a great difference between walking on the level in well-made shoes, and dragging through deep sloughs and acres of thick clayey mud in heavy ill-fitting jack-boots, particularly when the boots appear unwilling to proceed in your society, and one or other of them is continually disengaging itself, as if wishing to be left behind regardless of expense.

I found that the Carillo family had left Santa Rosa, and the valley had been purchased by Americans for the purpose of cultivating grain, for which many parts of it were well adapted. The Carillos had departed, with horses, dogs, Indians, and Quilp, for the south,

144

where the wine came from, where the temperature was better adapted to their " far-niente " dispositions, and where in particular Quilp was likely to enjoy a longer lease of life than his undisguised hatred of Americans would probably have permitted had he remained much longer at the valley. As slothfulness and ignorance stepped out, intelligence and industry usurped their place, and on the rich plain the wild waving oats fell to the ruthless scythe, whilst the plough upturned the maiden soil on every side.

And so must other lands and other people of this continent succumb to the increasing wants of Anglo-Saxon man. As the red-Indian retires before the pale-face, so will inert bigotry in the new world disappear before the march of energy ; and the bounteous riches with which the Creator has strewed this portion of the globe must some day be under a rule that will admit of these benefits being extended to mankind, no longer to be closed to the world, through the petty warfares or restrictive seclusion of a people too inert to seize the advantages around them, and (with a full sense of this) too jealous to admit others to do so.

*　　　*　　　*　　　*

About five miles from Sonoma is an " embarcadero," or landing place, situated on a mud creek, which is navigable for small boats, and communicates with the bay of San Francisco. Here are three houses, which conjointly represent the town of San Luis; opposite the town some fishing-boats lay at anchor, and in one of these I bargained for a passage to San Francisco, in company with eight live bullocks, that were now lying on the strand, bound neck and heels together, moaning piteously, as if impatient to get to the butcher's and have it all over.

With the exception of the owners of the three houses, the population of San Luis was a particularly floating one, being represented for the most part by the crews of the fishing-smacks, of which there were at times a great number in port.

From the centre house there proceeded the sound of a fiddle, and, as no one could be perceived outside, it became evident that the floating population had here assembled to wile away the hours until the tide served to enable the boats to leave.

I entered the house and found it to consist of a store and drinking-shop combined; and, in virtue of its latter attraction, it was filled, as I had anticipated, by the men belonging to the boats, who, already half drunk, were tossing off champagne,* out of tin pannikins, and drinking to a speedy voyage

* As it would be inferred from this that champagne must have been cheap, I may mention that at this period the prices ranged from 2*l.* to 4*l.* the bottle, and the quality was execrable.

across the bay. The proprietor of the establishment was not only an Englishman, but he was one of those plump, rosy-cheeked, good-natured-looking fellows that attract the eye at once, and whose smile is sympathetic; he was a gentleman, that is to say, he had been educated as one, and had lived as one, and was none the less one (as I found afterwards), now that he kept a grog-shop. I shall call him Ramsey; he was one of those men who never make money, for they cannot save; so that when Ramsey left, as he did, a high and very remunerative position of trust on the Pacific coast, and came up to San Francisco with a cargo of flour, in the expectation of making a fortune; and when he determined on taking the flour up the river Sacramento, and the flour was caught in a squall in the bay and went down, Ramsey found that he had done a very foolish thing. However, all smiles and good-humour, he took the grog-shop and store at San Luis, where I found him.

Ramsey had related these adventures to me before we had been an hour acquainted; and on my presenting myself as a countryman (for there was no mistaking his Anglo-Saxon physiognomy), he had immediately relapsed into beaming smiles, and placing a bottle of champagne under each arm, he had ushered me into his little bed-room, leaving his assistant to attend to the wants of the fresh-water sailors.

Understanding from him that he had lost all his personal effects when his cargo disappeared, I was surprised to find so many evidences in his bed-room of an English establishment;—a well-browned hunting-saddle and bridle, the stalk of a whip and a pair of spurs, a double-barrelled gun and fishing-rod, with some pairs of " cords," were observable about the little pig-sty he called his room. In answer to my inquiring look, he said he had just had time to save *these only* from his wreck, and that they were pleasant things to have about one as reminiscences of old England and happy days spent in fishing and hunting there; the smile forsook his face, as it did mine, when he said this, but it soon returned again to both of us, and as we chatted away I found much to like in my new acquaintance, who was not only intelligent and well-informed, but very humorous. There was to be a ball that night at Sonoma, at the house of one Judge White, and as the boatmen had (from the effects of the champagne) delayed their departure until the next morning, I agreed to accompany Ramsey, who had been especially invited, to this festivity.

At the ball everything appeared to be conducted with great propriety ; but the company was composed of honest mechanics, who, with the best intentions, danced quadrilles on a peculiar principle, inasmuch as they cut capers to such an extent as obliged the spectator, however disinclined, to smile. In no uncomplimentary spirit I made a remark in French to Ramsey on the subject, and this being overheard and but half understood, was retaliated in the following manner.

During a pause in the dances, a small gentleman, who had overheard my remark, and who was one of the most active of the *chassez-croisez* dancers, and was a blacksmith, though apparently small for his profession, informed me audibly, with fire in his eyes, " that if I did not like the company, I might leave it, and that d—d soon." To this I could only bow my assent, and shortly afterwards, being unable to find Ramsey, I left the room, intending to wait for him at our hotel, that was close by. I had not proceeded very far, when I was suddenly attacked by the small blacksmith and three other gentlemen—blacksmiths, too, I presume ; if so, they evidently mistook myhcad for an anvil, for they so belaboured it with bludgeons and other weapons that they almost killed me, and left me for dead, before I had time to strike a blow in defence.

When I recovered my senses, I found myself alone on the grass, and I then managed to crawl to the hotel, where I found Ramsey awaiting me, quite unsuspicious of the cause of my detention. I returned with him to San Luis, and soon found that, further than having been stunned, I had not suffered any material damage. This delayed, however, my departure for San Francisco; and during this time a circumstance occurred which is characteristic of the easy state of the law in the provincial districts at this time. The house next to Ramsey's was occupied by a choleric old fellow, who also dispensed "notions." This old rascal coolly shot a man over his bar on the most trifling provocation; the man died, and the murderer was taken before Judge White (who also kept a store, by the by, and gave his ball with an eye to business); the Judge not only (good, merciful fellow!) refused to detain the prisoner, but discharged him without bail, which, he said, was not requisite; and this was all that justice ever exacted at the hands of this cold-blooded villain.

I started at last, with fair wind and tide, for San Francisco, in a small yawl, with a crew of three men, who were not only half-drunk, but were about the greatest lubbers that ever went afloat. Before we reached the mouth of the creek, they managed to run the boat on the bank, where the ebb tide soon left her high and dry.

Under these circumstances, I cannot do better than introduce a sketch of the early history of California, which, however uninteresting, must be brought in somewhere; and there is no better place, I think, for imposing it on the reader, than whilst we are waiting for the flood tide to take us off, and are spitefully pelting, out of a bag of beans, the muddy little crabs that surround our stranded bark.

It was about the middle of the sixteenth century that stories of the existence of untold wealth first inflamed the minds and excited the ardour of the Mexicans and Spaniards. The expedition of Hernando de Alarcon and Francisco de Ulloa had returned in safety to Mexico, after having visited the river Colorado, and the Pacific coast as high as 30° North. Many and wondrous were the tales these bold adventurers related of precious stones, and gold and pearls; of Amazons, and wealthy cities; so that naturally the attention of the adventurous was turned in one direction only; and the dream of the young, the ambition of the aged, was to discover this Cibola—this undeveloped El-Dorado. The Viceroy of Mexico at this period was one Mendoza, a jealous opponent of the renowned Cortes. This man was sufficiently sagacious to perceive the advantages of obtaining, if possible, possession of the reported gold regions, and fitted out an expedition in the port of Natividad, consisting of two vessels, which were placed under the command of Juan Rodriguez Cabrillo, who had with him as lieutenant Bartolomé Ferrelo.

It is no honour to the viceroy that this expedition was set on foot by him, for in those days the discovery of new lands, as is well known, conferred large benefits and rewards on the potentates under whose rule the expeditions originated; whilst the brave fellows who risked their lives in carrying out the work were not only unrewarded then, but in few instances have been considered worthy even of a *name* in the history of the countries they have discovered. It was no slight proof of courage to undertake this voyage, for it will be remembered that not only were the vessels in use of such a class that the wonder now is that they ever rode out a gale; but the impression was strong in the minds of the mariners of that day, that the world was square, and that to arrive at its limits would bring down the punishment of Heaven for their presumption, even if they did not tumble over the edge. Nor need we wonder that such a belief existed in those superstitious days. Are there not many now among the civilised and enlightened who refuse to investigate the palpable evidences of the power of animal magnetism, from the fixed belief that there should be a limit to man's inquiry into the mysteries of nature ?.

The expedition sailed, it appears, in 1542, jogging on at the rate of about ten miles a day. Cabrillo discovered in succession the southern ports of California. At some of these he touched, and found the inhabitants to consist of a half-civilised tribe of Indians, who treated him with kindness. The existence of these Indians is confirmed by later writers. Vizcaino, who visited these shores in 1602, mentions having discovered idolatrous temples on the island of Catalina.

The surveys of this expedition are not of much value to the present age, as the nautical instruments of that period were not very true; but Cabrillo's explorations none the less assisted those who came after him, who, with instruments equally defective, hit his points with tolerable accuracy, although there was generally an error in *his* latitude by observation of about a hundred miles.

Cabrillo at last worked up towards San Francisco, but the heavy surf and iron-bound coast, together with the thick fogs that hang about the bay, no doubt prevented his entering, and he resolved on returning and awaiting a more favourable season ; but anchoring for repairs in one of the harbours of the Santa Barbara Islands, the old sailor died, probably from fatigue and exposure to the damps and north-west winds.

The command of the expedition then devolved upon Ferrelo, who bravely made another attempt ; but failing in effecting a landing, he returned to Natividad, after a voyage of 283 days. Sir Francis Drake next visited California in 1579 ; Juan de Fuca in 1595, and Sebastian Vizcaino in 1602. This latter entered the bay of San Francisco, though probably he was not its discoverer, and proceeded in boats as far as where Benicia now stands.

In 1769 the settlement of Upper California was commenced by Spanish priests at San Diego, and several small expeditions followed in succession until 1776, when the Roman Catholic missionaries Palou and Cambon landed in San Francisco, and established their head-quarters in that place. The settlement at this period was known by the name of Yerba Buena, from the presence of a medicinal herb which abounded in the neighbourhood, and which was held in high estimation by the Indians. Here the missionaries erected a church and other buildings, of " adobes," or sun-dried bricks. The Mission flourished rapidly. The Indians soon learnt, under the tuition of the Padres, the advantages of cultivating the earth; and those of them that embraced the Catholic religion began to drink rum, and value beads, as is usual with converted savage tribes. Mexican settlers also made their appearance, and the richest portions of the country were soon appropriated by them. Gradually cattle and sheep were introduced, which in their wild state increased rapidly without much trouble to their owners, who, having nothing to do but to kill their meat and eat it, basked in the sun like lazy dogs as they were, and thought themselves the happiest of men;—and it is difficult for any one to prove they were not.

By the year 1831, the number of Christian baptisms amounted to about 7000. After this period, the Indians, from some cause or other, perhaps from a scarcity of rum, altered their minds on the subject; and although a fresh supply of priests arrived, the number of converts rapidly decreased, so much so that in the eight years preceding the discovery of gold, only 400 savages were caught and converted. And if one may judge from the specimens of converted Indians that are to be found here and there in California at the present date, one has no reason to regret that the efforts of the priests were unattended with success; for, however we may deplore the abject misery and degradation of the aboriginal tribes, it is not by the mummery of a form that such souls can be redeemed, or such unhappy natures be remodeled.   On the contrary, their small glimpses of civilisation offer to their view both virtues and vices equally unknown before ; then, left untrammeled to choose between the two, we see the baptised savage follow his impulses until he sinks so low in the scale of men, that his original degradation stands out almost as virtue beside him.

A holy task is that of the missionary, and bravely carried out.   Let him still strive to reclaim the savage, and bring his soul to God ; but yet take heed that the work be finished, for I have seen in my day converted tribes that were a mockery on all that sanctifies the missionary work, and had better, one would think, have eaten each other's bodies in primeval irresponsibility, than, having been only *half* awakened to a sense of right, but fully so to a knowledge of all that is wrong, have been left to grovel in the vices that most debase humanity.   How much more care does it not require to avert the steps of the *converted savage* from crime, than that of others of your flock !—is he not naturally more debased, more prone to adopt the broad and easy path that ever lies plain and palpably before him ? Can you take a young tiger from the jungle, and having caged him, soften his natural propensities easily? You can do so only by unceasing watchfulness and coercion; cease these, and your tiger is a tiger again, as nature asserts her sway. Somewhat so it is with the savage you allure from the freedom of his hunting-ground; you show him the advantages of domestic life, and the means of applying to his benefit the soil around him; you adapt to his comprehension the simple outlines of religion, by pointing out to him that, to live in brotherhood and amity is good (and beneficial); that to wage war and hate and eat one's enemy is bad (and detrimental); that a good Supreme Being, who can reward or punish, has said so, and that the evidence of this Supreme Being reigns, as even a savage can see, in all around. The simple aborigine accords you his belief; regretfully, perhaps, he leaves his wild prairie and the baked heads of his enemies, and will worship the " Great Spirit," whose presence the poetry of his nature enables him to understand; sooner or later you baptise him, and you have your savage in the first stage of Christianity. But now you have a savage nature on your hand; you have implanted innocently what with his impulses may grow to avarice if you leave him to himself; for if he cultivates the land among the *civilised* he will cheat—

if cheat, wrangle—if wrangle, murder ; for the steps to crime are rapid 'in such a constitution ; but if he drinks, the savage ever becomes too brutalised for reclamation.

In what does this fault lie ?   Not so much that the man is so constituted that he must thus err, but that, like the tiger I have used for illustration, his propensities must be ever *watched* and *guided*.   The converted savage is never so alienated from his natural impulses that he can be left ;—yet he *is* left.

If there is fault in this, it is not, I know, on the part of those who *work ;* but to those who direct these things it might be said that it is better to convert a few, and *in reality increase Christ's fold*, than sign a million with His holy symbol, yet bring their souls no nearer heaven.   Yet how fruitlessly one may argue.   To whom is the reproach, that while we *may* add our mite to aid the propagation of the Gospel abroad, we dare not relieve gaunt misery in the street at home, for fear of encouraging systematic mendicity ; as if, forsooth, the blame of this belonged by right alone to those who practised it.

There are black missionaries who work as faithfully as white, and it is a startling fact to find that many of these, leaving their coloured brethren at home to the care of our white missionaries, are in our midst, attempting to alleviate, by God's help, the misery and ignorance that exist in our great towns; and if the most festering wounds have the first claim upon the surgeon's skill, the place of these black missionaries is here, God knows!

Why shall it still be said, and said again of us who are not loth to *relieve*, that our aims are misdirected from want of judgment and from ill-government? And why are the talents and energies of so many churchmen, whose beck and nod the charitable, to a great extent, obey, still turned to the Propagation of the Gospel abroad, when it requires but the opening of a proper channel at home to rid us of this great reproach?

We may condemn the love of political power, that in the main actuated the Jesuits in their efforts to propagate their faith; but how much has not the love of power, equally reprehensible, been a bar to the cure of our evils at home? Would the young and energetic of our young clergy seek a field abroad in which to work, with little reward and great privation, if the field at home was open to them?

*   *   *   *

About the year 1845, some Americans began to congregate at Yerba Buena, and these increased so rapidly, that San Francisco was in fact an American settlement before California became a territory of the United States.

During the war that broke out between the United States and Mexico in 1846, the settlement appears to have increased in population and prosperity, although the exportation of hides never seems at any time to have been of much importance. In 1847, the population of San Francisco amounted to eight hundred, and everything gave promise that the country would soon be sought for its agricultural advantages ; the attention of the Californian settlers was directed towards the supposed mineral wealth of the country, but gold was the last metal thought of. Quicksilver had already been found and worked at San Jose ; and the reported existence of veins of copper, silver, coal, and limestone, caused a feverish excitement to disturb this small community.

The first discovery of gold was made in December, 1847, when some of the labourers employed at Sutter's Mill, near Sacramento, discovered some flakes whilst constructing a ditch ; ample evidence soon existed of the truth of the first reports, and the whole population flocked to the gold fields, and shortly afterwards the country became the property of the United States. Events now followed one another with great rapidity :

adventurers poured in from all quarters of the globe, and ships arrived in harbour freighted with merchandise which realised tremendous profits.

The rainy season of California commences about November, and the winter of 1849 was more than ordinarily wet. It is said that nine inches of water fell on the night of the 6th of November; the whole town, which had now become important in extent, was a perfect quagmire; all rubbish and hard materials that could be procured were thrown into the streets to form a pathway, but to no purpose, for owing to the peculiar soil of the place, the mud was unfathomable. The streets were impassable to mules, for there were mud-holes large enough to drown them; in those streets which had been connected by means of a pathway of bales of damaged merchandise, it was necessary to exercise great caution in crossing, for one false step would precipitate the unwary passenger into a slough on either side, in which he stood a chance of meeting a muddy grave.

The amount of rain that fell in this winter was undoubtedly so great, that it is much to be regretted no careful record was kept, by some of those who now so eloquently narrate their adventures in connection with it.

The first of the conflagrations for which San

Francisco has become so famous, occurred in December, 1849. By this, fifty houses and an immense quantity of merchandise were destroyed. Another occurred a month afterwards, causing an almost equal amount of damage.

The great fire of the fourth of May, 1850, commenced at four in the morning, in a drinking-house, and spreading with great rapidity, was not arrested until it had consumed three hundred houses, and about a million sterling of property.

These were hard blows for the young city, but nothing daunted, the citizens renewed their exertions, and in a few weeks the burnt district was again covered with buildings. Every effort was now made to secure the city against future similar calamities; many brick houses were erected, fire companies on a large scale were organised, and reservoirs for water were constructed in different parts of the town. But on the 14th of June, fate again was relentless, and a fourth conflagration, aided by a high wind, razed three hundred houses to the ground, and scattered three million dollars of property to the winds. It was whilst this fire was raging that (as the reader may remember) I arrived at San Francisco; so here ends my digest of the early history of this brave young city, and as the flood-tide is coming in, I take a parting shot at a little crab that has not taken his eyes off me since we arrived, and wonders, I suppose, why I don't pelt one of my own size, and gliding off our mud bank, we make sail for San Francisco.

CHAPTER IX.

April, 1851.

AT daylight the next morning we found ourselves among the shipping that lay moored in crowds in front of San Francisco. Whilst threading our way to the wharf, we narrowly escaped being swamped by one of the Stockton river steamboats, which, in fact, did graze our stern. The Yankee freshwater skippers of those days expected everything to get out of their way, regardless of any difficulties that might prevent a small boat doing so; but one of these go-ahead commanders received, to my knowledge, a check. A fisherman of the bay had his smack damaged, and his trawling apparatus unnecessarily carried away by one of the river boats. His application to the captain for compensation was met with the remark, that the next time he got in the way he would swamp him. But might did not so easily triumph over right,

164

and for this reason. The small river-boats are very low in the hull, and as the steering apparatus leads forward, the helmsman stands prominently (under a booby hatch) near the bow of the boat. The old smack, as usual, was bobbing about with her trawls and lines out, when down comes the steamboat one day, the fishing-boat evidently directly in her course, and showing no disposition to move. " D—n that old crab-catcher ! " said the Captain. " I'll give him a close shave this time." But the " old crab-catcher," standing up in his boat, levelled a long wicked-looking Kentucky rifle, and " drew a bead " on the Captain, who, having taken the helm, formed a splendid target. Upon this, that brave sailor thought better of it, and not only dispensed with the close shave, but " concluded " to allow the small smack to bob about in peace from that time forth.

On landing at San Francisco, I found so many changes on every side, that my knowledge of locality was at fault ; wharves extended on all sides into the sea, and the spot where I last had landed was scarcely recognisable, it was now so far inland ; the steam-paddy had worked incessantly, and the front of the town still advanced into the bay.

The winter had been (compared with that of 1849) a dry one, and some of the streets having been graded

and planked, the town was under the worst circumstances navigable for jack-boots.

What first struck me, among the many changes of
a few months, was that the inhabitants generally were
less eccentric in dress. When first I arrived, the
people were most capricious in this respect ; they
wore, in fact, whatever pleased them, long hair and
beards included; sobered down by circumstances,
however, they had now quietly relapsed into the
habits of ordinary mortals.

Places of rational amusement had sprung up, and
replaced in a great measure the gambling saloons,
whose fortunes were rather on the wane from over
competition. There were clubs, reading-rooms, and
a small theatre, called the Dramatic Museum. This
last was sadly in want of actors, and as my time hung
very heavily on my hands (I was awaiting the arrival
of a vessel from England) I gave way to a vicious
propensity that had long been my bane, and joined
the company as a volunteer. For about a month,
under an assumed name, I nightly " Used Up " and
" Jeremy Diddlered " my Californian audiences, who
never having fortunately seen Charles Matthews, did
not, therefore, stone me to death for my presump-
tuous attempts to personate that unrivalled actor's
characters.

I became, at last, so used to seeing my "last appearance but one" displayed on the advertising posters, that I began to associate myself with the profession altogether, and to believe my name *was* Warren; and what with the excitement of acting in leading parts, and the pleasant parties, and pic-nics, with our troupe, I forgot all about Russian River Farm, and became a very slave to the buskin.

The dreadful experience of the place had made people so nervous respecting fire, that the sound of the fire-bell would cause every man to rush to his house, and get ready for the defence of his property; and as small fires on the outskirts of the town were of continual occurrence, there was scarcely a night but the deep-toned bell would keep the citizens on the alert. On these occasions the theatre would be deserted rapidly, whilst every other man would vociferate fire, but almost immediately the leading columns would return, with cries of "all over!" and "all out!" and the theatre would refill, and the performances proceed, until the "fire-bell" took them off again, which occasionally it would in ten minutes.

The market at this time was so overstocked with merchandise, that goods sold at auction at less than cost-price. Ready-made clothing, in particular, was cheaper in San Francisco than it was in New York or

London.   So that the storehouses being everywhere crammed with goods, great depression in trade existed. The city of San Francisco at this time was in debt, about a million of dollars, and the Treasury being empty, scrip was issued bearing the ruinous interest of thirty-six per cent. per annum.   But this state of affairs was remedied by funding the debt, and issuing bonds payable in twenty years, bearing interest at ten per cent.   The citizens cooperated in this movement, and submitted to a heavy tax, and thus, in spite of repeated conflagrations following on a state of apparently hopeless bankruptcy, the energy of the San Franciscans not only enabled the municipality to redeem annually a portion of their bonds, but placed the credit of the city on a firm and secure basis.

There were seven or eight churches already in San Francisco, all of different denominations—these were well attended on Sundays, but the price of pews was very exorbitant, reaching as high, sometimes, as ten pounds a month.   Some of these churches were built entirely in a spirit of speculation, and on asking an acquaintance once what security he had for some money he had lent, he told me, so many shares in —— Church ; and the same building was afterwards sold, I think, by auction, to satisfy its creditors.   Now that ladies begin to flock into California so rapidly, the churches are crammed to overflowing on a Sunday. The Americans are rather strict observers of congregational worship, which has this drawback, however, that it here imposes the necessity of so many becoming hypocrites on the Sabbath, for as regards the amount of religious feeling that exists at this time, one can neither judge of it by the attendance or the absence of the people from public worship. But I will say this for them, that as a nation they are most charitable, and that they are true friends to one another in adversity ; *once* your friend, the American will share all he has with you, and risk his life in defence of your honour and name—more, he will not even permit merited censure to be passed upon you in his presence, and however suspicious of others worldly contact may have made him, he will repose his confidence in you like a child. And so common are these friendships, that the true generosity which cements them forms a prominent feature of the American character; but whether it springs from deep religious feeling or not is a question I do not care to argue. A great portion of the working-classes of America are Methodists, or of somewhat similar persuasions ; they have their camp-meetings, read their Bible very generally, are given to psalm-singing, and have the appearance of being a religious people.

I attended one of these camp-meetings. My old friend of the English Barque, who wished to " rip up the cook," was officiating with " tears in his eyes." There was a great deal of excited praying, but the greater proportion of the people seemed to have come out for any purpose but that of worship—in fact, the scene was very lively, and if it had not been for the weeping priest, it would have been a merry pic-nic.

*   *   *   *

There are now seven daily papers at San Francisco, and each mining town of importance in the country publishes its weekly sheet. If the Americans were not thirsty people for news, warm party politicians, and all able to read, so great a number of periodicals could never be supported.

There is an independence about American journalism in strict accordance with the character of the institutions of the country, but which, in my opinion, detracts greatly from the value of the press. As, for instance, many journals of wide circulation, conducted by men of ability, enforce injudicious opinions that not only closely affect the vital interests of the state, but, to a great extent, the passions of the people. For this reason the American press has not so much weight with the highest class of Americans, and there is no leading journal of sufficient influence to direct and *admonish* them ; or which, from its impartiality and justness, can give a healthy tone to the thousands of minnows that follow in its track—none, in fact, that occupies the position of the " Times " with us.

The Americans are prone to throw in our teeth that we are led by the " Times," and form no opinion for ourselves ; but they forget that our faith in the practical essays of that journal is not the result of a blind adherence to custom, but of the confidence that, among the rational, will ever cling to opinions that are seldom proved, under the strongest test, to be fallacious. *Socially*, the " Times " is our expounder and monitor, and if, in this respect, it leads us, it leads us by conviction, as we should be led, and when you hear a man say that " he doesn't care what the ' Times ' says on this or that subject," he is generally one not open to conviction, or not sufficiently noble to surrender to it his own false impressions. In political matters the " Times " may be strategical, as great statesmen have been.

The press of England has not hitherto been widely disseminated among the working classes (fault we will say of their narrow means and education) nor were it so, would they, as in America, be so influenced politically by its tone ; but that *which is* disseminated either takes its tone from the " Times," so far as to echo weekly the strictures which that journal passes on our *home abuses*, or otherwise is conducted in the same spirit. Therefore there is an unanimity of opinion in the English press, and as its expositions are by no means flattering, as a general rule, to the public, and meet no contradiction, we may presume, from that fact alone, that the principles it inculcates on these matters are sound. Putting aside the slave question, the great proportion of the American press by no means devotes itself to the exposure of abuses : in the first place, the Americans are not fond of having their faults pointed out, and an editor is naturally anxious to place before his readers only what is palatable. Therefore the press declines to admonish, and following no just and truthful leader, each provincial journal disseminates its own doctrine, whatever that may be ; and thus, in a country where all read, the press exercises its power to excite the passions, but seldom to control them. For instance, at the time I write the press of California upholds strongly the doctrine of forcible annexation ; some of these journals inform the public (many of whom, by the way, are ripe for novel enterprise) that the Sandwich Islands *must* become subject to the United States ; whilst the more ambitious point to Mexico on one side, and British

Oregon on the other—undecided only, which first should bow to American rule. The higher classes, it will be said, disregard these "fillibustering" doctrines; but of the 200,000 souls in California how large a proportion does not foster them until a spirit is diffused that can never be countenanced even by the warmest admirers of the "Munro Doctrine."

For although one may admit it to be probable that in time the American people will add to their dominions the Sandwich Islands and the sickly independencies of South America, they will do so, it is to be hoped, only as becomes a great nation, and not through piracy or intimidation. In fact, to sum up, I think a great part of the press of the United States studies the foibles of the people instead of correcting them, when they most need correction, which leads to this result, that the Americans hear of their faults through the press of other countries, and attribute those strictures to a feeling of injustice and envy.

An American gentleman of great intelligence assured me that the good feeling which now exists (and I trust ever will) between the two countries, would have been induced long previous had the "Times" (I use his own expression) been *less silent* on the subject of America.

"What," he asked, "did your leading journal ever

say *in our favour* fifteen years ago, when this country was making the most unexampled strides towards prosperity? Were we ever written of but with an open allusion to the Pennsylvanian debt? Was anything connected with us thought worthy of record but our steam-boat explosions and Lynch law?"

There is great truth in this—the press of Europe *has* treated America until latterly with silence if not contempt, and it is no wonder that the Americans, who are the first to feel a slight, should retain some bitterness on this score.

But this has passed away, the superficial travels of prejudiced Englishmen (and women) no longer regulate our judgment of this country, which indeed, even if their views were correct, has long outgrown, in its rapid prosperity, the features they depicted.

The American newspapers are conducted with talent, and warmly encourage and keep alive the spirit of energy and progress, from which the country's greatness springs; their moral tone generally is good, and the amount of useful information they disseminate renders them of great value to the greater proportion of readers; but it is to be deplored that so many are connected with the press, whose feelings prompt them to keep alive a jealousy and hatred of the mother country. The best of us need at times to have the scales removed from our eyes, and the fallacies we hug so stubbornly must be made to fall before conviction. Therefore, with so large a mass of readers of the lower class dependent almost on the press for information ; among a people of warm blood and quick impulses, but a people, whom it is as easy to mould to think calmly and dispassionately as to inflame and excite until the judgment falls before the power of doctrines flattering to national vanity ; is it not to be lamented that that portion of the press to which the bone and sinew of the country looks naturally for guidance and advice, should in few instances be directed by a wise and sound policy, principally from the absence of leading journals sufficiently courageous to *chastise ?*

*　　　　*　　　　*　　　　*

There is nothing more pleasant than to revert to the good traits of a country, particularly after having recorded what in one's judgment appears an infirmity. I allude therefore with pleasure to the educational system of the Americans, honourable as it is to the good feeling of the country, although it must be re-remembered I am speaking of the Americans as *colonists*. The base of the American system of education is simply to educate everybody, and to develope the natural faculties ; thus the way is opened to all to raise themselves by assiduity and talent to independence and mayhap renown. How is it that great and wise countries in the matter of education discuss so much and so idly the manner of the doing ; leaving the patient unrelieved whilst the wise doctors disagree ? Or how is it that it requires a Bishop and his staff to plant a school in certain colonies, and why is so much fuss made about the matter when the Bishop comes home and informs the public, as bishops always do at some meeting or other, of the glorious success that has attended his labours, and how he has called together twenty-five small Carribean children in a wooden building forty feet by twelve, as if a sacrifice had been offered up to Heaven, the incense of which should diffuse itself gratefully over the whole land ?

Now if one turns to the accounts of San Francisco in 1848, they will be found to convey a tolerably truthful account of the society of that then city of tents. It was scarcely a fortuitous commencement for a colony, that its earlier inhabitants were for the most part maddened to excess by the easy acquisition of wealth ; and that under the influence of an all-absorbing pursuit (such as few of us, I venture to say, could under such circumstances entirely have resisted); the worst passions were exercised without control, and

selfishness, as is natural, reigned paramount; what idea
of the intellectual or moral cultivation of the young
would be expected to intrude itself on the thoughts
of a community occupied solely in the pursuit of
selfish gratifications?

Yet in *this* year a public school was opened in San
Francisco supported by the people, and this school was
shortly placed in the charge of an intelligent clergyman.
What better illustration can we find in proof that
the Americans stand out in strong colours on this
point? what better proof that they are good colonists,
when under such adverse circumstances, in the midst
of riot, dissipation, and ungodliness, the first and only
approach to a sense of responsibility was shown in a
fostering care of the young and helpless children *not
their own*.

There were no bishops here, no staff, nor was the
school organised by reverend men; it owed its foundation and support to the one sense of duty that no
circumstances could erase from the American mind;
and in this earnest desire to open to all the path to
future prosperity, the grand principle of equality is
better carried out than by any other feature of the
people of America. If this feeling exists, as I believe
throughout the United States, what stronger foundation-stone, speaking in a worldly point of view, can

a people naturally intelligent lay down as a basis for increased prosperity? for, putting aside religion, with this education is inculcated self-reliance; self-reliance in a nation leads to mutual support and unity, and this in colonists overcomes difficulties apparently insurmountable, as ants united move the dead body of a lizard from the doorway of their home, or sailors par-buckle a gun up some apparently impracticable mountain.

The proportion of children in California was naturally small as compared with the population, yet I find that in 1853 the City of San Francisco expended the monthly sum of seven hundred and fifty pounds on its schools, in which were educated fourteen hundred children; and excellent institutions now exist there, also, for the relief of orphans and the sick and destitute. It will be remembered that the city is already deeply in debt, and that the population are averse to taxes, which render the maintenance of these establishments a burden.

*   *   *   *

The book stores of San Francisco drive a thriving trade after the arrival of each mail, but the importations consist for the most part of novels, which are greedily bought up, and find a ready sale in the mining regions.

Apparently, every Californian can read, and judging from the fact that the mails take an average of fifty thousand letters to the United States every fortnight, we may presume that there are few among them that cannot write.

CHAPTER X.

———•———

May, 1851.

THE Central Wharf of San Francisco, which is nearly
a mile in length, is for some distance occupied on
either side by Jew slopsellers; and, as these indefa-
tigable gentlemen insist all over the world upon ex-
posing their wares outside their shops, the first
glance down Central Wharf impresses you with the
idea that the inhabitants of the district have hung
their clothes out to dry after a shower of rain.
Scattered among the Jew shops are markets for
vegetables and poultry, fishmongers, candy-sellers,
(the Long Wharfers are very fond of sugar-
plums), gambling-houses of the worst repute, and
drinking-shops innumerable. Being narrow and
crowded, and full of loaded drays, drunken sailors,
empty packing-cases, run-away horses, rotten cabbages, excited steam-boat runners, stinking fish,

180

Chinese porters, gaping strangers, and large holes in the planks, through which you may perceive the water, it is best to be careful in walking down Long Wharf, and to turn neither to the right nor to the left.

This busy street terminates at the city front; and from thence the wharf, which extends for half a mile into the sea, is flanked on either side by ships discharging their cargoes with great order and rapidity.

Here may be seen a fleet of those clippers to which the Californian trade gave rise. The " Queen of the Clippers " is one of the finest and largest of these ships, and is a beautiful model; she is extremely sharp at either end, and, " bows on," she has the appearance of a wedge. Her accommodations are as perfect as those of a first-class ocean steamer, and are as handsomely decorated; and, as it is worthy of remark that great attention has been paid to the comfort of the crew, the sooner some of our shipowners copy that part of her construction the better. Nor should they overlook any longer that the Americans have long economised in ship labour very materially by the use of patent blocks, patent trusses, and more particularly in patent steering-gear.

It gives cause for reflection to observe how on board these mammoth clippers, one man, comfortably protected from the weather by a wheel-house, can steer the ship with ease in any weather, and to recall recollections of big English ships beating up against the monsoon, with three and even four men at the helm, tugging to get it up, or pulley-hauling to get it down, exposed on the deck in heavy sou'-westers and painted canvass frocks, while their faces are cut to pieces by the salt spray that the wind sends drifting along the deck.   Yet comparatively few of our merchant vessel owners have availed themselves of these improvements.   Scotland, as far as we are concerned, has most distinguished herself in the production of clippers, and the small class, similar to the " Marco Polo " and " Stornaway " stand first as specimens of mercantile naval architecture.

The building of clippers, if not originated by, was encouraged by the discovery of gold in California, for the valuable market that was so shortly afterwards opened to the United States afforded a field for the employment of ships that could perform a journey round the Horn in a space of time that would enable them to land a cargo, not only clean and in good order, but with a certain degree of regularity as regarded time.   The ships that have sailed from English ports for San Francisco have been selected from a particularly inferior class of tubs, principally from the erroneous supposition that anything was good enough for the diggings. Then observe the mistake ! The expensive dashing clipper leaves New York, and, after a three months' passage, lands her cargo clean and dry in San Francisco (where the sale of packages depends very much on their outward as well as internal appearance) ; the English ship, which false economy has picked from about the worst in dock, after a passage of from eight to ten months, arrives in San Francisco, with *her* cargo. The market has not only gone by for the articles she brings, but these, from long confinement, and her unseaworthy qualities, are landed in such an unprepossessing state as to be almost unsaleable. Nor is this all—the clipper ship having discharged, sails for China, and takes home the first teas at a high rate of freight, discharges at London, and returns again to New York, full ; having accomplished a rapid voyage round the world, and, in all probability, cleared a large portion of her first cost in her first voyage. But our English clunbungy can find no cargo to take home from San Francisco, there being no export ; she knows better than to present herself in China as a candidate for teas, there is little chance of her getting guano, so she either goes home empty at a great expense, or, as is more often the case, is knocked down by auction for less than her value, and is converted into a floating store-ship.*

It was said, I remember, when these clippers first attracted attention, and before Australia had been found to be auriferous, that we had no field for the employment of such vessels, and that our own "A 1 for thirteen-year" ships were better adapted for our trade; that they were stronger and more *lasting*. Where we enjoy a monopoly of ship-transport, as for many years in some places we have done, the argument of "let well alone" is excellently prudent.

That our vessels are strong no one will deny who ever saw a teak-built ship with her heavy beams and prodigious wooden knees; that they are *lasting* follows as a matter of course, but this very qualification is at this moment our drawback to improvement. We are something like a man who has determined not to get a suit of clothes adapted for the dog-days until he has worn out his old winter garments, and has been unfortunate enough to have had these made of that imperishable article known as corduroy.

It is plain enough that we shall have comparatively few clipper ships until our enormous mercantile navy is worn out; and all we have now to regret is the stubbornness of that heart of oak

---

* This fact alone proves the truth of my remarks.

whose durability we have been wont to laud in speech and song. In the meantime, unless Aberdeen and other ports work cheerily, the Californian clippers will bid for the carriage of the teas, and take the bread literally from between our teeth; and, what is still more galling, the Yankee clippers will take our Australian trade, if they have not already done so. We have a bold competitor on the waters now, and I regret to see that almost at the moment that the projected Panama and Sydney steam-line is withdrawn for want of *government support*, measures are being taken by the American government to connect San Francisco and China, and thus complete the first steam communication round the world; whilst the " Sovereign of the Seas " and " Golden Age " are conveying our emigrants from Liverpool to Australia. On the other hand, the spirit of speculation in building clipper ships in America has been so far overdone as to cause many of them to be too hastily "run up," and a few of these have arrived in San Francisco, and in London, much strained and with damaged cargoes.

*   *   *   *

The Chinese have emigrated to California in great numbers. Those in San Francisco are mostly engaged in mercantile pursuits, and supply their countrymen at the mines with necessaries. There has been great outcry in the gold regions here respecting the rapidly-increasing numbers of the Chinese miners, and it was proposed forcibly to stop their immigration; it was argued, rather dog-in-the-mangerly, that they collected vast quantities of gold from the soil that of right belonged to the Americans only, and that they carried their gold-dust to their own country to spend. The last objection had some justice in it, for undoubtedly it is contrary to the spirit of a young colony to encourage the immigration of a class of people who bring their own rice with them, and impoverish the auriferous soil without leaving a "*pice*" behind them for the permanent improvement of the country.

I believe there are few men who have been thrown much among the Chinese who believe that many honest ones can be found among them; old Whampoa of Singapore, who gives champagne dinners in a most orthodox manner, may be one; but I confess, for my part, that from the Emperor down to the fellow in the blue shirt who begs in Piccadilly, and looks as if butter wouldn't melt in his mouth, I don't believe in them. They are a people whose natural propensities lead them to cheat, and whose natural cunning aids this object most materially.

A short time ago it was discovered that a clique existed in San Francisco composed of a few of the wealthiest Chinese, and that these self-constituted mandarins exercised so much influence over the Chinese population of the country as to subject them to fines and bastinado, and they even went to the length of shipping some of them back to their own country; this, however, having been brought to light by the police, was temporarily checked, as these punishments were applied only for the purpose of extortion.

The Chinese themselves are so used to this kind of despotic rule that they made no effort to resist it even when it was assumed by those not in authority; but they behaved better under the infliction of fines than they would otherwise have done, and indeed I am puzzled to know what such a race would become, with their natural cunning, under a freer government than that they enjoy.

    *   *   *   *

On the 3rd of May, at eleven in the evening, the fire-bell again startled us; but on this occasion the first glance at the lurid glare and heavy mass of smoke that rolled towards the bay evidenced that the fire had already a firm grip on the city. The wind was unusually high, and the flames spread in a broad sheet over the town. All efforts to arrest them were useless ; houses were blown up and torn down in attempts to cut off communication ; but the engines were driven back step by step, while some of the brave firemen fell victims to their determined opposition. As the wind increased to a gale, the fire became beyond control; the brick buildings in Montgomery Street crumbled before it ; and before it was arrested, over one thousand houses, many of which were filled with merchandise, were left in ashes. Many lives were lost, and the amount of property destroyed was estimated at two millions and a half sterling.

No conception can be formed of the grandeur of the scene ; for at one time the burning district was covered by one vast sheet of flame that extended half a mile in length. But when the excitement of such a night as this has passed by, one scarcely can recall the scene. The memory is confused in the recollection of the shouts of the excited populace—the crash of falling timbers—the yells of the burnt and injured—the clank of the fire-brakes—the hoarse orders delivered through speaking-trumpets—maddened horses released from burning livery-stables plunging through the streets—helpless patients being carried from some hospital, and dying on the spot, as the swaying crowd, forced back by the flames, tramples all before it—explosions of houses blown up by gunpowder—

showers of burning splinters that fall around on every side—the thunder of brick buildings as they fall into a heap of ruin—and the blinding glare of ignited spirits. Amidst heat that scorches, let you go where you will—smoke that strikes the eyes as if they had been pricked by needles—water that, thrown off the heated walls, falls on you in a shower of scalding steam—you throw your coat away and help to work the engine-brakes, as calls are made for more men.

At daylight you plod home, half-blind, half-drowned, half-scorched, half-stunned, and quite bewildered ; and from that time you never care to recall one half of the horrors you have witnessed on the night of the conflagration of the 3rd of May.

The Dramatic Museum was "burnt out" on this occasion ; and about the same time the ship I had awaited arrived. I had expected to receive an iron house in her, but as this tenement (which I had taken great pains to have constructed in England) was landed in the shape of several bundles of bent and rusty iron plates, and irrecognisable rotten planks, I deserted the property, and allowed the owners of the wharf to throw it overboard, which they eventually did after six months' reflection.

Iron houses under most circumstances are a failure, and I write from experience in the matter. I have sat in churches made of iron, and have been glad to get out of them for that reason. I have thrown down my billiard-cue in disgust in iron club-houses, have paid my bill incontinently and left iron hotels, and have lived in misery in an iron shooting-box of my own, which was supposed to be *very complete*.

I could live comfortably at all times in my little log hut at the " farm," but never could I endure myself inside my iron house. When the sun shone it was too hot ; as night advanced it cooled too suddenly, and at daylight I shivered. When it was too warm the hot iron, with its anti-corrosive paint, emitted a sickening smell; and when the rain came down on the roof it sounded like a shower of small shot.* I lined it with wood throughout, that is to say, I built a *wooden house* inside my iron one, and then it was only bearable. But it would have been cheaper, it seemed to me, to have built the wooden house first, and then have put the iron on if it was wanted, which it was not.

In this age, when so many of our countrymen are emigrating, it becomes almost the duty of a traveller to recount any experience that may tend to the benefit of those who go after him ; and therefore I trust that

* The intelligent reader will observe that this was not the same house that was thrown overboard.

in remarks similar to the foregoing, which may or may not affect a peculiar branch of trade, I may be exonerated from any other intention than that of benefiting others by my experience. I have seen so many metal and wooden houses thrown away (I have seen in one heap of rubbish the value of ten thousand pounds), that I would recommend to the emigrant of moderate means not to purchase either the one or the other. If new gold fields are discovered, as most probably they will be, and reports are rife of house room commanding enormous prices there, never for all that let him take his shell out, snail-like, on his back ; let him take the money that would buy the house— the cash will be the scarcest article there, and will find him house-room and a profit too. Perhaps nowhere has my argument been better proved than in California. Large numbers of iron houses were shipped to that country when first reports arrived of the scarcity of building materials. Had they been capable of resisting fire they would perhaps have been less generally condemned, but of those that were erected, not only did the thin corrugated houses first expand and then collapse, and tumble down with astonishing rapidity before the flames, but in the fire I have just recorded the American iron house of Taeffe and M'Cahill, of which the plates were nearly an inch in thickness, and the castings of apparently unnecessary weight, collapsed like a preserved-meat can, and destroyed six persons, who, believing it to be fire-proof, remained inside. And, in connection with this subject, it is worthy of mention that when these houses arrived in California there was no one to be found who could put them together; not but that the method is very simple, but simple things, as we all know, present great difficulties at times in their solution.

A friend of mine employed a man for a long time at four pounds a day, merely to superintend the erection of an iron hotel; it was completed at last, and, although it had a somewhat lopsided appearance it looked pretty well under the influence of light-green paint; but the fire came and it "caved in," as the Americans say.

This discussion on iron buildings would have found no place here, had not these cheerless tenements been connected with a speculation into which I was at this time induced to enter: nor would the speculation have been alluded to, particularly as it turned out a failure, were it not again inseparably connected with a peculiar feature of the country.

It appeared that the state was looking about at this time for a site on which to erect a capital, where,

free from the busy hum of men, the representatives of
the people might meet and do their country's work.
Upon the condition that General Vallejo would expend
a large amount in the erection of public buildings, a
part of this gentleman's property was selected by the
then Governor as the " seat of government," and upon
that, a few scrubby-looking hills that bordered on
the bay, were surveyed and staked off, and there was
your town of " Vallejo."

About this time a store-ship, laden with iron houses,
belonging to a friend of mine, sunk at her moorings
during a heavy gale.   When raised she was so full of
mud, clay, and small crabs that there was no possibility of rendering her cargo fit for sale at San
Francisco.   The bright idea occurred to me of landing
these muddy materials at Vallejo, and, after allowing
the tide to clean them, to convert them to some use
in assisting to erect this capital that was to be " made
to order."   Landing my cargo on Vallejo beach at
low water mark, Canute-like, I ordered the tide to
complete the very dirty work I had set before it,
which it did, and, to finish the story here, in the
course of six months I erected a very handsome hotel
out of the materials.   I felt rather pleased when it
was finished, and painted, and handsomely furnished,
to think what a butterfly I had turned out of the

very dirty grub I had found in the hold of the old hulk. But the moral of the story lies in the fact that at this juncture the government altered their minds relative to the site of the capital, and selected Benicia in preference.

The city " made to order " was then pulled down and sold for old materials, to the great delight, as may be imagined, of myself and the other speculators who had worked so assiduously to raise it, and who had received no compensation. It is quite like the story of the Enchanted City, that was up one day and down the next; but somehow I don't find so much pleasure in recalling the history of Vallejo as I did as a boy in reading the fairy tale.

The hills of Vallejo are destitute of game, but abound in coyotes, who lead a predatory life, not altogether, I suspect, free from care or anxiety, as, excepting in the calving season, they are dependent for food on the chance carcase of some poor mired bull or over-driven mule; and, as these casualties are not of very frequent occurrence, I feel satisfied that hunger and the coyote know each other. And indeed he has, in a great measure, himself alone to blame that his stomach is always either too empty or too full; for this fellow, when he gets a meal, raises such a hue and cry in the dead of night as effectually warns all savoury animals to avoid his presence.

In the calving season the coyotes are in clover, and the little veals fall an easy prey to a pack of these nocturnal robbers. In winter, when the wild geese cover the hills, I doubt if the coyote gains much permanent benefit, judging from the fact that I have seldom found feathers. The geese encamp in vast armies, and at times perhaps outlying picquets and sentries asleep on their post get cut off by the enemy; but the wild goose, fool as he may be, has just so much keen relish for a good joke as to allow the coyote to reach a point where expectation has resolved itself into certainty, and then the goose decamps, harassed undoubtedly, but whole in body. The coyote has more of the dog than the fox in his composition, and is a bungling poacher at any time; one feature alone of his character proves this, inasmuch that, when suddenly disturbed, he runs but a few yards, then stops, turns round and looks at you. A Norfolk poaching lurcher knows better than that, *he* would never turn his face to you for fear you should *identify him*, at least so Barnes tells me, and he ought to know; but the most satisfactory proof that the coyote is a weak forager exists in the conclusive fact that you seldom shoot one that has anything in his stomach.

As, therefore, there was no employment for my rifle
at Benicia, I was thrown on my resources for amusement.   Fortune again favoured me; fortune, by the
way, always has favoured me when I have been in
pursuit of amusement, but she snubs me amazingly
whenever my designs are in the least degree mercenary,
which leads me to infer that that divinity is of rather
a jovial disposition than otherwise.

In one day's search I secured two horses, one gig,
three well-formed Australian kangaroo dogs, and
three blood-hound whelps, just arrived from Hobart
Town; these being shipped in a small schooner, in
company with my iron shooting box, I started for San
Luis, and called on Ramsey, who had probably forgotten me.   I urged him at once to come and be a
Vallejo-ite; he demurred at first, but, alas, we are all
mortal; pointing with one hand to his buckskins and
hunting saddle, rotting from disuse, with the other I
directed his attention to my greyhounds, then I
uttered one word, " coyotes," and Ramsey struck his
flag in passive submission to his destiny—and followed me.

CHAPTER XI.

———✦———

June, 1851.

OUR first duty, on arriving at Vallejo, was to erect a temporary shanty, and before we had been long there the materials for about fifty houses were scattered over the ground by various speculators. Ramsey laid the foundation of a small village on his own account, and built a dwelling-house, a livery stable, and another grog-shop, in which his champagne and tin pannikins were soon rattling away, as of old, to the sound of the fiddle.

As soon as I had erected the iron house, to which I have already alluded in terms of bitterness, we tried the projected coyote hunt. I had two horses; one was an old grey "Texian Ranger," who had seen so much hard service that, when once adrift, he was neither to be caught with chaff or the best of oats, but had to be lassoed and dragged home by

197

main force; once assured, by means of spurs, and bottles of water broken on his head when he reared, and sticks broken on his side when he buck-jumped, that he was "bound to go," as they say here, "the Old Soldier" (for so I named him) proved an animal of great speed and endurance, and afterwards performed his eighty miles in a day with me without flinching. The other was a handsome bay that I had bought from a retiring watchmaker, and he retained the name his last master had bestowed in honour of his shop, "Main Spring."

My Australian Kangaroo dogs were a cross between the bull-dog or bull-mastiff and the greyhound; like the generality of cross-bred greyhounds, they differed only from the thoroughbreds in increased size, muscle, and breadth of chest; they ran of course from sight, but were not devoid of nose.

Of the three I had procured but two proved of any value, Tiger and Bevis, and these I coupled for an experimental hunt. I trust I may be excused from the charge of egotism in thus mentioning these animals in detail; they were my companions up to the very day I left the country; and being associated with the adventures I am sketching they will appear in my narrative from time to time. With all his faults I owe a debt of gratitude to the "Old Soldier."

Stealing quietly away to the surrounding hills, with Ramsey on the "Old Soldier," we soon found a coyote, and I slipped the dogs; he made a straight run, but there was no chance for him, and in less than five hundred yards he was caught and worried without a fight, and I whipped the dogs off. I was disappointed; I had hoped that the coyote would not only run well, but would make some kind of stand at the finish; but we found him invariably devoid of any pluck. Some that we afterwards saw would make an excellent start and then turn round and attempt to fraternise with the dogs, and these, after a time, began to recognise something of the nature of the cur in this conduct, and, after rolling the coyote over, would turn back without injuring him.* So that our coursing was deferred until we reached the hare country, where the dogs showed to better advantage, and generally killed, the hare of the country being rather a fool than otherwise.

It became necessary now for me to return to Russian River, and, as Ramsey and a Mr. Bottomly were anxious to accompany me, we made up a four-in-hand out of a pair of Ramsey's horses and mine, and, throwing our blankets into the old waggon that

* In which it will be observed they were more merciful than I was; but the "coyote" comes under the head of vermin.

constituted our drag, we put Tiger and Bevis inside to save their feet, and started.

We arrived without accident at the river, and I found that now the rains were over, settlers were flocking in from all sides. The river was still very high owing to the melting snow at its source; and when the waggon floated for a minute or two as we crossed the centre of the ford, and then filled to my companions' knees, they evidently viewed with great interest this, to them, novel feature in " tooling a four in hand."

The sun was intensely hot, and when we had reached the opposite bank of the river, we pulled up in the shade to dine, the provisions having been secured against all injury in crossing the river. Ramsey insisted on drinking an immense quantity of the river, which, however, he qualified with brandy; and after having in consequence expended a large amount of second-hand poetry on the surrounding scenery, nothing would please him but he must alter the tails of his two Canadian switch tail ponies, to make them match with those of Mainspring and the Old Soldier, which were banged. I remonstrated with him on the folly of spoiling two valuable animals, whose chief beauty consisted in their manes and tails, but he would do it; and having cut one tail about a foot shorter than the other with a blunt table knife, he left them pretty objects. Imagine my disgust when the fellow remarked, after gravely contemplating them, " Sh'no consequence, s'hey don't b'long to me." I got into trouble about them afterwards, as will be seen.

In the cool of the evening we arrived at the farm, where I found everybody well, and glad to see me back. As I had foreseen, settlers were beginning even to invade *my* dominions, and not only was the romance of the place destroyed, but the game was retiring very rapidly, and it required a long day's walk to find venison. This of itself would have determined me to leave the valley, but other causes hastened my decision—firstly, *the onions were a failure;* they had come up, but the ground squirrels had proved so numerous as to destroy all vestige of the young plants ; secondly, I had on one occasion disclosed at March's not only that I was *not* a naturalised American, but that I had no intention of bringing myself into contempt by deserting my own country from interested motives, as too many I regret to say have done. This had become known among the crowd of settlers that were now hunting for pre-emption claims ; they also knew, as of course there were a few Philadelphia lawyers among them, that as an alien I had no right to the valley. Some of them called upon me to tell me so, but these left however quicker than they came. Under all the circumstances, and particularly as I never could have resided among such a set as were now "locating" themselves about the place, I made a virtue of necessity, and gave the farm as it stood (excepting the cattle and my books and shooting materials) to one of the backwoodsmen I had known there for some time.

During this last visit to the old place, however, we enjoyed ourselves; the green peas had arrived at perfection, and the young fawns were excellent substitutes for lamb. Tiger and Bevis afforded us some coursing, and Ramsey found out for the first time in his life what it was to stand knee deep in a running stream and wash a flannel shirt without soap.

Whilst we were absent one night on an excursion, Thomas, who remained at home, distinguished himself by shooting a valuable milch cow, that had been brought up by one of the new settlers, and which, having strayed near the house, he mistook in the dark for a wild bull or a bear. When we returned in the morning, Thomas, in great trepidation, had just completed burying the carcase near the house, and we were still laughing over the matter, when a tall settler appeared amongst us and inquired if we had seen " e'er a cow," to which Thomas, knowing that the settler had followed his cow's trail, fortunately replied in the affirmative, and suggested a distant hill as a celebrated rendezvous for strayed cows in general, on account of the fine quality of its spring water ; thither the settler wended his way, after satisfying himself with a few rapid and suspicious glances that we had venison hanging about instead of beef, and that no symptom of cow was stamped about the place. As he turned once more to call three wiry-looking, gamboge-coloured curs, that he had brought with him, and which had been sniffing about, I observed with horror that the brutes were on the cow's grave, scratching away bravely—" Seize them, Tiger ! At them, Prince ! Bevis !" and these disturbers of the dead flew for their lives, and as I called the dogs off, evidenced no disposition to return, although my brave defenders immediately had a battle royal over the dainty morsel which had thus been brought to light.

I have already alluded to Barnes's physical strength ; in Norfolk he was always an expert axeman, even with the stupid broad-headed Flemish axe, that we still adhere to in England, but his six months' training at the farm with the American axe had so improved on his former strike and natural powers of

endurance, thet he was induced one night to boast
of his prowess whilst in company with some backwoodsmen at March's shanty. It had already been
proved that no one of the party was a match for him,
as I had given him permission to fell for March's
saw-mill in his leisure hours, (at which work I may
mention he often made his thirty shillings a day,)
March therefore undertook to bring a man called
Alexander, to take "the shine out of Barnes," and
during our stay this man arrived. He was a Hercules
in muscle though spare, and when, a tree having
been selected, the men "stripped for work" as *Bell's
Life* would say, there was little to choose between
them in appearance, though I thought I saw an
advantage on Barnes's side in point of loins. To me
it is delightful to witness a fair trial of skill and
dexterity between two picked athletes, where, as in
this instance, the pleasure is unalloyed by any brutal
exhibition of inflicted punishment. Our party and
that of the Americans were equally excited, but no
bets were made, and there was no boastful confidence in the issue on either side. I have mentioned
elsewhere that the redwood tree retains in its growth
sometimes so perfect a perpendicular that it may be
cut round its centre, and yet remains erect on a calm
day, supported but by a few inches of the heart. A

tree having therefore been selected of about eight feet diameter, as nearly as I can recollect, the men were placed on either side, and a few straight lines for their guidance having been chalked on the bark, they commenced work, the man on whose side the tree fell, to be declared the winner, as he of course would have cut the deepest. For the first part of the day the champions worked manfully stroke for stroke, and the issue seemed to the last doubtful, but at length the strokes became weaker and slower, and then Barnes seemed to have kept something back for the finish, for after a few vigorous drives, the huge tree fell over on his side, and came thundering to the ground. It was a touch and go victory; and caused no ill feeling; but Barnes on returning home was very unwell from over exertion, and during the night he wandered in his head; the next day, however, he was quite well; but the " shine " was taken out of him although he won.

I bade farewell to the little valley before its charms had so palled upon me by use as to render me indifferent to its possession, but its great charm of seclusion that first bound me to it was lost, and in my eyes it was as much " cut up " by the presence of fresh settlers, as is your country villa, sir, when a rushing railway, marking out its track directly through your favourite clump of weeping willows, sends its hot cinders on to the very lawn in front of you ; but you were compensated for your villa being smoke-begrimed, and sold it, moreover, on good terms to Styles, who likes living near a railway, and being hourly reminded that his country is making " giant strides," whilst I, equally a victim to the march of improvement, walked out without any other reflection than that I had gone to a great deal of trouble for the sole benefit of an utter stranger.

We arrived at Vallejo without accident. The appearance of the tailless Canadian horses brought forward their indignant owner, who demanded of me, as conductor of the expedition, an exorbitant sum, which I of course refused to pay, upon which he went to law ; and about the time that the hotel was completed, an execution was put on it by the sheriff for the amount claimed for two horses' tails that I never touched.

We had very little sport at Vallejo ; a few wild-fowl hung about the marshes, but were very hard to secure ; snipe and curlew also were tolerably plentiful; but the sun was hot, and the yellow treeless hills dazzled the eyes too much for shooting. Our guns therefore were shelved for the present ; but I found another source of amusement by fortunately making the acquaintance of a young Englishman of the name of Rowe.

Rowe was a surveying engineer of good ability, and had, previous to leaving England, scarified that country to a considerable extent in the shape of tunnels and cuttings on railways. His present business in Vallejo consisted in surveying and laying out the plan of that city, which having completed, he was now transferring to a gorgeous map, on which the Botanical Gardens, Orphan Asylums, and *Schools for the Indigent Blind* were already traced and lettered.

Rowe possessed about a dozen small Californian and Indian horses, and as these brutes were not only now wild, but were of that peculiar breed that can neither be tamed or fattened, I could not at first conceive what object Rowe had in keeping them, especially as they were all small, gaunt, and painfully ugly. I perceived that almost daily my new acquaintance, dressed in Californian spurs and leggings, would mount the horse that he generally kept by him (with the saddle always on), and proceed in search of the others which he had turned out to graze on the hills the night previous.

In the evening he would return as usual, driving his ill-looking pack before him, and these, after being enclosed for a short time, would be again turned out. On my suggesting that his animals seemed to cause him more trouble than they were worth, he at once elucidated the mystery.

It appeared that he had received these scarecrows from time to time in payment of bad debts, contracted for surveys of the surrounding farms; they cost nothing to keep, as they lived on the wild oats, and the reason he turned them out and brought them home each day, was for the pleasure of hunting and catching them with the lasso when he could. I soon joined him in this diversion, and the sport was most exciting. His band, as soon as they saw us coming, would have an appearance similar to this :—

ROWE'S LOT

They would stand in a crowd together, looking at us

out of the corners of their eyes; then as we approached they would go over the hills and gulches, whilst we rode after them, shouting and heading them back whenever we could.

After two or three hours of this exercise, they would allow themselves to be driven without much trouble into Rowe's corral. I believe they liked the sport; whether or no, they got it every day, and as it was all they had to do, they were better off than most of their race. In fact, the Old Soldier did the same work with me on his back, and liked it so much that I could not hold him at last when once he got sight of these scarecrows. He tried to catch them one day when in the gig, because they suddenly appeared in sight, and if it had not been for a deep gulch that brought us all up with a smash, I believe he would have "corralled" them on his own account.

Rowe had an Indian pony of great power and endurance; it was named "Chocktaw," after the American Indian tribe, to which of right it belonged. He had a head like a wedge of wood, and although tolerably quiet under a severe Spanish bit, he had the habit of never taking his eyes off you. He was always suspicious, if you walked round him, and would follow you with his wild colt's eye.

Chocktaw combined the sure-footedness of the mule,

with the speed of the horse, and the capability of the donkey of living and doing well upon comparatively nothing, which was so far fortunate for him as he was occasionally locked up and forgotten for a day or two, during which periods of trial he generally munched shavings, and upon being remembered and released became more suspicious than ever.

Chocktaw and the Old Soldier became fast friends, so much so, that the latter kicked other horses on Chocktaw's account, and took him under his protection generally, even to the length of eating Chocktaw's oats (which he got on Sundays), for fear, no doubt, they should disagree with his Indian stomach ; whether this made him more suspicious or not, I don't know, but Chocktaw never took his eyes off his friend for all their affection.

The unhappy Chocktaw is typical of a class of men who live continually in the torment of half-confirmed suspicions—innocents, who, stopping half-way in their study of the world, are ever doubting and fearing, yet never learning, force the lesson on them as you will ;— " Chocktaws " to whom " Old Soldiers " are neces- sary—these latter cheating them, yet preventing others from doing so ; finding brains for them ; kicking other horses for them, but eating *their oats as recompense.* Unhappy then the Chocktaw who wriggles, as it were, in the half-consciousness of being outwitted, and torments himself with vain suspicions. Far more to be envied he who can clap his persecuting protector on the back, and own him to be "necessary but expensive;" his mind is at ease from that time forth; he can pay his bully as he does his income-tax, and get more for his money.

News was brought in one day that a band of elk had been seen near the place, and upon this the whole population turned out. Independently of the fact that I feared being shot by some of the party, among whom were several boys, armed with rifles, I knew that the Elk does were heavy at this season, and I had no mind to assist in a butchery. The drove was headed about nightfall in marshy ground, and about *eighteen does* were killed.

I was sorry to have lost the chance of hitting the slot of these beasts, for the bucks might easily have been secured with care, whereas, approached as they were, whilst drinking in marshy and treacherous ground, the bucks being on the outskirts made for the hills, whilst the poor frightened does became quagmired, and fell an easy prey.

About this time I received a visit from Sir Henry Huntly, and we started on an exploring expedition, but losing our way, found ourselves at length near

Napa.   Pulling up temporarily at a small house at the side of the creek to enquire the road, we found it occupied by half-a-dozen fine-looking fellows, who were sitting over their supper.   The invitation to join them was too heartily offered to refuse, and Sir Henry and myself being armed each with a cast-iron knife and tin platter, attacked the provisions as men do who lose their way, and fall happily and unexpectedly on a savoury stew of antelope.   We were glad enough also to be so kindly invited to pass the night there, for a day passed in the hot sun is very fatiguing, and once down, a man has to be kicked up again, particularly after a surfeit of antelope stew. So we lit our pipes, and then, as a matter of course, we allowed gradually to leak out who and what we were.   Our entertainers consisted of four Americans and two Englishmen.   These latter were army-men, who had thrown up their commissions in Canada to seek a rough and adventurous life in exchange for the dull routine of barracks.   So far as roughness went, they had it in perfection, and they stood it well; but the *roughest* roughness palls, and an adventurous life, with its fevers and privations, and hard toil in the blistering sun, soon loses its charms, and then comes the yearning for home, and it is best then to have something *to fall back upon*.

There are few after all to whom either roughness or adventurous life comes aptly, although the proud man scorns to *own* he feels the privation he has sought as it were; but few of those who have sacrificed position, comforts, and friends elsewhere, for the pursuit of freedom and adventure, with wealth of course appearing in the distance, have realised their dreams, or have done otherwise in the long run than own their folly, and mourn it secretly. Some men are born for a wild and careless life—a happy liveliness of disposition, knowledge of the world, physical health, recklessness of personal safety, indifference to social position and home comfort, all fit them for it; their creed is to do as no one else does, (and they do *none* the worse for this); these men are few in number, and they can live when others starve. Observe the man in a hunting-field, who strikes out his own line of country, and that a new one to him; each fence may conceal a marl-pit, but he faces bravely all obstacles, and comes in right at last. Rash fool! says Jones as he opens a gate. Stupid ass! echoes Brown as he creeps through a gap! But no! Brown and Jones would be both fools and asses if they tried to do it, but to this man such work comes naturally.

As a rule the fate of the minnows who will pursue an unbeaten track is certain enough. It is generally a *great mistake* when men throw up on their own account a certain means of livelihood, to seek adventure and fortune in new gold countries. It is generally a *great mistake* when fathers with spendthrift sons, stupid sons, or lazy sons, say, "John, you are doing no good for yourself, here are five hundred pounds, go and try your luck in the diggings." It was a *great mistake* when a party of gentlemen left England in 1849 for California in a yacht of their own, and having arrived at the diggings got disgusted, and returned very much out at elbows, with most melancholy reports respecting the goldfields. And these are great mistakes, for this reason, that patience under disappointment, and a disposition that can ever look sanguinely into the future, are as requisite for "*rough life*," as strong *hands, willing hearts and* sound health.

Our entertainers occupied themselves in market-gardening, which is a peaceful and unexciting profession; and as the whole party were animated with a strong love of adventure, and were anxious for something more soul-stirring than weeding and watering beds of cabbages, soon after I last saw them they disbanded and dispersed, nor have I heard of them since.

Vegetables attain an unusual size in California, owing to the rich qualities of the maiden soil; but

I have observed an insipidity in everything that has thus rapidly matured, and size is attained at the expense of loss of flavour. Onions and tomatas as large as cheese plates are common. Melons have attained the weight of fifty pounds. Wheat and oats grow to the height of eight and ten feet, and are very prolific in the ear; potatoes reach dimensions unheard of elsewhere, and the diameter of a cabbage is sometimes so large that the cabbage has to be seen to be believed in.

A brutal murder had been committed at Napa previous to our arrival; the murderer had been sentenced to death, and without any ostensible reason, a free pardon for this felon was granted by the governor of the state. During our stay here some of the most determined of the citizens of Napa frustrated this act of ill-timed mercy, and the murderer was found hung in his cell. No further notice was taken of the matter; but this act cannot be justified under any circumstances, for as the people elected the governor, and armed him with the right, had he so chosen, of setting free every convicted felon in the state, their election was a farce if his decision was not binding in the pardon he dispensed to the Napa murderer.

CHAPTER XII.

———◆———

June, 1851.

SHORTLY after my return to Vallejo, a bright glare
in the direction of San Francisco indicated too surely
that the city was again in flames. The wind was
very high, and we had every reason to believe that
the conflagration was general. Having roused out
the Old Soldier to his intense disgust, I reached
Benicia in time to take a passage to San Francisco in
the last returning Stockton boat. We met steamers
going up river crowded, that stopped and confirmed
our worst fears; mine in particular, for I had felt
anxious respecting the property of a friend who had
shown me unceasing kindness since my arrival in
the country. I learnt that his stores had already
fallen, and knew that he was ruined. It was with
great difficulty we landed, for the fire had extended
to the water's edge, and in many places the wharves
had been disconnected; everywhere deep holes had

216

been burnt in them, and some were drowned that night from this cause.

The ruins of the fire were quite deserted, the inhabitants had sought the suburbs, sorrowfully no doubt, for a night's rest ; and the bright moon looked calmer than ever in contrast to the red angry embers which smouldered on every side.

I found myself alone after I had scrambled up a small hill that commanded a view of the fallen city, and I never remember feeling so solitary in my life. Small columns of red-tinted smoke rose lazily in every direction, the blackened shells of brick warehouses stood out here and there in bold relief against the moonlight, whilst every crevice and window in them was fantastically lighted by the glowing embers that still burnt within. Over the ruins of large drug stores ghostly lights of blue and green flickered in a supernatural manner. Where the fire had already been extinguished, dark pits seemed to yawn, and open wells, and deep cisterns, stood ready on all sides, their coverings being burnt, to trap the unwary adventurer who might be led to explore those regions. Not a sound broke the stillness of the night, and as the moon was overshadowed by a passing cloud, I turned and stumbled on what was either a very dead man or a very drunken one, and having seen all there was to see, I descended the hill and rejoined my companions.

Lodgings were scarce enough that night, as may be imagined, nor was there a sufficient number of houses standing to accommodate the burnt-out citizens. I was fortunate enough to meet an Hungarian geologist, who was probably the poorest man in San Francisco, for the science he professed could not at this time be put to much account in California. Were it not for the respect in which I hold a learned society at home before which "papers" are read, and by which laws are made for the better regulation of geology, I should say that the reason why the votaries of this science did not succeed in California, arose from the fact, that this eccentric country, had for ages past acted in defiance of the fundamental rules of the society in question : whether or no, whenever my friend set out in search of gold on scientific principles, he generally left that metal farther behind him at every step.

Wherever you go now you will meet a few Hungarians, and I have ever found them a superior class of men—quiet and unobtrusive in their habits, and of very liberal education. My geological friend had a small hut built among the sand-hills. As we walked towards it we were called on to deliver

by three gentlemen of the road, but as, happening to
be both armed, we made the usual demonstration in
such cases, we went on our way without molestation.
Not but what it would have been a kindness to have
robbed the Hungarian, for though he had no money
in his pocket, and his clothes were valueless, he was
staggering through the deep sand under the weight
of an enormous bag of quartz he had collected, every
ounce of which I foresaw was destined to be pulverised
in a hand mortar and tested, involving a great
amount of labour but *no profit*. I tossed up with my
friend who should have his bed, and having won it I
was soon asleep, it being now nearly daylight; when
I awoke he was gone, and I was at no loss to conjecture that he had sought elsewhere a softer couch
than the heap of rocks and fossils that had fallen to
his lot.

When I reached the burnt city all was again
animation, and on every side preparations were being
made for rebuilding it of brick and stone.

I have alluded to a friend; it was with sorrow that
I viewed the wreck of the noble warehouses that had
been his: but yesterday, as it were, he had pointed
to these buildings with pride as evidencing his
successful efforts, though never forgetful to whom
success was owing, while to-day a heap of ashes marks

the emptiness of human calculation. A week ago and his glorious hospitality assembled hundreds to commemorate the completion of a stately warehouse,—to-day the firm is hopelessly and irretrievably ruined.

He lies now in the cemetery outside San Francisco, and those who have not forgotten the warm grasp of a hand that was ever ready to succour—now that that hand is cold, will recognise this sketch, and will not blame me for recording this slight tribute to his memory.

After a diligent search I was directed by the appearance of sundry steel buttons to the ashes of what had been my wardrobe; everything had been destroyed, and among the papers I had lost were the notes and sketches of the country that I had collected to this date, which notes, after three years, I am re-writing from memory.

After contemplating mournfully the whitened remains of two little dogs that lay side by side, with the blackened ashes of my dress coat and patent leather boots, I turned from the spot, and shortly afterwards encountered Sir Henry Huntly, who in an equally melancholy frame of mind, had just completed a survey of his " ashes ; " we agreed to pay a visit to the northern mines, and made preparations for a start.

The wooden wharves had for the most part been

converted into charcoal, and the steamer was crowded with those who like ourselves were anxious to leave behind them so much desolation.

The mail steamer had come in from Panama, and ladies who had just arrived to find their husbands, houseless and ruined, were hurrying careworn from their toilsome journey sorrowfully to seek a temporary shelter in Sacramento. There were troupes of actors, who, forgetting all rivalry in their common adversity, felt the reality of tragedy. The fire bell had arrested their performances, and though they worked ever so manfully at the breaks, the temples of Thespis had been swept away in the storm, and with them their wardrobes and arrears of pay. There were professional gamblers for whom the losing card had now turned up, who, burnt out of their tinsel saloons, were starting for the mines, to commence life again in a thimble-rigging tent, until growing prosperous they could work gradually back again to San Francisco, where the tinsel saloons were already being rebuilt.

There were speculators who had a " snug lot " of flour or pork up country, and who were off to fetch it down and lock it up in store-ships, until the wants of the community should make it worth its weight in gold almost. There were small traders, whose debtor and creditor accounts had been, fortunately for them, buried in oblivion by the general ruin, and who talked furiously of their losses, and bespattered their hard fate with curses of the loudest and deepest character. And there were many who like myself had come to satisfy their curiosity, just as we go to the sea-shore and view the wreck of a noble ship; and these grew hilarious upon the strength of having lost nothing, and returned to their homes in famous good humour with themselves and all the world.

Passing Benicia we entered Suisun Bay, on the shores of which a city was attempted—New York by name—but failed. There is something to admire in the audacity of speculators, who finding themselves possessed of a few acres of swamp, wave their wands and order a city to appear. The working human tide of California ebbed and flowed past New York with great regularity, but all commands to arrest it, and direct it from its natural course were futile as regarded that city, which really presented no advantage that I could see. It is now dusk, and we enter the Sacramento river. Presently we pass a large steamboat going down, who gives us a close shave, and complimentarily strikes three bells, upon which we strike three bells; and in a few minutes we pass a small steamboat also going down, who gives us a closer shave, and shrieks three times out of something connected with her steam-pipe, upon which we groan three times out of something connected with our steam-pipe. These salutes are invariably observed, and the greater the rivalry between the boats, the louder they scream at each other.

The banks of the river are for the most part marshy, but in the fading light we catch glimpses here and there of small cultivated enclosures, with comfortable-looking shanties peeping between the oak trees. After supper everybody turns in, and at daylight we arrive at Sacramento.

Sacramento is built on the banks of the river, from the encroachments of which it is as often drowned as its sister city is burnt. The houses are gaily painted, and the American flag waves in every direction; the streets are wide, and some trees that have been left standing in the town give it a cheerful appearance.

It is an American town at the first glance; an immense quantity of sign-boards stare at you in every direction, and if anything would induce a man to purchase " Hay and Grain," " Gallego Flour," " Goshen Butter," or any other article for which he has no want, it would be the astounding size of the capital letters, in which these good things are forced upon his notice.

Every other house is an hotel or boarding-house, for with few exceptions every one is put out to "livery," as it were, in Sacramento; and in hard times, when cash is scarce, one half of the population may be said to feed the other half gratuitously, or on credit, which often amounts to the same thing, thus affording a beautiful illustration of mutual support and confidence.

Sacramento is terribly dusty; the great traffic to and from the mines grinds three or four inches of the top soil into a red powder, that distributes itself everywhere; it is the dirtiest dust I ever saw, and is never visited by a shower until the rainy season sets in, and suddenly converts it into a thick mud.

I was introduced to a club of Sacramento gentlemen, who had formed themselves into what they called a literary society. In their rooms was to be found what in those days was scarce, a tolerable collection of books and the periodicals of the day. They were very jovial fellows, well-informed, not so literary as I expected, and certainly quite free from pedantry. The most important ceremony at their meetings consisted in the members standing in a circle, upon which a Chinese hat of teetotum shape was spun in the centre, and the " literary savant," who was indicated by a black mark on the hat when it ceased to spin, stood " drinks for the crowd."

The weather was oppressively warm, and the iced

" drinks " * were necessary even to a literary society; —so much so, that the hat was kept continually spinning by public acclamation. There was no lack of sensible and entertaining conversation, and the evenings passed with these gentlemen were to my thinking none the less pleasant, although perhaps less literary, for the twirling of the Chinese hat.

A levée, or sea-wall, has been built in front of the city, to protect it from the river when it rises with the high spring tides ; but the river generally undermines these works, and flows over the surrounding plain as it has been wont to do for ages past.

A large number of old dismantled hulks, now converted into floating houses, are moored along the front of the levée, and it is from these probably the rats first landed that are now so distinguished at Sacramento for their size and audacity. These animals come out after dark in strong gangs, as if the town belonged to them, and attack anything that may happen to have been left on the wharf during the night ; being very numerous, the destruction they cause to merchandise is a serious loss.

Ten thousand dollars were offered, I was told, to

* " Drinks " are not necessarily composed of intoxicating liquors : on the contrary, the principal ingredients are ice, syrup, and herbs. I mention this, because *we* mean by a man who " drinks," a drunkard, or the next thing to it.

the man who should clear the town, and seduced by this bribe, some one in the rat-catching line volunteered to draw all the rats into the country, and there enclose them in a paddock, to be publicly exposed previous to a massacre; but whether the rats thought it best to leave well alone, and be content with the comfortable quarters and nice pine-apple cheeses they enjoyed in the city, or whether they objected to country air, does not appear; but they never went out to the paddock, except one, who is reported to have approached within a reasonable distance of the vain-glorious rat-catcher, and then standing on his hind legs, after the manner of rats, and scratching the tip of his nose contemplatively with his paw, he turned tail for the city, causing grievous disappointment to five terrier dogs, who ineffectually chevied him in.

The conflagrations of San Francisco had been attributed to incendiarists, and as many attempts to fire the town had been frustrated, it is probable that this was the case. A Volunteer-Guard, therefore, patrolled the city of Sacramento at night, to guard against this evil, and to protect the inhabitants from the wholesale plunder of organised bands of burglars. Crime had increased so rapidly of late in San Francisco, and robbers and incendiarists had become so emboldened by the impotence and venality of the justiciary, that the citizens organised a society styled the Vigilance Committee, for the purpose of affording the protection to life and property that the law would not bestow.

So far was well ; but this society, composed of men who *smarted under personal loss,* attributed *perhaps unjustly* to incendiarism, took upon themselves the dispensation of life and death.

Men detected, as was supposed, in the act of *felony only,* were tried, sentenced, and executed, without defence, in the same night.

It is useless now to dwell on the summary executions that were put in force in half a dozen cases by the Vigilance Committee ; no one would defend their acts, and they met with opposition at the time from the better class of citizens ; the memory of them may pass away, but they certainly had the effect at the time of ridding the country of a set of desperate men, and of restoring a degree of security to the inhabitants of San Francisco that had never previously been enjoyed.

Colonel D——, a friend of Sir Henry's, had control of a quartz vein at a place called Volcano, in the northern mines, and we determined upon an inspection of this vein, which was reported to be highly auriferous.

We started at daybreak, in a light spring waggon,

and, taking with us our blankets, we were soon five miles from Sacramento, and pulled up at the young town of Brighton.

Colonel D—— appeared to be the owner of Brighton; and, being a sporting man, he had constructed a race-course here; with the exception of the race-course, and one or two stables, there was not much of the town developed as yet; but being really advantageously situated, I have no doubt that it is well populated by this time.

The road was straight and level, and on either side, enclosed by fences, were well-cultivated farms; numerous dwelling-houses lined the road, and it was difficult to believe that the signs of civilisation and industry, that met us on all sides, were the result of two years' occupation of the country by gold hunters.

As we left Brighton we overtook long lines of waggons, heavily laden with stores for the mines; and these, drawn by innumerable oxen, ploughed up the deep dust to such an extent as obliged us to cover our faces as we passed them. We met waggons coming in, containing miners, on whom, to judge by their appearance generally, a bath, a shave, and a new suit of clothes would not be thrown away; and I have no doubt they indulged in these luxuries on their arrival at Sacramento.

We stopped to breakfast at a house of entertainment kept by one Crockett, who had a very pretty wife; but the possession of this luxury, so far from humanising Crockett, appeared to keep him in a continual fever of irritation; for he was jealous, poor fellow, and used to worry himself because there was ever a dozen or two of hairy miners gazing in a bewildered manner at Mrs. C.; but, if report speaks truly, the bonnet and boots of a " female " had been successfully exhibited in this region at a dollar a head, (a glimpse of them being thought cheap even at that price) surely therefore Crockett might have excused the poor miners for regarding attentively the original article when presented gratis in the shape of a pretty woman.

Crockett carried a revolver of disproportionate size, he not being a large man, and this instrument he occasionally used upon provocation. A great number of miners had looked at Mrs. Crockett on the morning of our arrival, and her husband had not quite finished foaming at the mouth in consequence, when we entered the house. It was some time before he condescended to be civil; but having at length informed us that he was " so riled that his skin cracked," he added that he was a " devilish good fellow when he was ' *right side up*,' " and commanded us to drink with him. After this he procured us a most excellent breakfast, and, on the strength of our respectable appearance, allowed Mrs. Crockett to preside at this repast, which she did in a nervous manner, as if momentarily under the expectation of being shot.

We left our host "right side up," and, proceeding on our way, we soon lost sight of the cultivated country and began to traverse undulating plains studded with the dwarf oak. The road now gradually becomes worse, and has long ceased to be level; we pass road-side houses, whose names indicate the localities in which they are placed: " Rolling Hills," " Willow Springs," "Red Mountain," and so forth.

After travelling twenty miles we ascend the first range of hills; the pine-tree appears, and here and there we catch glimpses of the American Fork River. As we leave the plain, and ascend the wooded hills, trails may be observed indicated by blazed trees, leading to mountain gorges, where diggers are at work. Flowers clothe the hills in the richest profusion, and most conspicuous is the yellow poppy, which lightens up these desolate red hills for a few weeks each spring; growing in rich masses that, in contrast to the bleak and stunted herbage, are like sunbeams, and like sunbeams leave every spot they cheer more gloomy, when, under the influence of the first hot summer wind, they droop in a night and pass away.

CHAPTER XIII.

July, 1851.

WE reached the Salmon Fall diggings about noon,
and, without halting, crossed a wooden bridge that
had been built here on the north fork of the American
River ; we paid five dollars toll to its enterprising
owner, and ascended the opposite hill. The road
here became so uneven that we got out of the waggon
in preference to being pitched out, and we were kept
very busy in locking the wheels when it went down
hill, and pushing behind when it went up. We
passed no houses now, but trails led off on either
side, whilst occasionally we encountered solitary miners
" prospecting " near the road. " Prospecting " is the
term applied to a pursuit of knowledge under difficulties, that is, searching for gold where no trace of it
is apparent on the surface.* There are plenty of

---

* Looking, in fact, for new diggings.

231

" prospectors " in the mines, but the profession
scarcely pays, for the " prospector " is the jackall who
must search for many days, and, when he has found,
the lion, in the shape of the old miner, steps in and
reaps the benefit. So that there is something to
be learnt in the diggings, for undoubtedly one of the
first principles in life is to look on while others work,
and then step in and cry " halves."

We stopped at dusk at a house a little off the trail,
and, having had supper, we spread our blankets on
the ground, and being tired were soon asleep; but we
soon awoke again, for, separated from us by a canvas
screen, was a young goat, whose dismal bleatings
made " night hideous: " vain were the imprecations
that were showered on the goat's head; daylight discovered him still crying, and us awake and unrefreshed.

As we prepared to start, in rather a sullen humour, what was our astonishment when our host accosted us smilingly thus : " I had an addition to my family last evening, gentlemen, and as fine a boy as ever you saw ! " So he must be, thought we, to have a voice like a goat ; and, as we went on our way, we recalled the compliments with which, during the night, we had greeted the new-born babe, under the innocent impression that it was a kid ; and conjectured to ourselves the feelings of the mother when she heard herself alluded to as an old she-goat !

As the waggon followed the trail, we walked through the forest at the side ; the botanist of our party had now ample employment, and tortured a new flower at each step ; whilst our mineralogist pocketed specimens with such fervour that their accumulated weight began at last to tell severely on his frame, upon which he discharged his gleanings surreptitiously, to our great amusement, for we insisted that he had dropped them by accident, and made him pocket them again. If the people of this world had but to carry their hobbies up a dusty mountain, under a hot sun, in the shape of a bag of quartz, how soon they'd cast them off!

At noon, having reached the ridge of the mountain, we had an extended view of the gold country as it stretched away for miles beyond us in a succession of steep red hills; through these the American Fork rushed impetuously, and huge masses of red-woods clothed the highest mountains ; while, in the distance, the white peaks of the Sierra Nevada were perceptible ; those famous mountains of which the reputed wealth is still as much the Dorado of the Californian diggers, as were the placer fields before me once the dream of the Mexicans of the sixteenth century. "Prospectors" visit these cheerless snows never to return ; but, like the discontented squirrel of the fable, who would ascend the sun-lit hills that looked so much like gold, reach them, utter a moral and die.

A turn of the road presented a scene of mining life, as perfect in its details as it was novel in its features. Immediately beneath us the swift river glided tranquilly, though foaming still from the great battle which, a few yards higher up, it had fought with a mass of black obstructing rocks. On the banks was a village of canvas that the winter rains had bleached to perfection, and round it the miners were at work at every point. Many were waist-deep in the water, toiling in bands to construct a race and dam to turn the river's course ; others were entrenched in holes, like grave-diggers, working down to the "bed rock." Some were on the brink of the stream washing out "prospects" from tin pans or wooden "batteas;" and others worked in company with the long-tom, by means of water-sluices artfully conveyed from the river. Many were coyote-ing in subterranean holes, from which from time to time their heads popped out, like those of squirrels, to take a look at the world; and a few with drills, dissatisfied with nature's work, were preparing to remove large rocks with gunpowder. All was life, merriment, vigour, and determination, as this part of the earth was being turned inside out to see what it was made of.

The air was so still and clear that the voices rose to us with startling distinctness, and when a head appeared from a distant pit, and its owner vociferated, "How are you, Frank?" I thought at first he meant me, and was on the point of replying, "Well and hearty, thank him. How was he?"

Small patches of garden surrounded the village, which bore so palpably the stamp of cheerfulness and happy industry, that I was disappointed on learning that its name was "Murderer's Bar;" though the appellation was justly conferred in memory of a brutal murder that had been committed amongst its earliest settlers.

Had all the diggings been named in accordance with the circumstances that ushered them individually into public notice, there would be more Murderer's Bars than the traveller would well know what to do with, unless they were numerically arranged like the John Smiths in the muster-roll of a marching regiment.

The name is unpleasantly candid; there are plenty of " diggings " that can record their tales of blood much more forcibly than Murderer's Bar, but under such peaceful titles as " Diamond Springs," or " Happy Valley," they bring no shudder to the traveller. So that we learn another thing at the diggings, which is, that it is ridiculous to be a Publican and make a clean breast of it to every stranger, when such great immunity is gained under the garb of the Pharisee.

One would ask how it is that Murderer's Bar, despite its name, is a peaceable village, where each man's wealth, in the shape of ten feet square of soil, is virtuously respected by his neighbour; it is not because there is enough for all, for every paying claim has long ago been appropriated, and the next comer must go further on. There is a justice of the peace (up to his arms in the river just at present), and there is a constable (who has been " prospecting " a bag of earth from the hill, and been rewarded with a gold flake of the value of three cents); these two, one would suppose, could scarcely control two or three hundred men, with rude passions and quick tempers, each of whom, as you observe, carries his revolver even while at work. But these armed, rough-looking fellows themselves elected their judge and constable, and stand, ever ready, as " specials," to support them.

If a man wanted a pickaxe or a shovel, and thought to help himself to one of those that lie about at all times at Murderer's Bar, he would find it inconvenient if discovered; for, as there is no extenuating clause of hunger or misery in the diggings, theft is held to be a great crime; in all probability the offender would be whipped at the tree; and this brings us again to the perplexing subject of Lynch law as relating to the miners.

I venture to say that it will puzzle the theorist to determine how far the roving population of the mining regions in California have been justified in taking measures to eject the bad and worthless from among them; for all rules and precedents fall before the strong argument of self-preservation. When Christian and his shipmates landed at Pitcairn's Island and made laws for the regulation of their small colony (happily little needed) they acted as much upon the principle of Lynch law as did the miners; for these latter were equally without the reach of the laws under which they had been born. Where, after all, was the great difference in the first trial by jury and the Lynch execution among a colony of men living far from civilisation? Was the peace of a community of honest men to be disturbed by crime and bloodshed, unpunished, when, from circumstances, the law of their country was unable to protect them? These and similar questions would form the basis of the argument in defence of Lynch law in the mountains.

On the other hand, the opponent would point to the fearful instances on record of men being hurried to eternity without preparation—victims to the overwrought feelings of an excited mob. The defence of self-constituted law is untenable, yet there are instances in which small communities have seemed to me justified in enforcing, by the only means at their command, the order so necessary in such a state of society as that of the mountain gorges of California.

But when we see this law "subverting law" in a city like San Francisco, then we are forced sweepingly to condemn, once and for all, all that bears the name of Lynch, and we feel loth to admit that in any case the end can ever justify the means. Still it is a question, taken from first to last, that one may split straws on, when we see how peacefully Murderer's Bar progresses, not under the *execution*, but under the *fear* of Lynch law. In most mining villages public indignation has been confined to ordering men to "leave the camp" in twenty-four hours, or otherwise take the consequences; and after being thus warned, the nefarious digger invariably "slopes."

The mining population have been allowed to constitute their own laws relative to the appointment of "claims," and it is astonishing how well this system works. Had the Legislature, in ignorance of the miner's wants, interfered and decided that a man should have so much, and no more, of the soil to work on, all would have been anarchy and confusion.

Whereas now, every "digging" has its fixed rules and by-laws, and all disputes are submitted to a jury of the resident miners; excepting in those instances where twenty men or so are met by twenty men, and in these cases there is first a grand demonstration with fire-arms, and eventually an appeal to the district court. The by-laws of each district are recorded in the Recorder's Office of the county, and these laws are stringent although self-constituted; ill-defined at first, and varying as they did, they were conflicting and troublesome, but though they have been jumbled as it were in a bag, they have come out like Mr. Crockett, " right side up."

I have had my claim in the digging more than once, of ten feet square ; if a man " jumped " it, and encroached on my boundaries, and I did'nt knock him on the head with a pick-axe, being a Christian, I appealed to the " crowd," and my claim being carefully measured from my stake and found to be correct, the " jumper " would be ordered to confine himself to his own territory, which of course he would do with many oaths.

It is customary to leave your mining tools in your claim, to indicate to all new comers that it is occupied, and as this rule is recognised it saves a great deal of unnecessary explanation ; but it has often struck me that if in the quiet and virtuous hamlet of Little Pedlington, a market-gardener were to leave his spade outside as a sign of occupancy, he would not detect that implement in the morning, spite of the vigilance of the one policeman, who guards that blissful retreat.

We descended the cliff by a short cut ; the miner-alogist took a shorter, for a ledge of earth gave way beneath his weight, and enabled him to reach the base about three minutes before us.

Gongs sounded at this moment, and the red clayey

population flocked in to dine, looking disproportion-
ately dirty in contrast with their white houses : I
did not see a woman in the " camp." But these things
are being better ordered now, and I can foresee the day
when the traveller from Murderer's Bar shall speak of
anxious mothers rushing from the white tents with
soap-sud arms to rescue embryo miners from the
gutter ; and when flaxen-headed urchins shall gaze
suspiciously at the approach of such as I, and running
back to their parents, will exclaim, " Oh ! daddy, here's
a Britisher ! "

The gold is found here in coarse flakes, and the
bank washings, from all accounts, average five or six
dollars a day per man.

The days had passed when diggings were abandoned, so soon as they ceased to reward a day's
toil with less than an ounce or two of gold, and
" chunks " and " big strikes " * were now exceptions
to the rule ; but the days had passed, also, when to
obtain these prizes men laboured painfully under the
influence of fever, produced by bad food and poisonous
spirits, to die at last, perhaps, disgorging every hard-
earned flake of gold to some attendant quack.

Much happier the miner, when, as at Murderer's
Bar, his toil is regularly rewarded with a smaller gain,

* Deposits of Gold.

for his health is no longer impaired by feverish excitement and drink, and the necessaries of life are placed within his reach, at prices that enable him to save his gold scales as well as his constitution, for the "rainy day," that in one form or the other comes to all at last.

Leaving the village and passing some hills, the sides of which were overgrown with the white azalia, we reached another part of the river, where was a ferry-boat, and here we found our waggon. On the opposite side of the river the ascent was very steep, and would have been impracticable for waggons, had not the owner of the ferry excavated a portion of the mountain, and otherwise constructed a road.

For this outlay of capital the ferryman was reaping a rich harvest; having thus opened the only practicable trail at this time to the more northern mines, he had secured to himself the toll of every waggon passing to or from those regions, and these tolls amounted in one year to sixty thousand dollars (12,000l.). The original capital was, I understood, the result of successful digging; and I mention this circumstance as it proves two things, first, that fortunes in the mines are not dependent on the discovery of little nests of gold, as some suppose, but on the judicious application in a new country of the small capital which a little steady work with the pick-axe will ensure to any industrious and healthy man ; and, secondly, that a large portion of the gold amassed in mining regions is expended upon the permanent improvement of the country; so that the export of the " dust " is no criterion of the yield.

Bridges, ferries, roads, watercourses, dams, hotels, and stage coaches, have nearly all been started by means of the capital obtained from the soil over which they run, or on which they are constructed.   No one knows what a waggon will undergo, until he has mastered Californian trails and gulches.   The worst places are the steep descents that skirt the base of a mountain, where the road has an inclination of about thirty degrees towards the precipice beneath.

In such places you may fasten a rope to the axle of the waggon, and passing the other end round a tree or rock as a check, you may let her " slide," which she will do without any further trouble on your part.

We were now approaching a spot where a few days previously the Indians had made some successful descents upon mining parties, cutting off some of their number.   The Indians of this region promise to be a great annoyance, for they are mounted and brave, and are gradually becoming possessed of rifles.

There is an Indian commission in the country, and

portions of territory, called "Indian Reserves," have been marked out as in other states, and presented to the Indians from their good father, the President. These "Reservations" the Indians accept and occupy, but the lurking idea still remains, that the rest of the country is theirs also, and in the mean time they "lift hair," * from time to time, to keep their hands in.

When Indians, labouring under the ridiculous notion that anything can belong to them that the white man wants, become troublesome, it is customary to drive them back; but the Indians of this region when so driven, will find their revenge in carrying on an exterminating warfare against the overland emigration—at least so it appears to me.

Still, the policy of conciliation pursued by the " Commissioners " is the only one that lies open, and if they can persuade these savages " that half a loaf is better than no bread," they will have carried out their diplomatic mission to its full extent. But it is easier to lull Indian suspicions than to eradicate them; and unfortunately for all parties, these aborigines cherish morbid ideas relative to the " graves of their fathers," from which, under the influence of diplomacy, they have been induced to retire: and certainly in those cases, where their progenitors have been buried

* Scalp.

in auriferous soil, their remains are not more religiously respected than would they have been had their fate consigned them to some of our intramural burying grounds. For although, in a civilised country, one's great grandmother's skull may be thrown up with impunity, when her lease of the grave is out, these Indians cling to the absurd superstition that the great " Manitou " looks wrathfully on those who wilfully disturb the dead !

We ascended hill after hill, and by noon, being hot, tired, and dusty, the scenery had no longer charms for our eyes; we passed gigantic red-woods only to sneer at them ; we pooh-pooh'd cascades that fell from masses of black basaltic rock ; the honeysuckles that lent their sweetness to the air around us, were pronounced disgusting ; and even the botanist reproached the yellow poppies with being " stinking," as if *he* couldn't have borne with them.

But when we pulled up at "Smith's ranche " and bathed and dined, we dismissed these unhealthy feelings, and took the honeysuckles to our bosoms again. We now began to experience the change of air consequent on our increased elevation, and the ascent was so rapid here, that thirty miles ahead of us the snow was reported to be lying fifteen feet in depth.

Where we now were, the main trail was little worn, but at a certain point we struck off to the right through the forest, and following the "blazed trees" we suddenly emerged on a clear and rocky ledge on the side of the mountain. Here was the quartz vein we had come to see, and its thirteen American owners lived upon the spot in a couple of log huts.

We were received with great hospitality, although this was of less substantial kind than it would have been, had not our entertainers been "out of everything" but flour, water, and tea. We had fortunately brought some provisions with us, otherwise we might have indulged in the luxury of a mountain appetite longer than was conducive to comfort. During two days we inspected the quartz mine, and having to the best of our ability satisfied ourselves of its wealth, we retraced our road to Sacramento, taking care to avoid the residence of the "old she goat," but calling on Crockett, whom we again found with his "skin cracking" at some imaginary insult to his wife.

When we reached San Francisco we found that preparations were going on, on all sides, for erecting brick and stone buildings in lieu of combustible shanties.

The style of architecture in vogue was less remarkable for cunning design than for its sturdy fireproof

qualities; and although the square houses, with
their thick walls and double doors, and shutters of
strong iron, and bomb-proof cellars underground,
added little towards the embellishment of the city,
it was no time to think of elegant façades or imposing
friezes when the first object was the security of life
and property. Each building, then, was intended to
assume the character of a fortress to resist the common
enemy of the place; and from that day to this, this
end has been fortunately carried out, and the heart of
the city is impervious to fire.

LIST OF PLATES

Drawn on stone by messrs. hanhart,
from designs by Frank Marryat

HIGH AND DRY.

CHAGRES RIVER

THE WINTER OF 1849.

BAR ROOM AT SONORA

HORSE AUCTION

SAN FRANCISCO—A FIREMAN'S FUNERAL

CROSSING THE ISTHMUS

CHAPTER XIV.

———•———

September, 1851.

So many reports had reached San Francisco at
this time of the discovery, in various parts of the
mining regions, of auriferous veins of quartz of
immense wealth, that all that portion of the population who were in waiting for something to turn up
had already departed for the mountains in search of
gold rock.

Although not exactly belonging to this class, it was
my destiny to hear from one Joe Bellow an account of
a certain mineral district, a portion of which, it
appeared, had been showered by Fortune into his lap.
His description was resistless. His natural volubility,
trained as it had been by his professional duties as an
auctioneer, overcame all obstacles that I could raise,
and I succumbed to his earnest entreaty that I would

visit the mine in question and feast my eyes, as he had feasted his, on the glittering wealth which nature had here exposed to view, and of which he extracted a specimen from his pocket of the most satisfactory description.

The mine was situated in the vicinity of Sonora, the chief town of the southern mines; and as, independently of my curiosity to inspect it, I wished to visit that section of the country, we started at four o'clock one evening in a small river boat called the " Jenny Lind," bound to Stockton, a town situated on the San Joaquin River.

On starting from San Francisco for the mines, it was but natural to bid adieu to cleanliness and comfort for the time being, and, having so fortified myself, I was better able to withstand the intolerable filth of the "Jenny Lind." She has since " blown up," which is about the only thing that could have purified her.

At daylight we arrived at Stockton, which I shall allude to more fully by and by, and at once landed and secured our places in the stage then about to start for the town of Sonora.

The stage coach was of American manufacture, and of the class known as " Concord " coaches. It carried nine inside and two out. Our driver was a colonel, and his name was Reed.   He was one of the best of whips, and, as proprietor of the line by which we were now travelling, he was making money very fast. Having been forestalled in the box seat by a very hairy miner, I completed, in company with Mr. Joe Bellow, the complement inside, after paying the gallant colonel an " ounce " for passage money.   This was a " reduced fare," occasioned by an opposition having lately made its appearance on the Sonora road; the bare mention of this emulative vehicle raised the colonel's " dander." With a crack of the whip we started at a good pace, behind four well-built, active beasts, not over-groomed, or " turned out " very expensively as to harness, but famous goers, and good for ten miles an hour over the plain.

Lines of stages now traverse the country in every direction, and there is scarcely a canvass mining village that is debarred from communication in this way with the principal towns.   The horses used by these lines are of the best quality, for a Yankee stage driver knows wherein true economy lies ; but the capital required to start a line is very considerable, and as soon as the profits begin to " tumble in pretty freely," as Colonel Reed remarked, up starts an opposition ; for stage-driving is a favourite specula- tion ! Our inside passengers consisted of a young

Canadian woman, who travelled under the protection of an ill-looking dog, a kind of Irish Yankee, who was very quarrelsome and bumptious, and carried his revolver in a very prominent position. We had two or three miners, who, as a matter of course, brought their rifles and blankets with them into the coach, and who squirted their juice at passing objects on the road with astonishing accuracy. We had, however, one decided character. This was a man who, as he gratuitously informed us, was professionally a bear hunter, bear trapper, and bear fighter; who, in fact, dealt generally in grizzly bears. When he shot bears— and it appeared he lived in the mountains—he sold the meat and cured the skins; but when he was fortunate enough to trap a fine grizzly alive, a rich harvest generally awaited him. The grizzly was immediately transferred, bound head and foot, to a large and strong cage; and this, being mounted on the bed of a waggon, the animal was despatched to some large mining town in the vicinity, where notice was given, by means of handbills and posters, that "on the Sunday following the famous grizzly bear, 'America,' would fight a wild bull, &c., &c. Admission, five dollars."

A bull and bear fight is, of all exhibitions of this description, the most cruel and senseless. The bear, cramped in his limbs by the strict confinement that his strength and ferocity have rendered necessary, is placed in the arena; and attached to him by a rope is a bull, generally of fine shape and courage, and fresh from the mountains. Neither animal has fair play, and indeed, in most instances, each one avoids the other. The bull's power of attack is weakened by the shortness of the tether, whilst the bear, as above mentioned, has scarcely the free use of his muscles.

The bull invariably commences the attack, and the immense power of the bear's fore-arm is then exemplified; for, raising himself on his hams, he meets the coming shock by literally boxing the bull's ears; but this open-handed blow saves his entrails, and the bull swerves half stunned, whilst his horns graze Bruin's skin. But if the bull approaches in a snuffing, inquisitive kind of manner, the bear will very probably seize his enemy's nose and half suffocate him in his grip. The fight generally ends without much damage on either side, for the simple reason that neither of the combatants means mischief.

I was sleeping one night at Campo Seco, a mining village in the southern mines, the houses of which were, for the most part, composed of canvass, the " balance," as they say here, being of muslin. The camp was very full, as on the day previous, Sunday, a long-expected fight had come off between a grizzly bear and a cinnamon bear. I had heard that, after an uninterrupted embrace between the two of about four hours, the grizzly had been declared the victor, which was not so extraordinary, considering that he weighed about 1200 lbs., and that you could not have driven a tenpenny nail through his hide, whilst the cinnamon's weight was quoted at 400 lbs. I was "putting up" with an acquaintance who kept a store in a small canvass house, and he having, with true mining generosity, opened a bale of new red blankets for my temporary accommodation, I was soon asleep. About daylight I was awoke by what I imagined to be the moaning of a man in pain, and the occasional disturbance of the canvass wall nearest my sleeping-place satisfied me as to the locality. The moaning soon became deeper, and occasionally the canvass yielded to some heavy weight that pressed against it. Presently was heard a smash of crockery and a tremendous roar; upon which my host started up, and, placing a revolver in my hand and seizing his rifle, he rushed out of the tent, vociferating, "Come on." Following him into the adjoining room, which formed his kitchen and occasionally a stable for his old mule, my eyes at once lit upon the cinnamon bear, whom my host had provided with lodging at the nightly charge of one dollar. The bear was fortunately chained to a strong stake in the centre of the hut, otherwise, "all smarting, with his wounds being cold," he looked, judging from as much of his eyes as one could distinguish in his swollen face, as if it would be grateful to him to set-to with something as much smaller than himself as he was smaller than his late antagonist. Upon an after inspection of his chain I ascertained that its length would have admitted his gratifying this desire on my carcase, had he tumbled through the canvass partition which had separated us for the night.

The weather being at this time fine and the roads in good order, we passed, throughout the whole length of our journey, innumerable waggons laden with winter provisions for the mines ; and droves of mules—patient little brutes, some as small as donkeys, staggering under barrels of liquor and cases as big as themselves ; each drove led, as a matter of course, by an old white mare with a bell.

As we neared the Stanislaus River, distant thirty miles from Stockton, every one inside became sociable, except the Irishman, whose jealousy had been aroused to a fearful pitch by J. Bellow, who entertained the fair Canadian in French, a language unknown to her protector. During our journey J. B. had not been inactive, having already disposed, conditionally, of sundry bags of sugar to the miners, and a box or two of German cigars to the bear hunter; samples of these articles having been extracted from his capacious pocket. Crossing the river Stanislaus at a fordable spot, we pulled up at a large wooden house, and alighted to dine and wash off the dust with which we were covered.

The immense traffic carried on on the roads that lead to the mining regions affords an extensive field for the profitable management of houses of entertainment. These may be encountered at almost every mile throughout the whole country, and they vary in size from a wooden two-story house to the very smallest kind of canvass shanty.

There seems to be a certain hour of the day for every traveller in California to breakfast, dine, or sup; and should he not arrive at a roadside house at one of these specified hours, he will get no meal; and could the traveller by any possibility be present at each and every hostel at the same moment, he would find a stereotyped bill of fare, consisting, with little variation, of a tough beefsteak, boiled potatoes, stewed beans, a nasty compound of dried apples, and a *jug of molasses*. He would then sit down at the summons of a bell in company with all the tagrag and bobtail of the road who might have congregated for the repast in question : and, if inclined to follow the custom of the country, he would, with the point of his knife, (made blunt for this purpose) taste of the various condiments, butter included, that were ranged before him, and, selecting as many of these as were suited to his taste, he would pile them on his plate, demolish them with relish, and depart on his way in peace.   Travel where you will in California, you may rest assured that of the foregoing will your meal be composed, and in nearly such a manner must you eat it.

Dinner over, we mounted a strong spring waggon in exchange for our covered coach, which had too much top hamper for the mountain trail we had before us.   We had now six horses, all American, good sound cattle, that had come to California across the plains, and were well broken in to crossing gulches and mud-holes.   We were soon in a different style of country.   Hitherto we had been crossing a level track across the Stockton plain, interrupted by an occasional dive into a dry gulch ; now we commenced at once to ascend the hilly country which first indicates the approach to the mining regions.   The road to Sonora, as indeed to most places in this country, has never been laid out by Government, but is, in fact, a natural trail or path marked out by the first pioneer waggons that passed that way, deviated from, from time to time, as experience indicated a shorter cut; receiving no assistance from the hand of man, and encountering a vast number of obstacles from the hand of nature.

For instance, we arrive at a part, that, skirting the base of a hill, presents a rapid declination to the left, which is a very hard and rocky-looking ravine. Colonel Reed exclaims, as he places his foot on the break, which works from the box, " Hard up to the right ! " upon which the insiders loll their heads and bodies out on that side of the vehicle to preserve its equilibrium. We had to " hard up " a great many times either to one side or the other, during which time J. Bellow always considered it necessary to assist the fair Canadian ; whereupon the Irishman looked fierce and talked large, but finally one of the miners told him, in a quiet but unmistakeable manner, that " if he didn't ' dry up ' he'd chuck him out of the stage." Whereupon the Irishman did dry up for the rest of the journey ; and shortly after arriving at Sonora we heard of his being detected attempting to pass off *bogus*, or imitation gold dust, and he narrowly escaped being lynched by the mob. In the course of the afternoon I obtained the box seat, and engaging the colonel at once on the subject of horseflesh, I soon obtained from him a great amount of useful knowledge on the subject of American stock, of which I am a great admirer. As we neared Sonora, the colonel's attention was almost entirely occupied by his team, for in many places the trail led through deep gulches, into which previous volcanic eruptions had showered an infinity of small cindery rocks, which, close enough together to prevent wheels getting through them, were just sufficiently high to capsize the cart if the wheels went over them. We arrived at the summit of a "used up" crater, and, having a long descent of this description before us, the inside passengers were ordered out; the break was put on, worked by the colonel's leg on the box. I held on according to orders. We slided down in famous style, first over on one side then the other, the colonel occasionally addressing his team with "D—— you, don't touch one of them!" meaning the rocks, through which we were picking our way. But, near the bottom of the hill, we got our off-wheels into a *mud-hole* and declined gently on that side, a fine specimen of volcanic formation preventing the waggon from going over altogether. The colonel, without hesitation, made all his passengers hang their weights to

THE SONORA
STAGE

the near side of the waggon, and, sitting on my lap, with a crack of the whip he started the whole concern, and sent it flying and swaying from side to side to the bottom of the hill. Here we pulled up, and the colonel, relieving me from his weight, observed, in extenuation of what might otherwise have appeared a liberty, "that he was obliged to be a little *sarcy* on this road."

Fleas are very prevalent in the southern mines, and my first introduction to the species was in this wise. The colonel turned suddenly to me, his hands being occupied with his ribbons, with "I guess there's a flea on my neck;" and I perceived on the instant that there was a large, broad-shouldered insect, refreshing himself on the place indicated, in apparent oblivion of all around. As in duty bound as box seat, I pulled him off and put him to death, the colonel remarking as he nodded his thanks, that he generally had three or four of the "darned cattle put through" in that fashion during the journey.

With so many teams and waggons on so narrow a trail, there is occasionally much disputing for the right of way. Men carry arms on the road as a general rule; but very seldom use any worse weapon than their tongues in these disputes. In a very awkward descent we found the road entirely and unnecessarily blocked up by a waggon, drawn by eight yoke of oxen. The Colonel at a glance recognised a teamster with whom he had previously had many words on the same subject, and he opened fire by ordering him to his own side of the road; to which the teamster sulkily acquiesced after some delay, our driver, as he passed, threatening him with a "lamming" on the next convenient occasion; to which the teamster replied by a promise of blowing the top of the colonel's head off; which so incensed the colonel, that he forgot himself, and rising in his seat, solemnly assured the driver of the ox team, that at some future period nothing should deter him from "spiking" him; to which the driver replied with such a shout of derision, that, believing as I do in the colonel, I have no doubt that before this the teamster has met his fate, and is a *spiked* man. The colonel felt very "ugly" for some minutes after this, but soon recovered his equanimity of temper. And here I shall take leave of him, for we now approach Sonora; the sun was disappearing behind the red wood trees that capped the surrounding mountains; we began to pass rapidly through mining villages and mining populations, of which more anon, and after dashing through several bad places, in which, as the colonel remarked, the best driver might get *mired*, or stuck in the mud, the town of Sonora appeared in sight; and dashing in at full gallop, we pulled up at the principal hotel.

It was dark when we entered Sonora; and as the habits of the people here are nocturnal, the evening may be said to have commenced as we alighted. It certainly had commenced, for Greenwich Fair might be spoken of as a sober picture of domestic life, compared to the din and clamour that resounded through the main street of Sonora. On either side were gambling houses of large dimensions, but very fragile structure, built of a fashion to invite conflagration, though offering little of value to the devouring element when the invitation was accepted, which it was about every other night or so.   In most of these booths and barns the internal decorations were very glittering; chandeliers threw a brilliant light on the heaps of gold that lay piled on each monté table, whilst the drinking bars held forth inducements that nothing mortal is supposed to be able to resist.   On a raised platform is a band of music, or perhaps some Ethiopian serenaders, or if it is a Mexican saloon, a quartet of guitars; and in one house, and that the largest, is a piano, and a lady in black velvet who sings in Italian and accompanies herself, and who elicits great admiration and applause on account of the scarcity of the fair sex in this region.

Each gambling house is full; some are crowded, and the streets are full also, for it is Saturday, a night on which the miners flock into Sonora, with the avowed intention of purchasing necessaries for the ensuing week, and returning the same night; but, seduced by the city's blandishments, they seldom extricate themselves from its temples of pleasure until very early on the ensuing Monday morning, when they return to their *camps* and *long toms*,* and

* Gold washers.

soothe their racking headaches by the discovery of chunks of gold.

The Mexican population preponderates in Sonora and its vicinity, and nearly everything is stamped with their nationality. The gambling tables are surrounded by them; and, dirty fellows as they are, they are very picturesque at a distance with their slouch hats and long serapes. The American population, between whom and the Mexicans a rooted hatred exists, call the latter " greasers," which is scarcely a complimentary sobriquet, although the term " greaser camp," as applied to a Mexican encampment, is truthfully suggestive of the filth and squalor the passing traveller will observe there. Sonora has a large French population, and to this Gallic immigration is attributable the city's greatest advantages; for where Frenchmen are, a man can dine, which is very important. The " *Trois Frères Provençaux*," has its namesake here, where good cooking and excellent light wines are at all times to be relied on; but where Frenchmen are, there are also good bakers; and there is, moreover, a great deal of singing and gaiety, and good humour, which is a pleasant contrast to the coarser hilarity of a generally very drunken population.

The long bar of a saloon is always actively engaged,

and the bar-keeper must be prepared for all demands in all languages. Here he serves a Mexican group with *agua diente;* now he allays a Frenchman's thirst with *absinthe,* in the pouring out of which he displays much art; again he attends with rapidity to the demands. of four Americans, whose *orders* embrace respectively, a "gin-cocktail," a "brandy-straight," a "claret sangaree," and a "Queen Charlotte;" these supplied, he must respond with alacrity to the call of a cockney miner, whose demand is heard even above the surrounding din :

"Hain't you got no hale hor porter?"*

J. Bellow expounded a great deal more than I have attempted to describe, before we had been many minutes at Sonora. As soon as we had bathed and freed ourselves from the dust with which we were covered, and which, perhaps from its having been ground off an auriferous soil, resembled a fine rich plate powder, we dined at a French restaurant and commenced our perambulations: not before J. B. had conducted me to his residence. This was situated in the main street, and was a small canvas house rather ostentatiously placed between two glittering saloons. The interior consisted of one large room,

---

* But when a couple of China-men make a demand for sam-schou, then the bar-keeper is puzzled.

filled with stores and provisions, and another very small apartment in which J. B. slept. The front of the house was entirely occupied by black letters, more than a foot in length, which, so soon as you got far enough off to read them all at once, informed you that Joseph Bellow carried on the business of auctioneer. In one of the saloons, a very interesting and well-looking young girl was attending at a part of the bar where confectionary was sold. I should not have supposed her to have had black blood in her veins; but J. B. assured me that she had been a slave, and had been once sold at New Orleans at a very high price, which he mentioned, and I ascertained this to be true; she was free now, but freedom had come too late, I suspect, to bring much value with it to her. J. B. knew every miner in the place, and to each he had something to say, and with most he took something to drink. It was, "Well, Jones, how did those pickles suit you?" and if Jones disparaged the condiments in question, as he probably did, it was, "Well, let's have a drink: allow me to introduce my friend, Mr. M——;" and if I had not managed to elude him, I should have had to shake hands with every man in Sonora on the first night of my arrival.

I had been directed to a place called Holden's

Hotel as a sleeping place. The lower floor formed the gambling saloon, in which were the Ethiopian serenaders already alluded to; the upper being converted, as I had understood, into sleeping apartments. On applying at the bar for a bed, I was requested to pay a dollar and enter my name on a slate opposite a vacant number; 80 it was. I wished to go to bed, and was directed to mount the staircase and find No. 80 for myself. On reaching the second storey, I found myself in a long and dimly lighted room of the same dimensions as that below, and round and about which were ranged about a hundred wooden stretchers, covered with canvas, and furnished each with one dark-blue blanket, and a small bag of hay to represent a pillow. It is satisfactory to me to remember, that, so far from expressing surprise, I displayed a stoicism that would have brought the blush through the vermilioned cheek of a Pawnee warrior; I wound my way through the settees, most of which were occupied, until I arrived at one on the head of which was a card bearing my number. A glance assured me that the bag of hay that rightfully belonged to me was there, but that the blanket was not. A momentary inspection further developed the fact, that on all the occupied stretchers were two or more blankets, whilst the unoccupied beds had been denuded of this covering. Having been educated as a midshipman, it is needless to say that to be in possession of *three* blankets, for it was cold, and an extra bag of hay, was the work of a moment; and making myself as snug as I could in No. 80, I was soon asleep, notwithstanding that the chinking of the monté-bankers, and the noise of the crowd below, and the calls for brandy-smashes, and the chorus of the serenaders, were by no means "fainter in the distance;" and no wonder, for close to No. 80 there was a chink between two planks, so wide that I could see "Bones" lolling out his tongue at the public, as he accompanied the chorus to the popular song of "Charlestown Races."

I awoke about daylight, very chilly, and found that my blankets had disappeared. The law of reprisal had been fairly enforced, and one cannot always be *wide-awake*. It was a comfort to me to reflect, that he who took the blankets, took the fleas that belonged to them; and as these creatures feed about daylight, *I had the best of it after all.* It was a capital idea of the landlord's, to have all the blankets of the same colour, for as every man deposited his revolver under his head before retiring for the night, it prevented all possibility of the joke becoming serious.

As I have already observed, the Spaniards enclose

their wild horses in a " corral." Here, closely packed,
the best horse kicks himself into the best place, and
keeps it.   These wholesale human dormitories are
also called corrals, and the principle is much the
same as regards the occupant ; you must kick or get
kicked—and indeed for that matter the whole world
is conducted on much the same principle.

CHAPTER XV.

———

September 1851.

EARLY the next morning I proceeded on horseback
with Joe Bellow and an engineer to the mine, which
was situated near a mining village called Tuttle-Town.
To reach this spot we had to cross a table mountain, so covered with the débris of former volcanic
eruptions, that it was a perfect cinder-heap upon a
large scale. The ground reverberated as we passed
over concealed craters, and for two or three miles we
were confined to a foot pace, as we picked our way
through the rough boulders that lay half buried in the
earth, like a field of winter turnips.

The Tuttletonians were not actively employed at
the time of our arrival, principally from the fact that
the diggings had "given out."

The quartz vein, however, was there, and after a
day's inspection, I was satisfied that in external

269

appearance at least it bore out the report that Joe Bellow had given of it. To the man who wants more money than he has (and few of us are free from that craving), the sight of massive veins of rock, peppered with specks of gold, is a trying spectacle.

As he sits upon a boulder on the outcrop, and extracts a piece of pure metal with the point of a knife, he is subject to a thrill which I am afraid is indicative of the sordid ideas of his nature;—when he descends the shaft, and by the aid of a candle still beholds the specks of gold, he draws a long breath, in mental contemplation of the wondrous wealth before him; then when the wealthy seam is placed at his service, on terms so easy that it appears quite thrown away, in all probability he will do as I did, swallow the bait, hook and all. The opinion of the engineer was highly satisfactory, as engineers' opinions generally are; we therefore returned to Sonora, where I plunged at once into the subject of mining statistics. I remember now how ridiculously plain the whole matter appeared; here was the gold,—you could see it and feel it,—well, all you had to do was to get it out! Argument would have been wasted upon any thick-headed fellow who looked upon the matter in any other light. But none such existed,—all Sonora was quartz-mine-mad,—and although no machinery had as yet reached this region, shafts were being sunk, and adits cut, in every hill around the town. One mine, which extended from the rear of the principal hotel, was owned entirely by Cornish miners; these had sunk two deep shafts, and connected them by a gallery, by which means two or three hundred yards of the vein were laid bare.

This vein was called the "Englishmen's mine," and it had not only the merit of being sufficiently rich to all appearance to justify the erection of machinery, but it was about the only lode that had been scientifically opened by miners, and which was ready without further expense to supply any amount of ore. But up to the time of my leaving the country, the owners of this vein, although Englishmen, had not been able to exert sufficient interest to get it "looked at," and if this incident should be read by any victim who has had two and twopence returned to him in exchange for the sovereign he invested in California Mining Companies, let him not as he contemplates his "small returns" lay the blame on the quartz rock of the country, for I assure him that the cause of failure is much nearer home; but of this I shall speak in its proper place.

Sonora is dependent for existence on the surrounding mining population; it is a town with a resident population of about three thousand souls, but with accommodation on the corral principle for about ten thousand more. Sonora is advantageously situated in one respect, inasmuch as it is irresponsible for the morals and conduct of its floating population; if Sunday is desecrated in Sonora by five thousand pleasure-seeking miners, Sonora washes its hands of that.

Sonora is one large house of entertainment for bonâ-fide travellers; and although nearly every one makes a point of travelling thither on a Saturday, to have a " burst " on Sunday, and return in penitence on Monday, Sonora washes its hands of that,—otherwise I should say that Sonora in 1851 was as loose a community as was that of San Francisco in 1849.

No church bells here usher in the Sabbath; but auction bells arouse the inhabitants equally to a full sense of the duties before them,—the sun shines for Sonora on this day alone, and in accordance with wise maxims, the population commences early to make hay.

The miners prefer buying everything at auction, and although I imagine the purchasers suffer in the long run by this principle, the " loafers " gain by it; for (supposing you are a loafer) you have only to mix with the crowd of bidders, and take out your clasp-knife; you can then make an excellent meal from

the samples exposed to view, presuming always that
your constitution will stand a mixture of salt butter,
Chinese sugar, pickles, and bad brandy. Joe Bellow
was an auctioneer, and certainly he understood his
business. Long before his sale commenced he would
place a keg of butter, or a bag of dried apples, outside his store, and the miners would surround these
luxuries like flies. Joe Bellow's object was to get a
"crowd" and this accomplished, the auction would
commence in this style :—

Joe Bellow takes his stand on a cask in the midst
of his samples, and startles you suddenly with "And
I'm only bid one dollar for a dozen of mixed pickles ;
one dollar, one dollar, one doll—try them, gentlemen."
In the meantime Joe nods to an imaginary bidder in
the distance, and rattles on, "One and a half, one and a
half, one and h—" "Doo," says a Dutchman, with
his mouth full of pickled gherkin. "Two dollars I'm
offered for a dozen of mixed pickles." "Dos y medio,"
says a Spaniard, under the influence of a green bean.
"Ah! Senor Don Pacheco," says Joe, "son los
escabéches d'Inghelterra, muy buenos, muy finos ! "

"Have I any advance on two dollars and a half ? "
"Trois piastres," says a French restaurateur. "Three
dollars I am bid for a dozen of pickles that cost five
dollars in the States, Tenez! Monsieur Leon voici

des cornichons comme il faut. Three dollars, three doll's, three doll's"—" Dree-and-a-half," says the Dutchman, to whom they are finally knocked down, just as an old miner observes that "darn him if his knife aint turned blue with the darned vitrol juice." No description, however, can do justice to the rapidity with which Joe Bellow knocks down his lots, or to the easy impudence with which he meets all disparaging remarks from his tasters; and such is human nature, that even in the mines, where few simpletons are to be found, there was no butter so rancid but Joe Bellow could dispose of it on a Sunday by means of his volubility and soft-sawder ! I heard a Dutchman enquiring very anxiously one day for some one in Sonora whose name he did not know ;—" What is he like ? " said one, but the Dutchman was apparently not apt at description, and no clue could be gained; at last he spluttered out, " Tyfel ! I mean dat man dat cries always ' bickel, bickel, bickel,' " and everybody knew at once that Joe Bellow was the individual required, and directed the Dutchman accordingly.

The auction extending as it does across the street will be interrupted most probably by a Mexican funeral procession, headed by a brass band, playing dolefully ; scarcely has this filed by when the same band will return to an inspiriting tune, accompanied by merry-andrews and torredores, who proclaim the day's amusement in the bull arena. A man goes rapidly by on a lean horse he is selling at auction ; he is bid twenty dollars for a flea-bitten roan, " Will anybody say twenty-five ? " Half-an-hour elapses, and back he comes, will anybody advance on thirty dollars ?—By-and-by he is seen tearing through the street, scattering Joe Bellow's pickle-eaters to the right and left, and sending the mud flying into the sample keg of butter,—going for forty dollars, going for—and-as he does not appear again upon the scene, it is presumed that the animal has either been sold, or withdrawn until the ensuing Sunday.

The horses that are sold this way are not very showy, nor do they fetch much, but it may be remarked that if the high-priced horses that are occasionally sold with us on account of their owners " going abroad," were first subjected to a four hours' galop, over a stony road, in presence of the bidders, many of them would be " knocked down " for even less than are these Californian ponies.

For these animals have at least the advantage of possessing four sound legs, and unless my experience much misleads me, three are as many as you can reasonably expect in any animal whose pedigree will admit of a gentleman mounting him. Civilisation has done for horses, what in some instances it has for their masters, improved their exteriors at the expense of a ruined constitution. I wonder what Choctaw would think, if he could be made to comprehend the fact, that there were horses of twice his size and strength who couldn't " feed " without the aid of gentian, just as their masters take a glass of " ver- meuthe " before dinner to " gammon an appetite."

In Sonora, every man carried arms, generally a Colt's revolver, buckled behind, with no attempt at concealment. In countries where men have no protec- tion from the law, and the vicious preponderate, this is necessary. And although it is much to be deplored, that this necessity did exist, its consequences were less deleterious to society than would have been expected. For the fear of the law, in the best regu- lated community is not so strong as the fear of sudden death ; and if quarrels and assassinations were rare, comparatively, in the mountains, it was owing to the fact that every man was able to protect himself. It is generallly inferred, as a matter of course, that where all men carry arms, blood is shed on the first passionate impulse, and life is not safe. This is not so ; it is where all carry arms that quarrels are less rare, and bullying less known than elsewhere, although the population may be be more vitiated and intemperate than that of other countries.

From the fact of all men being armed, robberies are less frequent in the mines than would be expected, and in most cases where murders have been perpetrated, the victims have been unarmed.

There are many countries where the carrying of defensive weapons is imperative as a preventative against outrage, but to those who from choice or necessity visit such places, this Californian rule may be of some value :—

" Never draw your pistol unless you intend to use it."

Previous to the last San Francisco fire I have recorded, burglaries were so common, that it became necessary to carry fire-arms after dark, more particularly as the streets were not lighted. An acquaintance of mine was walking late one night through a street which was apparently deserted, and in which one dim light alone shed a sickly ray from over the door of a closed restaurant. As he reached this spot, a man started from the obscurity, and requested with the politeness of a Claude Duval to know the time. With equal civility, my friend presented the dial of his watch to the light, and allowing the muzzle of his revolver to rest gracefully upon the turnip, he invited the stranger to inspect for himself. Slowly the latter advanced, and the sickly ray gleamed likewise on the barrel of his " six-shooter," as with some difficulty he satisfied himself respecting the time.

Both then prepared to depart, and for the first time the light fell on their faces ; then these desperate fellows discovered that they were no burglars, but old acquaintances, who had dined in company on that very evening.

But this is not the only part of the world where it is prudent to look on every man as a rogue until you know him to be honest.

Having completed my mining calculations to my entire satisfaction (unfortunately), I returned to Vallejo, and on my arrival there discovered that the order for this young city had been countermanded by the government. Everybody was preparing for departure, and as the place owned a justice of the peace, writs were being served in every direction. My hotel *

* The reader will observe, if he pleases, that in erecting this hotel I had no view to becoming its landlord : had I taken any situation in it, it would have been in the capacity of " boots," which berth a " handy young man " can turn to better account in this country than even the head cook. That a cook's situation, with or without tea and sugar is lucrative, the following anecdote will attest :—In '49 the captain of a merchant brig at San Fransisco having engaged a crew, regardless of expense, in lieu of that which had run away, regardless of their contracts and arrears of pay, found himself still in want of a cook. Meeting a negro on the beach he offered him the situation, and to the enquiry of the latter respecting

was placed under execution on account of the two horsetails, before-mentioned; the law was arrayed against me, but as in Vallejo the law's authority was represented by one man, and the individual supposed to be amenable was represented by another, the law did not always get the best of it, and as far as my own case was concerned, it consisted in requesting the sheriff to leave the premises, which he did gladly enough, having business of his own to look after. Many of those who come overland to California, bring one or two young blacks from the plantations with them; these of course if not previously freed, become so on their arrival, but they are in all cases much attached to their masters, and are very useful servants, so much so, that they assume great importance and begin to think that nothing can be done without them. I was amused one day at overhearing one of these young niggers, who being aroused from his sweet slumber, under a waggon, by his master's reiterated cries of "Bob," drew himself slowly out and muttered, "Bob here, Bob there, Bob everywhere; b'lieve, by Gad, you could't come to California

salary, the captain said he could give but two pounds a day. Having cocked his hat, folded his arms and adjusted his legs as niggers do, this fellow laughed musically and said, "dat if de capten wish to hire heseff out for five pounds a day to fill dat occupation, jes walk up to the restaurant and he would set him to work *immediently*."

without Bob." "What's that you say, sir," said his master, who unluckily heard the last part of the speech. There was no reply, but Bob made for the hills there and then, and his guilty conscience would not permit him to appear for three days, when he returned very thin, but set himself to work so assiduously, that it really did appear as if nothing could be done without him.

I paid a short visit to San Francisco, and returned with such stores as I thought necessary, and with these, Barnes and Thomas started at once for Tuttle Town.

Among these stores was a bale of canvas, of which I determined my next Californian house should be built, and a barrel of gunpowder, with which I contemplated disturbing the bowels of the earth.

Rowe had decided upon accompanying me, a circumstance which I shall never regret, for he was in every respect an excellent companion to the day I parted with him. In mountain life, a friend whose tastes are congenial to your own is indeed an acquisition; for each happiness is doubled then, and let misfortune come as it will, its sting is ever allayed by the sympathy of one true heart beside you.

With the "Old Soldier," "Choctaw," "Tiger," and "Bevis," we embarked late one evening on board a Stockton steam-boat; this latter was naturally a slow boat, but she managed to perform her journey in as good time as the rest, for her engineer was a famous fellow, who held life cheap, and maintained as his creed that " she was bound to go anyhow ; " so she went anyhow, trembling fore and aft, with an engine-room full of steam, and a blaze from her funnel that lit up the banks of the river on either side. There were few passengers on board, which was fortunate, as there were few sleeping bunks.

It is not customary to undress when seeking repose in these bunks ; in fact, decency forbids you doing so ; for they are openly exposed on either side of the saloon, and this latter is generally filled up, for the best part of the night, by card-players.

A placard informs you that " gentlemen are requested not to go to bed in their boots ; " but as the proprietors do not guarantee that your boots shall not be stolen if you take them off, this request is seldom complied with. I remember attending a political meeting in a little church at Benicia ; in each pew was a poster, which requested that you would neither cut the wood-work, nor spit on the floor, but the authorities had provided no spittoons, so, as a gentleman observed to me whilst inside the sacred edifice, " what the something was a man to do who chewed ? "

At daylight we were at Stockton, and landing our horses we were soon in the saddle and making the most of the cooler part of the day. Nothing worthy of mention occurred on our journey, excepting that at the end of forty miles our animals were as fresh as when they started. We pulled up to dine at the Stanislaus, which river we crossed in a ferry. An acquaintance of mine once crossed at this spot under peculiar circumstances. He was proceeding from one digging to another, and had three quarters of a pound of gold dust sown up in his pantaloons; he was an Englishman, and after the manner of many of his countrymen, he carried an umbrella, which nothing could induce him to part with.

There was no ferry in those days, and when he arrived at the banks of the river, he determined to swim across; but then his clothes and the *umbrella*, how was he to get these across, and how could he go over without them? He was seized with an idea, and at once acted upon it; extending his umbrella, he placed his clothes inside, and fastened a line to the handle; with one end of this in his mouth, he plunged into the current, and struck out manfully with his boat in tow for the opposite bank. But the gingham, like most experimental vessels, leaked so much on her first cruise, that when the centre of the stream was

reached, nothing could be seen above water but the
vessel's mast head, which was represented by an
ivory hand clasping a round ruler.   Now the order of
things became reversed, for the current was strong,
and having taken firm hold of the umbrella, the
question was whether to go down the stream with it
or let it go.   The latter course was adopted, not on
account of the gold dust or the clothes, but from a
pure and unshaken attachment to the parachute
itself. After some effort, not unattended with danger,
" gingham " was safely brought into port, but on
beaching it, the cargo had vanished.   Madam, our

adventurer had a straw hat on his head with a very narrow brim, and with this article of attire and his umbrella, he proceeded for about seven miles without encountering a soul, when he reached what had been an encampment. The diggers had left, but there was as much second-hand clothing lying about as would have furnished a regiment. Selecting the best of this and washing it, my friend was soon equipped, and went on his way rejoicing; rejoicing for this reason, that although gold dust and clothes had gone to the bottom, he had not only saved his precious umbrella, but had newly equipped himself from a "ready-made clothing mart," with no bill to pay.

The road was very dusty and the heat intense, but nothing seemed to tire our beasts. The last part of our journey consisted of a gradual ascent, and in many places the ground was covered with small round rocks, that would materially have impeded the progress of most horses ; but Choctaw allowed no obstacle to arrest his long swinging " lope," and the Old Soldier, with his tongue lolling out of his mouth, followed his protégé unflinchingly. I have sketched these two worthies ; the Old Soldier, it will be perceived (to show that he has still a kick left in him) is expressing his disgust at the shadow of a crow that is thrown on the road, whilst Choctaw, still suspicious, plants his Indian legs among the loose rocks with an accuracy really marvellous. Before night we arrived at Sonora, having by a circuit that we purposely made, completed a journey of nearly seventy miles.

CHAPTER XVI.

Sept. 1851.

In less than a fortnight we had a couple of canvas houses erected at Tuttle Town ; each of these had a large fire-place and chimney, built of mud and stones, and surmounted by an empty barrel for a chimney-pot, after the popular architecture of the mines. Rowe and I occupied the small shanty, whilst in the larger one I had Barnes, Thomas, and a couple of English miners.

Our houses faced the main street of Tuttle Town ; this at the time was indicated by stakes, there being as yet but three buildings in the place. Higher up the hill and near the main shaft were eight Mexican miners, whom I had hired for the purpose of quarrying the ore ; having supplied these with about twenty yards of canvas, half a dozen raw bullock hides, an

286

unlimited quantity of beans and a frying-pan, they made themselves very comfortable in their own way. I must not omit to mention that I had a canvas stable for our four horses, not that these required any shelter during the warm dry nights, but simply because I wished to avoid the inconvenience of losing twelve of my party at once, and finding some morning that my four horses and eight Mexicans had departed in company. Most of the Mexicans of California are from Sonora,* and horse-stealing is a characteristic weakness of that country. These people become such adepts at this trade, that I dare say if a party of them were to visit New York, they would steal the woolly colt out of Barnum's Museum, although to lure a dead horse from a man of that gentleman's acuteness, would require a great amount of ingenuity and patience.

Having now established myself at the mines, it is incumbent on me to explain to the patient reader my exact position there, as otherwise I shall be accused of having attempted to accomplish that for which I was incapacitated, a censure which I do not wish to be applied to me otherwise than as an author, in which quality I must perforce admit its truth.

My object at Tuttle Town was to test the value of

* In Mexico.

the quartz vein there, and if with the assistance of
such miners as I had engaged, I could satisfy myself
that the vein held out sufficient promise of remuneration, it had been agreed between myself and a friend
at San Francisco (he whose death I have recorded)
that sufficient machinery should be erected to give
the ore a fair experimental trial.

Amateur performances are seldom successful ; and
whether he wishes to fatten short-horn bullocks for
an agricultural show, or take the helm of his yacht
in a race for the cup, your amateur in one way or
the other, generally " comes out wrong."   " Chacun
a son metier," is a motto more generally applicable
than we are willing to admit, although there are few
of us who have not tried something that we had no
business with.   Still man is emulous and vain, and
until the end of the world fat Muggins will waltz,
ignorant Foodle will talk, and travellers like myself
will appear in print, and let us appear ever so ridiculous to others, we cannot, and will not, acknowledge
that " every one to his trade " applies in any degree
to us.   But where a new course is opened for emula-
tion, all may start in the race, and former experience
bore so little on the subject of the quartz mines of
California, and the means of extracting the gold there-
from, that I entered upon my new employment with no

more difficulties to contend against than others in the same field. And this, be it understood, should always give courage and confidence in a new country, for although a little more retiring modesty would become both Muggins and Foodle (not forgetting myself in a literary capacity), the same diffidence in the mines of California would act as a bar to the research and experience so necessary for that country. And however we may fail in our exertions we ought not on that account, as is too often the case, to be ridiculed, for the failure of one brings experience to the many, and some one must "pioneer" the road. The prudent wait until the track is clear and the way is easy, and when every tree is blazed and every obstacle removed, they advance chuckling, of course, as the miner does who follows the prospecter; thus the pioneer and his follower resemble two boys, one of whom will not enter the river until his companion has tested the temperature of the water and the depth of the stream.

The quartz mines of California were discovered and opened almost entirely by men who had no previous knowledge of gold mining, therefore in many respects they worked in the dark, and from want of capital their hard bought experience served only to benefit others.

But the more fortunate of these bands of pioneers are now receiving an ample compensation for the privation they suffered, the toil they underwent, and the ridicule with which they were assailed. Auriferous quartz has been found in numerous cases to yield a rich return, even to the unscientific miner in California; how great then must be the wealth amassed, one would suppose, by those experienced gentlemen, who, with capital at their command, have been deputed by English companies to do the same work on a larger scale. Yet experience has proved that the great mining captains of the age have nothing to laugh at, even in the unsuccessful efforts of such a worm as I.

Unity and goodwill had been so long established amongst my little party, that we were soon comfortable in every respect, and actively employed. The vein extended for about half a mile, and the three spots I selected for exploration had each its band of men sinking a " prospecting " shaft.

Rowe and I had ample employment in superintending the operations, and testing the samples of ore that were daily selected from each pit; so with windlasses and buckets, crowbars and drills, gunpowder and fuze matches, pestles, mortars, retorts, and quicksilver, we each of us had our occupation, and were happy as the day was long. The quartz was sharp and cut like glass, so we wore deer-skin "trowserloons," our beards grew, our muscles increased to an alarming extent, our manners were less toned down than was usual, in fact they were *swaggering*, our appetites were very large, but for all that we were so happy that even the pleasures of the "little valley" fell into insignificance before those of our Tuttletonian life; and this arose in a great measure from the fact that we all entertained a strong belief, that one day or other our labour would be rewarded.

Who talks of hope and disappointment in the same breath? Shall a day of the one efface or tarnish the recollection of a year's happiness brightened by the other?—Not with me whilst I live. "See here, now, boys," said a Tuttletonian miner, one day, as he held up to an admiring crowd a small and well-constructed lady's boot. "The chunk aint found that can buy this boot; 'taint for sale, *no-how!*"

A lady's boot to you, or I, reader, is not much unless we are married and have to pay for a pair occasionally; but so long as we can associate our hopes of earthly happiness for the future with some emblem held out to us even at arm's length, as was the miner's "lady's boot," we may go on

our way to work as did his gratified spectators more cheerfully and light of heart.

When a man recals some sensation with more than ordinary pleasure, it is very usual for him, particularly if he is a writer of travels, to ask you if you have experienced the same. Says one "reader, did you ever witness a sun-set from Chimborazo?" Says the other "reader, did you ever eat a mangostein?" Unfortunately the reader is unable to reply until the description of these wonders has been perpetrated. I have alluded to this custom in excuse for asking the reader if he ever groomed his own horse and derived pleasure from it? If not, I recommend him after he has managed Chimborazo and the mangostein to try it. Mainspring's coat was daily rubbed by me, when my own coat hung neglected on a peg; but the fact is, he was a very handsome horse, and in the mines such a rarity is a passport. With the natural vanity of man, I found that Mainspring attracted more attention than I did, so I allowed my beard to run to seed, and bestowed all my pains in beautifying the dumb animal.

You, madam, who have viewed with pleasure the envious glances that have been cast on the lovely bonnet you wore at Chiswick, will understand the emotions I felt when miners left their pits and claims to pronounce with less spleen upon the beauties of my steed.

The Old Soldier and Choctaw were seldom groomed; the mud in which, of course, they wallowed, was generally removed from their coats with a spade, and on grand occasions they were finished off with a broom. Rowe had a cream-coloured mare that was considered by the miners "some pumpkins," an expression which indicates great merit, and is equally applied to a chew of tobacco, or the President of the United States.

We generally rode into Sonora of an evening, for we were always in want of something, and our drills and pickaxes, in particular, soon became blunted by the hard quartz, and had to be tempered again by the Sonora blacksmith. We would return by moonlight, and had always to pass through a camp of Mexicans of the worst character; these fellows not only cast their covetous glances on our horses in open day-light, but on more than one occasion they attempted at night to entrap us into a position that would have left us unable to defend either our lives or our beasts. They had a quantity of curs in their camp, and these, as we rode through in the moonlight, would rush out, being set upon us, and worry us on all sides with their yelping; they would follow us, howling, for some distance, and our natural impulse was to shoot them with our revolvers, for they were like wolves, but we were soon wise enough to refrain from discharging our fire-arms, for we should thus have left ourselves defenceless, against the half-dozen mounted ruffians we would encounter higher up the road, waiting, undoubtedly, for this result.

Two armed white men need fear little interruption from Mexicans provided a proper amount of caution is exercised, and no sign of trepidation is evinced. But their first principle is to attempt to throw you off your guard, therefore the best rule in meeting such men is to insist at once that they do not approach within the distance at which they can throw their deadly lasso, a weapon more formidable in the dark than fire-arms. Whenever, singly or with Rowe, I met a party of mounted Mexicans in the mines, I drew up on one side of the road until they passed, and after dusk I took the precaution of warning them to a respectful distance, nor was this unnecessary, for the Mexicans encamped round Tuttle Town committed many murders, and my horse alone was sufficient inducement for them, independent of the sums of money that the necessities of my party often required me to carry of a night.

One morning on entering the canvas stable that adjoined my hut, I discovered that Mainspring was gone; his halter had been cut, and there was no doubt that he had been stolen. Fortunately a drizzly rain was falling sufficient to moisten the ground, and this had probably set in about an hour after the thieves had removed the horse at the risk of their lives. Without some knowledge of Mexican cunning, it would have been useless to have attempted to track a stolen horse of Mainspring's fleetness. We presumed at starting that he had been taken over the table mountain in our rear, as his foot prints could leave no trace behind for some miles in that direction.

Rowe and I then started on the search, and after crossing the mountain we halted at a gulch. With some trouble we discovered at last that the horse had crossed here, for he had one cutting shoe, the heel of which left a slight imprint ; from the gulch we traced him to a tree, and here the ground being covered with dead leaves and brushwood, all sign was lost. Accident favoured us, for a few miles further on we again hit his trail at another gulch, but here he appeared to be returning. A close inspection, however, proved that his shoes had been turned, for the heel of the cutting shoe was on the wrong side, still we lost him again among the trees, and as evening advanced we began to despair. But soon we arrived at a Mexican encampment, and here by some stupid oversight on the part of the thieves, Mainspring's rug was left lying exposed on the ground. All had protested their ignorance of the matter on our arrival, but now with the blanket staring them in the face, they soon produced the horse from a distant tent in the bushes, and assured us that a man had left it there that morning, and had gone on his way.

But a Mexican who was sleeping in a tent in mud-splashed clothes was the thief, I knew : he started when I roused him up suddenly and held the blanket before his eyes : but he swaggered out in apparent unconcern, and lighting a cigarito with admirable sang-froid, he began to play at cards with one of the others. I was too glad to recover Mainspring, to care about troubling myself by taking the Mexican back to Tuttle Town on suspicion, and I dare say he was not sorry when Rowe and I departed, for a horse thief in the mines has not much chance of his life when detected, and of this he is fully aware. It has ever puzzled me on reflection, that where so much pains had been taken to remove all trace of the horse, the glaring evidence of the theft should be left forgotten in open daylight, and I am inclined to think that the horse thieves considered themselves safe from pursuit, and were rather surprised at our appearance. From that day our horses were chained and padlocked every night.

The American residents of our mining village were very sociable and kind, and the good feeling they evinced towards us added materially to our comfort.

Englishmen and Americans are for the most part the victims of prejudice, and when they meet, too often each one expects to find in the other one who is prepared to depreciate and misunderstand him and his country. They approach each other like two strange dogs who stand head and tail, with bristling hairs, rubbing their ribs together with an angry scowl, for no reason on earth except that they are two dogs.

It may have been my fortune to have effaced some false impressions respecting my countrymen from American minds; but, at all events, I have had an opportunity of divesting myself of much prejudice by a social intercourse with them.

It is asserted that the Americans are great boasters, and I grant that retiring modesty is not the chief characteristic of the race ; but it is right to remember, that for a long period, the Americans have been rather depreciated than otherwise, and unmerited depreciation will probably induce a habit of boasting more than anything else. When we tell our friend reprovingly not to blow his own trumpet, we presume that such merit as he possesses will be fully acknowledged. Public opinion has not until latterly dealt fairly with the Americans in all respects, and it is perhaps for this reason that they sound their own praises with stentorian lungs; if they have not been justified in doing so they have at least practically overturned that old saw of our revered ancestors, that "those who *talk* most *do* least."

American character is necessarily very varied, and nowhere is this more clearly perceived than in California, where all classes, freed in a great measure from conventional restrictions, appear in their true garbs. I do not presume to write of American character, I can only record my experience of individuals as I have seen them in the shifting scenes of colonial life; but I think that I have had sufficient intercourse with Americans of all grades to warrant my asserting that foreign historians have too often unfairly paraded their faults, whilst their own writers have in many instances erred equally on the side of their virtues; I believe therefore that there is ample room on our bookshelves for one fair unprejudiced work on the people of the United States of America. Man is ordained to be charitable, and authors are not, that I am aware of, exempted from this command; if, therefore, in writing of a people, a little more pains were taken to discover their virtues, and a less wholesale principle was adopted in regard to the record of their vices, great good might be done to the nation written of and no harm that I know of would accrue to the author. The man who can kindle a warmer feeling in one nation towards another by displacing, with a little judicious reasoning, the prejudices that may affect the latter, waves a stronger wand than the most bitter satirist that ever lived and wrote.

Our vices are generally uppermost; this was exem-

plified in the " Old Soldier," for your first acquaintance with that animal might possibly be cemented,
as it were, by a kick in the ribs, or a bite on the
shoulder ; but, recovered from this shock, the longer
you knew him the better you liked him ; and the old
fellow, when once satisfied that you were *his* friend,
would appear to you in a very different light than
when under the influence of suspicion, justified, I'll
be bound, by the experience of his life, he attempted
to do you a mischief.

I do not wish to compare this poor beast with a
man, much less a nation, but the simile serves me so
far as to illustrate the fallacy of first impressions as
applied either to man or horse ; yet, while all acknow-
ledge this for a truism, we find that half the books
of travels that analyse so fearlessly the character of
the people visited are valueless as commentaries on
them, either from hastiness or unfairness of opinion,
on the one side, or laboriously-studied partiality on
the other.   But seldom does the work of an alien run
into this latter fault, and most books on America
remind me of a volume of Veterinary Surgery, of
which, open what page you will, you are met with a
description of a curb or a splint, a spavin or a ring-
bone, with the author's directions for a complete
cure !

*   *   *   *

How small a trifle will disturb, at times, the even current of one's life ; let me recal the sole drawback to our otherwise complete contentment at Tuttle Town.

One of our neighbours had two pigs, and these, like all four-footed animals in the mines, had a roving commission, and lived by nocturnal plunder. This practice we could bear with, as much from our reverence for pork, as from the fact that it was a free country for man or pig. But these wretches took a fancy to scratching themselves, in the dead of night, against the canvas shanty that Rowe and I inhabited; there were plenty of posts, but they preferred a shanty; now, as the only hard substances they could find were our recumbent bodies, as we pressed against the canvas wall, the pigs scratched themselves against us, and as this occurred for about four hours every night, accompanied by the satisfactory grunts which the temporary alleviation of cutaneous disease elicits from the pig, our rest was continually being broken upon. We kept water boiling, and waking up suddenly we would scald them, we harpooned them with crowbars, damaged the vertebræ of their backs with the sharp edges of spades, fired blank cartridges under their noses, and scarified them with a deadly fire of broken bottles; but to no purpose, they would come back and rub us out of bed again regardless of any injury we could do them. The owner of them was absent, and there was no " pound," honour forbade our shooting them, and we never could catch them to " corral " them. So, for the best part of a twelvemonth, we were nightly roused up by these intruders, who itched so badly that they rubbed our frail tenement out of the perpendicular. Soon they had a litter, and then, while they still rubbed, the little pigs would get under the house and squeal, and although we kept a long pole with a steel fork attached to it, with which we tried to " grain " them, as we do dolphins at sea, yet it was to no purpose, and they did as they liked with us up to the day we left. At first we used to set the dogs at them, but, being savage combatant pigs, rendered reckless by a free life, they would stand at bay with their sterns bulging against our tent, which they evidently mistook for the rock which was " to fly from its firm base as soon as they," which it nearly did on one or two occasions; moreover, the dogs had enough to do to keep off six donkeys and about a dozen curs, who were generally very musical when the moon was up.

I mention this circumstance because we hear so

much of the power of the human will, and I am satisfied that a pig's will is stronger ; and it is, moreover,
not only a traveller's duty to record a fact, but he is
expected likewise to discover something new.

CHAPTER XVII.

October, 1851.

THE diggings in our immediate vicinity were not
actively worked, as there was not sufficient water for
the purpose; this, however, was shortly to be remedied,
for companies composed of miners were at work in
every direction, conducting water from the rivers to
the dry diggings; and at this moment new plots of
auriferous soil are daily being added to the area of
"paying ground" in the mines by the artificial introduction of the water which nature has denied to them.
Most of these companies have received handsome
returns; the charge to each miner supplied with
water being about two shillings a day.

This affords another instance of the successful
employment of capital originally procured by gold
digging; and if you wanted a few shares in one of

304

these young companies, you could procure them without money, for by taking your coat off and helping to cut the ditch, you could in six months work yourself into a very respectable stockholder. I suppose each traveller who returns to his home from California, whether he is an Englishman or a Sandwich Islander, is questioned on all sides as to whether the " diggings " are nearly exhausted ?   This is easy to answer in the negative, but then follows a query far more difficult to reply to, viz., " when will they be ? " Conjecture must necessarily have much weight in determining this problem, statistics of the past or present yield of the placers being almost valueless for that purpose.   Yet this should be a question of very great financial importance, and not alone as regards the probable duration of the twelve million sterling now annually exported from California. For we must consider how far we are sustained by facts in presuming that the present yield of this country will be doubled, nay, quadrupled annually before the surface-soil is left again as once no doubt it was, valueless in gold.   Of course, the gold mines must some day be exhausted ; let us see then how far we are justified in supposing this day to be, comparatively speaking, distant, as regards California.   I offer the following remarks with the avowal that they are of worth only as the crude opinions of one who has had nearly all that practically bears upon the subject brought before his notice, but as they will necessarily be dull and heavy as a blue book, I recommend the generality of those who have followed me thus far, to skip this chapter, which they probably will do with all the rest of the book.

For you, reader, who have sent to the circulating library for the " Newcomes," and have had this book forwarded you as a " new work," (the " Newcomes " being out,) can scarcely be expected to peruse in your present state of disgust, a chapter on gold mines : I therefore dedicate this " paper " to two individuals, one of whom shall be the gold mine victim before alluded to, as contemplating the two and twopence he received for his invested sovereign, and the other is that unknown man, who, in the *ennui* of a long sea voyage, shall peruse, mayhap, as I have done before to-day, the pages with which his trunk is lined.

Mormon Gulch was the name of a ravine that was about a hundred yards from my tent, it was reported to have been the wealthiest digging in the mines, and according to rumour, half an hour's work with a clasp knife or tin spoon, had invariably enriched any of the fortunate Mormons who first discovered it in 1848. Since those days, however, the earth, or stones rather, for these preponderate, had been turned over again and again, each time yielding less, until the soil ceased to return sufficient remuneration to the only process of labour that could be at that time applied to it. But before now water has been conducted there, and by the more wholesale process of sluice-washing, the gulch claims are again up in the market.

By-and-by we shall hear of the sluice-washing companies having deserted the gulch, and perhaps for a short period the red stony gravel will lie idle; but soon steam-engines and some process of securing the gold by amalgamation with quicksilver, will brighten up old Mormon Gulch again, and there is no knowing how remote the day is, when its red banks shall for once and all, finally and for the twentieth time, be reported to have " given out."

The history of Mormon Gulch, and the future I have sketched for it, is applicable to every ravine in the country, so far as this, that each auriferous flat or gulch will be subjected to certain processes, until at last the appliances of steam and science shall have robbed every square foot of earth of the treasure it contains.

Now, if all the gold territory of this country had been seized upon and worked at the time that Mormon Gulch was first discovered, we might form some estimate of the time when machinery should be brought to bear generally upon the placers; but as yet we cannot ascertain the amount of gold-bearing soil that exists; for not only are fresh diggings still brought to light, in the vicinity of the original discoveries, but we have ample proof that plenty lies beyond in the direction of the Sierra Nevada, which now, from the presence of hostile Indians, cannot be disturbed, and indeed, for the present, is not wanted.

The number of those who are now actually collecting gold by mining in California, may be computed at about one hundred and forty thousand men.

The obstacles that are alike presented by the extremes of the wet and dry seasons, will not admit, probably, of these miners working for more than two hundred days in the year, and the average daily sum amassed by each man, may be fairly quoted at three and a half dollars, or fifteen shillings.

This will give an annual yield of twenty-one millions sterling from California, and I have no reason to doubt that this sum is obtained, although it does not (for many reasons) appear in the reported exports of specie from the country.

Now, if this sum can be annually realised by the exertions of comparatively so small a body of men, who have even at the latest dates no better plan of securing the gold than by a rude system of washing, what may we expect when machinery is employed, and labour concentrated?

Those portions of the placer fields that would reward manual labour with less than one or two dollars a day, are as yet unmolested, for as yet the ruling rates of wages in the mines is higher, being guided by the average yield. Therefore it is difficult to place a limit on the amount of auriferous earth that now, rejected by the miner, will, by the proper application of machinery and the reduction of labour, eventually produce a vast return. There is scarcely a hill-side but gives evidence of the existence of gold, but although this soil will not at present repay manual labour, no one can suppose that the metal will be allowed to rest there undisturbed.

The distribution of gold in the soil is most eccentric, and this is attributable probably to three causes : * firstly, that for the most part it was disintegrated from the matrix during the stupendous volcanic action to which all the gold territory of California has been subjected; secondly, that it has been carried to and fro by vast masses of water, the result of heavy rains,

* Independent of the probability of there having been more than one formation.—See Appendix.

or more probably of heavy falls of snow in the mountains, that have suddenly melted and carried all before them ; finally, from the land-slips and accumulations of upper soil that must necessarily result where steep hills of gravel have been for ages subjected to the sudden transitions of wet and dry seasons.

I tread very carefully whenever I find myself on the geologist's ground, bearing in mind my scientific friend at Murderer's Bar, who reached the bottom so much quicker than he desired ; therefore I can only suggest ; and the two readers to whom this discourse is dedicated, whilst they deplore the ignorance which prevents me leading them through a labyrinth of formations and stratas, must place something to my credit on the score of modesty.

Wherever gold is discovered in California, particles of quartz are found adhering to it more or less ; this quartz, even when found at great depths, is generally rounded by the action of water, for quartz, when detached by violent action, is naturally angular, and inclined to splinter, and from its hardness it must require ages to give it the form of a pebble, by the slow process of grinding it receives in a comparatively dry mountain gorge. This, taken in conjunction with the facts that the gold is found now on the surface, and now low down resting on the bed rock, here forced into clefts of granite, and again in clusters of small pear-shaped nuggets, as if the metal had been ejected by intense heat, and had dripped from the volcanic boulders that lie scattered around; tends to bear out the supposition that disintegrated gold has been cast into places that time and accident alone can reveal, and that the original opinion that the gold was on the surface only no longer holds good.

Tunnelling has already been applied to rich hills in the mines with great success, and this fact alone is of great importance, in so far that it leaves us powerless to place a limit on the amount of auriferous soil that is imbedded in the small round hillocks that extend over a space of nearly four hundred miles, north and south.

Where ingenuity aided by science is at fault, a very slight clue will often accidentally lead to the solution of a problem; thus much capital has already been devoted to the damming of those streams in California, of which the banks were found to be wealthy; but in few instances hitherto have the beds been found to be productive: yet they must be so at some point, unless we are to imagine, what is improbable, that gold has been carried by rain water to the verge of a swift stream, and then has been arrested there without any apparent obstacle.

There is something capricious about this metal in its released state ; a search for it, even where evidence of its existence has been shown, is seldom attended with success, yet every day almost chance brings to light some fresh gold field.

I remember a gentleman who, taking an early Sunday walk among the hills that surround the town of Sonora, struck his foot against a stone.   He should have found a sermon in it, for he was not likely to find one anywhere else, but in the agony of a muti-lated great toe, he turned and apostrophised the rock in unbecoming language ; but he suddenly checked his impetuous feelings, and we will hope from a good motive ; whether or no, the offending quartz was so richly coated with the dross that we make a point of despising when we can't get enough of it, that he took it home.   It was found to contain more gold than quartz, and yet within a few hundred yards of a populous city, it had protruded itself ostentatiously without notice for two or three years.

It is difficult to understand why gold remained so long undiscovered in California, considering that so much of it was on the surface, even in those parts of the country already inhabited by whites.   The

Indians, who will search assiduously for the flints
they require for arrow-heads, do not seem to have
been aware of the existence of gold on the plains,
although the savages of the as yet unexplored mountain districts, are found with gold in their possession.
The early Spanish priests evidently sought for it without success, judging from the old shafts that have
been sunk, on part of the banks of the Stanislaus
River; and yet these explorations were ineffectually made in the centre of a rich district, and by a
class of gentlemen who were never in the habit of
overlooking a good thing. Some of the best diggings
have been discovered by market-gardeners, who have
chosen some apparently valueless tract for the purpose
of cabbage growing, and it is a fact that one man
with more energy than agricultural experience, who
was abusing the earth for producing cabbages that
were all stalk, found on rooting up one very lengthy
specimen, that a piece of gold adhered to the roots.

Holden's garden, near Sonora, is a case in point;
this was found to be so rich, that the gamblers of the
town sallied out to take possession of it, and a fight
occurred, in which one or two lives were lost before
the " claims " could be adjusted.

For four years Holden's acre of cabbage ground has
been worked with great profit, pieces of gold of many

pounds weight each have been taken from it, and to
this day it is a rich digging, as times go.

It is possible that both my readers have heard of a
certain Irish pig that could only be induced to go in
one direction by being at the onset driven in another ;
it is somewhat this way with the search for gold.—
Start on a voyage of discovery for copper or coal, and
you will probably, if in a gold region, tumble down
and break your nose over a nugget as large as a
paving stone; but if you give chase to the seductive
metal itself, the toil of a lifetime will very likely not
counterbalance the first week's privation.

In respect to gold-fields, even if our argument leads
to no definite conclusion, it is something gained if
we can determine that no sign of diminution of yield
is as yet apparent,—as regards the future, the wisest
can only record an opinion. I believe for my part
that the gold-fields of California will certainly yield in
an equivalent proportion to their present produce for
many years, even if the diggers are left to their own
resources ;—what may be done with the soil eventually, when capital shall increase in the mines and
from the mines, is a question as impossible to solve
as that of the advance of science in other respects
within the next half century.

The miners of California are a highly intelligent

and determined race, possessed of a degree of *mechanical genius* that surprises me ; they have before them a large area of soil, which they, equally with myself, believe still to be most wealthy.   They may by-and-by have the advantages of foreign capital to help them ; but if not, the capital that their sinews can accumulate ounce by ounce from the gold soil will, in the long run, so far answer the end, that the hills will be burrowed and the streams turned, until the wealth is sifted from them, and then they have a gold territory, as yet partially explored, to fall back upon—the first range of the Sierra Nevada.

Now, like enterprising farmers, they sow again perhaps one half of the year's harvest, until each fertile spot shall be in cultivation, multiplying and fruitful ; and so long as we see that the gold from the soil is turned against the soil in the all-powerful form of capital, aided by science ; and so long as we know that what is separated to-day by the "long tom" may to-morrow be devoted to the erection of steam-engines and the sinking of vast tunnels ; we know that a great system of improvement is being carried out independent of *all external aid :* and in the facts that on every side attest the strong faith the miners hold themselves in respect of the inexhaustible nature of the soil, and in the evidences of success that meet us at all points, where fresh inventions are applied, we have the best guarantee that the "placers" of California are in a state of progressive improvement.

The reader will better understand this when I state that the miners of California have many of them had six years experience, are naturally men of ability, and are now in positions of independence, though still miners. The popular opinion respecting gold miners, is that of a body of rough, vagabond, long-haired men, who work one day with a tin pan and get drunk the next; this is perhaps what they were, to some extent; and San Francisco, which owes existence to the mines, was then a canvas village, given up to dissipation; but the tents have disappeared from Yerba Buena, and we have in their room a large and substantially-built city; equally have the mines changed, and the "vagabond population" stands forth in the shape of engineers, excavators, mechanics, and cunning inventors, and, better still, organised bands of labourers, who, under the guidance of these first, bring profit to themselves and benefit to the country generally.

The quartz mines of California must now be reviewed, for, in connection with the probable future yield of gold, they occupy a prominent position.

In that column of the " Times " which is expressly devoted to a review of the Share Markets, some half-dozen Californian quartz mine operations will be found daily recorded ; these, for the most part, are in a very sickly state. Why they are so is no business of mine; but the fact is no criterion of the value of the quartz lodes of California.

The quartz formation stretches in one great vein across the country for nearly three hundred miles in a north-westerly direction, and this main lode is throughout more or less impregnated with gold, excepting where it has been disturbed by volcanic eruption. From the main vein tributaries branch out on either side, throughout its length, and many of these possess undoubtedly sufficient wealth to repay labour, if this is properly applied. I say this cautiously, for I know something now of the traps and pit-falls that beset the path of the quartz miner. These are among them : you have rich and partially decomposed lodes that enrich you with a nest of gold on the onset, but lead you a wild-goose chase into the bowels of the earth before you find another ; you have broad lodes white as alabaster, speckled in parts with gold, but from which you must quarry more valueless quartz than the " paying seam " will compensate for ; and you have lodes that are liberally and evenly diffused

with gold, but contain so many properties antagonistic to amalgamation by quicksilver that the metal
you seek can only be secured by a most expensive
process. These are the lodes that do not pay; and
by this time probably the mining community here
know as much of them as I do.

But a great number of veins, worked unostenta-
tiously by American companies, are giving very satisfactory results; a *larger* number are paying their
expenses only, but with good prospects of improvement. But I must direct attention to this fact; the
amount of profit derived from quartz-mine speculations
is not of so much importance to my argument as the
number of quartz mines being worked. If many of
the lodes now open in California are bringing at
present a smaller percentage to their owners than was
anticipated, fault perhaps of imperfect machinery and
false economy, they are none the less of importance
as affecting the question of the yield of gold. For
although the hundred ounces per day that pass
through the stamping-mill may scarcely leave a profit
on the expenses, the hundred ounces are none the
less added to the gross daily yield of the country.
Palpably plain as this is, I mention it because we
are apt, when speaking of gold quartz mining as
comparatively profitless to speculators, to forget that

the gold is for all that compressed from the rock; and it is with this alone I have to do.

But as it may be observed that operations that combine so much risk of failure will shortly be abandoned, particularly in a country where money commands so high a rate of interest, I must mention these facts.

In the first place, many American mining companies are already paying handsome dividends, and those which are least successful have, in most instances, their machinery to blame more than the vein, on which it is erected; but everything is in favour even of those who are thus situated, for improvements in machinery start up on every side, labour and the expense of living is diminishing rapidly, whilst fresh developments bring new aspirants continually into the field. For there is something about quartz mining that is seductive; fail as you will, as long as some are successful around you there is a " never-say-die " feeling which ever prompts to fresh exertion in the same field.

I shall not attempt to draw conclusions from an estimate of the number of veins that are now being profitably worked, or the amount of gold that may be derived from them in California, as that country is still in a state of transition, and not yet ripe for figured calculations. I can only fall back again upon my belief, that where gold exists ready to man's hand, as it does in the great veins of California, the people of that region are not likely to allow it to remain slumbering.

Having now shown that the material, the capital, and the energy exist to warrant a belief amounting almost to a certainty, that an amount of gold will yet be produced from California that will throw into the shade the millions that have already been acquired, I leave it to others to argue how far the same facts apply to Australia, Oregon, and other gold-fields as yet less perfectly developed. I scarcely dare guess at the sum that the next ten years will see produced from California, but call attention to this fact, that seven years have elapsed since the discovery of gold, and as yet no apparent sign of exhaustion is manifest, although all predicted, from the first, that the auriferous soil was but superficial. Had this prophecy been borne out to any degree by experience we might have made a calculation; as matters stand, all tends to the belief that the best is yet to come. Nor should it be overlooked that the price of labour in California is still slightly *higher* than in Australia, one country being four years older (in gold discovery) than the other, and both necessarily regulating wages by the profits of the gold-field.

When I have stated that twenty millions sterling are annually produced from California, and that as yet no probability is apparent of a less yield for some years, I have said as much as comes within the province of my narrative.

How far gold may be eventually permanently depreciated by the addition of five hundred millions, to the specie currency of the world, is a question for financiers, and those who have gold enough to care about the value of it; but ten years of successful work in the gold-fields already discovered, may produce that sum, and in all probability will.

There is but one question more: is gold already depreciated in value? As measured by labour and property undoubtedly it is; for it matters not whether in speaking of a gold country, we say that gold is cheap, or labour is dear: as affecting the question the terms are equivalent. Like a stone thrown in the water, the effects of a gold country spread from it in widening circles; the increased value of labour there is diffused to places more remote, and consequently the depreciation of gold is diffused also. If the farmer here, affected by the extending influence of the gold-field, already pays more for his labour, he may individually counterbalance this loss by receiving a higher price for his wheat: still his gold (supposing these effects to be perceived) represents less labour on the one hand, and less property on the other. But it will be argued that such a depreciation is caused by the indirect means of emigration, and that this is temporary. Granted : but if it is a depreciation, may it not last, in a temporary way, as fresh gold-fields are discovered, until it is supplanted by the permanent depreciation which will arise when the vast influx of precious metal shall first make itself felt throughout the world ?

Already out of my depth, I leave the foregoing remarks as they stand, and the reader will observe that they are only suggestive. If I have allowed myself to plunge from a firm bank of facts into a small puddle of conjecture, with which I had no business, all I can say is that I am very sorry for it, and will wade out of it as fast as I can.

CHAPTER XVIII.

November, 1851.

In the course of three months we had collected two or three hundred tons of ore, and as the tests we daily made still bore out our preconceived opinions of the value of the mine, I proceeded to San Francisco for the purpose of procuring the steam power and machinery requisite for a trial of the metal we had quarried.

The life of the quartz miner at this date was tortured by doubts; he was ever in doubt as to the value of his rock; he was ever in doubt as to the depth of his vein; and he was ever in doubt as to the machinery best adapted for securing gold; nor is his position, taken generally, much happier in these respects at the present time; and I will be bound, sir, that the directors who led to your victimization,*

* Obsolete term revived.

323

and the subordinates that they employed, are as much trammelled by these doubts as any quartz miners I could mention.

I was profoundly meditative on the subject of machinery as I jogged along on the Old Soldier to Stockton. I recalled to mind that for pulverising the rock we had stampers, rollers, grinders, and triturators, which you pleased ; that for amalgamating the gold with quicksilver we had "trapiches," "erasteros," wooden tubs, and iron basins, which you pleased also. That we had design No. 1, that had been so successfully employed by Professor A, in the Ural Mountains ; design No. 2, that Professor B had made his fortune with (by selling the patent though), and which had never failed in the Swiss Cantons, where gold was rather scarce than otherwise ; and design No. 3, an infallible invention by Professor C, an American gentleman, who hadn't sold his patent yet, but was quite ready to part with it for a consideration. All this I knew, but I was also aware that none of these plans had been attended with complete success ; some were too simple in construction and too slow, others were too complicated in mechanism and too fast and furious.

One machine would catch every metal the quartz contained except the gold ; another would allow everything to give it the go by, except the refuse tailings that were not wanted; none secured the gold but those which required *more manual labour* than it would have been profitable to employ.

When, therefore, I arrived at San Francisco I determined on trying a newly invented machine which had not yet been proved in the mines, but which looked very promising for my experimental work; with this, and an eight horse power steam engine, I returned to Tuttle Town.

It was hard work to get the boiler of the engine over the mountains, for the rains had commenced to fall, and in many places the mud was very deep. Three or four days' rain entirely change the character of the Sonora road; and wherever there is a hollow in which the water can accumulate, there, throughout the winter, you have a quagmire which becomes deeper as each fresh waggon or mule passes through it, until at last having become impassable, it is avoided by a circuit, which one traveller having made every other traveller from that day follows.

Although I had given the boiler two or three days' start, I found it on arriving at Table Mountain, with the worst part of the journey still before it; however, we had sixteen yoke of oxen, and after a couple of days of great trouble, the machinery was at length

safely planted in Tuttle Town. Its arrival created
great sensation, and the town increased in size and
importance on the strength of it. A French baker
and a butcher established themselves in our main
street; and at the first general election a justice of
the peace and constable were legally elected; the
former was a worthy carpenter of good education;
the latter post was filled by Rowe. Whenever we
saw Rowe buckling on his pistols in a decisive manner
preparatory to a start, we knew that he was proceeding to collect a debt due to some Tuttletonian,
and this active constable invariably brought back
either the money or the man. And although our
own small population was very peaceful, our justice
of the peace had ample employment from the surrounding miners, and dispensed a great amount of
justice in a very firm but off-hand manner; and so
much respect was felt for the sagacity and impartiality
of our carpenter, that his decisions in those disputes
that came before his notice were invariably received
with satisfaction on all sides. The following incident
will illustrate the summary process by which one
judge and one constable could force obedience to the
law amongst an armed population in the mountains.
One evening as our "judge" was putting the finish-
ing touch to a shanty he had been engaged in

repairing, a messenger informed him that a murder had just been committed at an adjacent digging; the judge thereupon threw down his hammer, and, after taking the depositions, issued a warrant for the arrest of the murderer, who was a well-known desperado.   Constable Rowe was to serve this warrant and capture the delinquent; consequently, the whole population of Tuttle Town (about fifteen) armed themselves to protect constable Rowe, and accompanied him to the diggings in question. Arrived there, the accused was found to have entrenched himself in his house, with desperate intentions of firing his revolver at the law in what- ever form it might summon him.   I was not sorry to find on our arrival that he abandoned this design and surrendered himself at discretion, so we marched him off to Tuttle Town.   The judge heard all that was to be said, and that was sufficient for the com- mittal of the prisoner to the jail at Sonora to await a trial; so we mounted our horses, took him at once into the town, and had him locked up.   Whatever became of him afterwards I don't know, but he never returned to our vicinity, and this was the way that the law was put in force in every case that came under the authority of our carpenter judge.

A Sonorian was found one day in possession of a

mule not his own. Whilst the culprit quakes in the grip of our constable, our judge exhorts the villain to be more honest in his dealings. I have this scene before me so vividly that I'll place it on the wood at once before I write another line.

So! now if there is less benevolence beaming from the eyes of our carpenter than I would have you believe existed in his heart, the fault is in the spectacles.

We rid ourselves about this time of a bad character. There was a fierce brute of a man who often visited our camp, who was known to have committed a cold-blooded murder, although the law had acquitted him. He was called "Cut-throat Jack," nor did he object to the appellation; he was more feared in the mines than I should have supposed any man to have been, but he was always in a reckless, half-drunken state, and those who preferred to avoid a deadly quarrel would leave any house he entered. He was invariably armed, and always boastful.

One night as Thomas was watching a stack-fire near the tents, in which a mass of quartz was being purposely brought to a white heat for experimental purposes, Cut-throat Jack swaggered up to him, and informed him that he intended to pass the night in our shanty (Rowe and I being at Sonora). To this Thomas objected, upon which Cut-throat made such a warlike demonstration that Thomas very properly knocked him down. "Jack" unfortunately fell on the red-hot quartz, and the sensation was so new to him that, as soon as he could withdraw himself, he drew neither pistol nor knife, but was instantly lost to sight in the surrounding gloom, and never swaggered into our camp again from that night forth.

F M

In our immediate neighbourhood we had three
classes of miners, Mexicans, French, and Chinese,
and their peculiarities of race were so marked that I
shall record them.

The "Greasers," which term includes all Spanish
Americans, will pass the night and early morning in
working at their claims, and then devote the day to

gambling and sleeping, and the evening to a Fandango or a horse-stealing excursion; a Mexican in the mines has no idea of saving money, but, like the water-carrier of Bagdad, he will work one half of the day that he may spend the other half in indulgence.

The French, among whom are many Parisians, will work in a quiet and tolerably steady manner if nothing unusual occurs to disturb them; but, if by chance a strange Frenchman should arrive in their camp, or an old copy of the " Moniteur " should reach them, the picks and spades are relinquished for the day, and all devote themselves to discussion. Often I have passed some solitary Frenchman at a gulch, who, whilst elevating a tin pannikin of vin ordinaire, would be shouting out " L'Amour et la Patrie." Probably some of his countrymen had that day passed on the road, something of course had been said in allusion to the beautiful France, and the poor fellow was as happy under the influence of re-awakened associations, as if he had already reached his native vineyards to settle there for life, with a well-lined purse.

The Chinese are a strong contrast to the thriftless Mexicans and joyous Gauls.

The Celestial digger, with a grave, elongated face, is up with the dawn and at work, forgetting to perform his ablutions in his hurry. No laugh proceeds from his lantern jaws, but his thoughts are steadily bent on the pursuit before him; if ever he chuckles, it must be inwardly, to think how fast he is putting by the nice gold, and how cheaply he is living every day upon six pennyworth of rice and salt worms, whilst those around him are gambling away their substance. But the Chinaman is none the less a gambler, the only difference is that he plays for a small stake, and is, in fact, a good economist, for as he watches the wavering fortunes of his farthing, he enjoys pleasurable excitement if he wins, and is not materially damaged if he loses. Hundreds of these gambling houses are to be found in the Chinese " quartier " of San Francisco, and there is one or more at every Chinese digging, but with the exception of an occasional silver dollar, I never saw any thing change hands in them but the copper *pice* the Chinese bring with them to the country.

These people must feel very happy whilst daily fingering the Californian soil, where they acquire more gold in a week, than at home they would see in a year. John Chinaman knows the value of a dollar so well, that he will do anything rather than be without it: to gain so much, then, at such little trouble must indeed be a treat.

When a couple of Chinese dispute over the right to a claim, the noise and gesticulations are frightful ; arms (corporeal) are elevated on all sides ; fingers are extended in indication of numbers, days, or dates, whilst each disputant being supported by his friends, all talk at once so rapidly, that the wonder is how they can sustain the altercation, and it is only when breath is exhausted on all sides, that the argument is at last made comprehensible. Chinamen are a long time coming to blows, and I have seen them at Amoy and other towns, stand almost nose to nose, with arms extended, as if preparatory to a deadly struggle that was to end only with life ; but, further than making a dreadful uproar, no harm came of these rencontres.

A real fight, accompanied by loss of life, occurred in a Chinese digging in the north, but this was attributable principally to the fact, that a small party of Tartars compelled a larger body of Chinese, either to fight or relinquish the gold field, and this was driving poor " John " into a corner indeed.

Many of the Chinese at the mines have abolished tails, and when their hair has grown in its natural manner, it is astonishing how villanous an appearance they present. Their hair grows low down on the forehead, and is invariably straight.

An ordinary Chinaman, in his loose dress, with his head shaved and hair drawn back, is rather an intellectual looking being, at the first glance, but take the same man, and allow his hair to grow, and divest him of a picturesque costume, and in place of an apparent mild benevolence, you are struck at once with the small cunning-looking eyes and low forehead, which in the other garb escaped notice.

A Chinaman is supposed to regard his tail in a religious light, but those who have dispensed voluntarily with them in California, do not seem by any means to have placed themselves without the pale of society.

Some of them adopt the European costume, and patronise patent leather boots and gold watch-chains. I remember a very beautiful drawing, I think by Allom, of the "Feast of Lanterns," in China; the same festive day is observed at San Francisco, and if the accompanying sketch of two Americo-Chinese, celebrating this fête, on hired hacks, is less picturesque than the drawing alluded to, it is none the less a faithful delineation of the appearance of civilised Celestials.

All the Chinamen of San Francisco are fond of riding out on these feast days, and in whatever costume they may be, they invariably pursue one mode of horsemanship, that is, to ride at full gallop, shouting or screaming, and then to tumble off into the sand or mud, the last act being involuntary. There is no doubt that these people are excellent colonists as regards their own interests, for they have learnt the first art of colonisation, a systematic obedience to a chief, and wherever they go, they quietly submit to the code of discipline established among themselves, and submit even when this authority is abused, by the imposition of taxes and extortions, by their own head men. Part of Sacramento Street is entirely occupied by Chinese retail merchants, and it is similar in appearance to the Old Bazaar at Hong-Kong. Immediately a ship arrives in port with Chinese emigrants, these are taken in charge by the head men, and are supplied with stores and packed off to the mines, with great precision and regularity, there to pay a tax to these self-constituted chiefs as long as they are in the mines.

I have already alluded to the existence of a combination of three or four of the most powerful of the Chinese merchants, which being discovered, was interfered with ineffectually by the police. Now I have no doubt that this clique of wealthy Chinese not only supply the Chinese emigrants, as aforesaid, looking to their labour in the mines for a profit, but that they also invest money in chartering ships to bring the poorer classes of their nation to California, thus exercising a monopoly in the gold fields.

Much has been said and argued relative to checking by law the Chinese emigration to California, and believing, as I do, from such facts as I could gather, that this system of private taxation is on the increase, I wonder at the forbearance that has hitherto been shown by the authorities. "Live, and let live," is a capital creed, properly carried out, but when the mines of California are overrun with bands of poor fishermen, whose profits serve to enrich a clique, and these latter remove the money from the country as fast as they collect it, the principle is an unfair one, injurious to the country, and antagonistic to the principles which have made it a free state as regards black slavery.

An instance of the power these head men attempt to exercise came under my notice, for whilst staying with an English friend in the suburbs of San Francisco, there arrived one day a carriage, from which a gorgeously dressed " John " emerged. He stated in tolerable English that he was a " lawyer," and that he had come for a Chinese woman who, for many years, had been in my friend's service, and who, he said, had complained of being confined against her will. The woman had saved a large sum in wages, and could speak no language but her own, but she resolutely declined to go when an interpreter was procured. The Celestial lawyer was consequently well kicked for his pains, and departed, but we had no doubt that all that was wanted of the old woman was the money she had saved, and it was fortunate for her, that her master was a Hong Kong merchant, and knew something of the wiles of John Chinaman.

Much has been said, also, at home here, relative to the conversion of the Chinese, and no one would more gladly see this brought about than myself, provided it is done with *Chinese money*.

The Chinaman is highly intelligent, inventive, laborious and patient, be he where he will, but he is ever avaricious; it may or may not be that those are right who, knowing something of his character, hold that he would worship any god if thereby he can better worship mammon; * but I confine my opinion to this, that it is time enough to build colleges for the Chinese, when we have suitably provided for the instruction of our own ignorant poor, and until this is done, I humbly submit, with every respect for the Missionaries among the Heathen, that every sixpence that leaves our country for the conversion of the Chinese, is an injustice to those at home, whose claims

---

* A converted Budhist will address his prayers to our God if he thinks he can obtain any temporal benefit by so doing; but if not he would be just as likely to pray to Budha or to the devil.—Baker's "Rifle and Hound in Ceylon," page 85.

upon our charity ring daily in our ears, with a truth that ought to be more forcible than the energetic appeals that are raised for John Chinaman, but which unfortunately is not always so.

Never doubting that it is our first duty as a Christian nation to disseminate those truths that come from an inspired source, why should we, under the influence of a false sympathy, strive to do for the Chinese what so many of our own people yet require. The Chinese have an advantage over many of our lower classes; they are intelligent and reflective, and have Confucian maxims daily brought even in the highways before their notice, that enjoin most of the social duties that render man's life more in accordance with the Divine wish. *Morally* at least, the Chinaman is cared for; and although a heathen, ignorant in this respect he cannot be said to be. Let him therefore, for the present, study from gilded sign-posts the Confucian maxims that ordain him to be charitable, honest, and reverent to his parents; and let us first instil these commands given from a holier source to those around us who have never heard them, who could not read them if they were written up, and who are too ignorant, too poverty-stricken, and too much at war with the life that has entailed nothing but misery upon them, to accept them even as truths, until they first see charity in a more substantial form.   This done,* we may build colleges for the Chinese, in a full hope that He who has ordained us to love our brother, may bless the work of CONVERSION.

* If the reader will refer to the "Times" of the 29th of September, 1854, he will perceive that a liberal collection was made at St. James's, Piccadilly, for the Borneo Mission. In the same journal, three days earlier, the police magistrates express their regret that want of funds compels them to deny assistance to surviving sufferers from the cholera! All have, of course, a right to do as they like with their money; but after the hat had passed round at St. James's, I should have liked to have seen its liberal contents transferred at once to Bermondsey instead of to Kuchin. And for this reason, that I know, from personal experience, that my old friends the Dyaks are as fat and sleek a people as any in the world, well fed, well housed, and free from disease, whilst the stomachs of those at Spitalfields, charitable sir, are aching with the hunger that drives man to *crime!*

CHAPTER XIX.

—◆—

Christmas, 1851.

THE machinery was at length in its place, and we got the steam up for a trial; our engineer was one of the same school as he of the Stockton boat, and considered that engines were " bound to go," whether on sea or land; and when I remarked to him that ninety pounds of steam was about double the pressure the boiler ought to bear, he asked very naturally " of what use was an eight horse power engine if you couldn't make her work up to a *twelve ?* "

Having started the machinery, we awaited in a great state of excitement the result; this came soon enough, for in a few minutes the crusher broke down irremediably, and like some unfortunate two-year-old horse, ran its first and last race at the same time.

I returned, therefore, to San Francisco, meditatingly as before, and on my arrival there, I gave my mind

341

to the preparation of machinery that should grind and scrunch with a vigour that nothing could resist, and which should give ample employment to the four extra horses which my engineer managed to extract from the steam engine. The city presented a much improved appearance, the small sand-hills had now nearly all disappeared, and having been thrown into the bay, a level site was being rapidly extended on either side, where before was a shelving sandy beach, the least adapted in the world for building a large and substantial city. It is worthy of remark, that sand thrown into mud has not proved a bad foundation even in a country subject to heavy rains. The first brick building erected on this artificial foundation was the American theatre, this, on the first night it was opened, settled bodily two or three inches, but afterwards remained steady.

I found the people of San Francisco still very nervous about fire; and though the dreadful experience of the past had caused extraordinary precautions to be taken for preventing the recurrence of another general conflagration, still night after night as the warning bell hurriedly announced some fire in the suburbs, the whole population would turn out, and follow the engines " en masse " to the scene of conflagration. Not a night passed but one or more alarms were pealed forth by that dreadful bell, of which the tone was so familiar, and so associated with misfortune, and a shanty or two would generally be consumed in the wooden portion of the city. Sometimes an hotel or hospital would blaze and furnish a famous night's work for the firemen, but these were so active and vigilant, that the flames were always confined to a small space, and it was evident that the days of general conflagrations were over. The highest praise that I can accord to the San Francisco firemen, is to record the simple truth of them, and say that they are zealous and intrepid, and that their services are gratuitous. The fire department of San Francisco now numbers about fifteen hundred members and twenty engines. It is divided into companies, each of which is formed on a military principle, chooses its own name and uniform, and bears all its own expenses.

The companies are distinguished by such names as the "Monumental," the "Empire," the "Washington," and to see them in their smart dresses, as they turn out in procession on a gala day, one would not suppose that there was so much real work concealed beneath so much show.

There are also two or three " hook and ladder " companies, who do ample service in blowing up and tearing down buildings when necessary. Many of these young firemen occupy the best positions in San Francisco ; and it strikes a stranger as somewhat novel, if when the fire-bell is sounded in the day time, he sees the junior partner in the house of Mivins and Co. rush out of his office with a helmet on his head, and proceed at full speed to his engine house.

Sometimes some poor fellow loses his life in his exertions to perform his self-imposed duty, and then his brother firemen, in unassumed grief, pay him the last tribute of respect by following his body to the cemetery.

I have introduced such a scene in the sketch of San Francisco, and would draw attention simply to the deep significance of the motto on the banner that is lying low, emblematical of him they are burying— " We strive to save."

There is no boast, no ostentation in these words, no vainglorious confidence in what shall be done, no allusion to victories gained or deeds performed. Look on the motto, " We strive to save ; " now look on the coffin that contains all that is mortal of one who under that banner has found a death as worthy of the laurel as any soldier who at once brings pride and sorrow to the nation in whose cause fighting inch by inch he yields up life.

You and I, reader, can sleep comfortably in our

beds, and have no cause each night to be drenched by water and scorched by heat, no bell summons us to duty, nor need we risk life or limb when the glare ascends from a blazing manufactory, but turning comfortably over, we can again court sleep with the intention of reading of the fire over our breakfast table.

But you will agree with me, perhaps, that be we where we will, be our powers what they may, if we look around us we shall find no better standard to rally round and be faithful to than that which bears the fireman's motto, " We strive to *save*."

*   *   *   *

Gorgeous decoration is characteristic of San Francisco; the people pay high prices for the necessaries of life, so velvet and gilt work is thrown into the bargain. In the "shaving-saloons" this system of internal decoration is carried out in great force, and the accommodation these establishments afford is indispensable to a Californian public.

Let me suppose myself to have arrived at San Francisco from the mines early one morning. Having travelled down on the Old Soldier, I have no carpet bag of course, and I enter a shaving-saloon. At a counter I purchase any quantity of linen I may require for the moment, and with this I proceed to the bath-room ; when I return from my ablutions, I am asked if I would like my head "shampoo-ed." With a reckless feeling in respect of shampooing, the result of an intimate acquaintance with Turkish baths, I submit to this operation.

Seating myself on an easy chair of velvet, and placing my legs on an easy stool, also of velvet, I become drowsy under the influence of the fingers and thumbs of the operator, as they are passed over my skull, as if with a view to making a phrenological chart, and which produce a feeling at last as if hundreds of fingers and thumbs were at work, and the whole force of the establishment were scratching my head.

I am conducted to a marble washstand, and a tap of cold water is turned on me. I thought I had washed my head in the bath, but it appears not, judging by the colour of the water. My head is dried by hard labour, then it is wetted again by a shower of eau de Cologne and water, thrown at me when least expected. "Will I be shaved, sir?" Of course I will! "Take a seat." I sink into the velvet chair, and contemplate my dirty boots, that for days have not known blacking, but have known mud, as they contrast with the crimson pile velvet on which they rest. The back of the chair is raised by means of a screw, until my head is in the proper position for operation. First I have hot water on my chin, and a finger and thumb (generally the property of a coloured gentleman) feels for my beard in a dreamy way with a view to softening the stubble. Then comes the lather, and shave the first, and I am about to get up, when I am stopped by more lather, and shave the second; this is conducted in a slow methodical manner, the finger and thumb wandering about in search of any stray hairs, like gleaners after the harvest.

The operator says not a word to me, San Francisco barbers are not loquacious, but his eyes wander to the open door, and suddenly he leaves me with a rush, and apostrophising some one passing in the street, he says, " Say, how about that sugar ? " The reply is inaudible, but I observe that the barber produces a sample of cigars from his pocket, and says, " See here ! fifty dollars a thousand for these won't hurt you ; " and so, having failed to make a " trade " he comes back, and, as he " finishes " me, he observes, in a general way, that " Damn him if that (the gentleman in the street) wasn't the meanest man in all creation ! " I am then released, and this was a San Francisco shaving-saloon in 1852. From the barber's I proceeded to a boot-blacking saloon kept by Frenchmen. I seat myself on a comfortable fauteuil, two Gauls are at my feet, each Gaul has two brushes, and such a friction is commenced that my feet are being shampooed as much as my head was. The morning paper has been handed to me, and I have scarcely settled to the leading article when "V' la M' sieur," announces that all is over. What a change! my boots rival that famous effigy of Day and Martin, whose polish is ever exciting the ire of a contemplative cat; I pay the money with pleasure, one shilling, not before I am brushed though. Shall I exchange my battered wide-awake for a beaver hat? Certainly; and now reader I don't think you would believe, if you saw me, that I had just returned from Tuttle Town, and from a life of leather breeches and self-inflicted horse grooming. It is eight o'clock now, and, in an instinctive search for breakfast, I enter the Jackson House. Here are a hundred small tables nearly all occupied, I secure one and peruse the bill of fare. I could have wished for fresh eggs, but these were marked at two shillings each, and in the then uncertain state of the mine I considered economy a duty. "Fricassée de Lapin," that sounded well, so I ordered it; I didn't tell the waiter, when he brought it, that it was not rabbit but grey squirrel, but I knew it from the experience I had had in the anatomy of that sagacious animal. It was very good, however, and if it had been a fat Sacramento rat I daresay that, under the circumstances, I should not have turned my nose up at it; for I have eaten many things in my time that are not found on the " carte " at Verrey's; and when a man has once dined off monkey soup and has ladled a human-looking head out of the pot and has eaten still, regardless of that piteous parboiled look, he can stomach anything in reason ever after.

But the San Francisco bills of fare present at all seasons great variety, and no one has a right to complain who has but to choose from bear, elk, deer, antelope, turtle, hares, partridges, quails, wild geese, brant, numerous kinds of ducks, snipe, plover, curlew, cranes, salmon, trout, and other fish, and *oysters.*

It is not until you have been a long time without an oyster that you find how indispensable to your complete happiness this bivalve is; so soon as the want of it was generally expressed by the inhabitants of San Francisco, some enterprising individual gave his attention to the subject, and, after an adventurous voyage of discovery along the coast, he found a bed, and returned with a cargo of natives in triumph. This cargo, however, was not to be vinegared and peppered that year, but was transferred to a bed prepared for its reception in the bay; here the oysters were left to fatten on bran and other luxuries, and by next year the young colony had increased sufficiently to supply a small quantity to the restaurateurs. They were very small innocent oysters at first, and tasted like a teaspoon-full of salt water, they also cost six-pence a piece, which was about their weight in silver; but they were oysters; a victory had been gained; an imperious want had been supplied: we thought of this as we swallowed them, and were grateful for them even at the price. Since then the submarine colony has thrived so well that oysters in San Francisco are not only large, but comparatively cheap, so that many of the inhabitants gratuitously supply the city with pavement by throwing the shells out into the street as oyster-venders do in every city in the world where the law permits. And, by the way, it is not inappropriate that the law should wink at hecatombs of obstructive oyster shells, if, as they say, that part of the fish alone falls to the share of the public; and indeed it strikes me that any man who has been unfortunate enough to inherit a chancery suit in this country, should be allowed to pile his oyster shells before his door, for in this way he would denote the number of shells that, figuratively speaking, had been returned to him, and might thus exemplify the *certainty* of the law of equity in a manner suited to the meanest capacity.

Places of amusement were springing up rapidly in San Francisco, and these were of a better character than would have been supposed. It was pleasant to observe that gambling houses, and those low haunts which in every country minister to degrading appetites, were rapidly being swept away in this young country, and giving place to rational recreations. Theatres, reading rooms, and gymnasiums; these are good sources of amusement, be you where you will; read for the improvement of your mind, exercise the clubs and dumb-bells for the benefit of your body, laugh or cry over a good play, and in a colony you are safe for a cheerful, and perhaps grateful man.

My old schoolmaster, I remember, was wont to characterise the theatre as the house of the devil; if so, this personage is a very temporary lodger, for often when the devil is in a man, the merriment a farce excites, or the moral a drama displays, will drive it out of him; and perhaps before to-day a comedy has done more for a man, in the way of correction, than the best sermon that ever was preached to his inattentive ears. For, when you can interest a man, his feelings and judgment are open to your appeal, and I dare say a great many of my readers have, like myself, felt deeply moved at a drama, the moral of which would have been unheeded in a sermon, as inapplicable to our own cases or positions in life; just as, when children, we can only stomach a powder when it is presented to us in the fascinating shape of jam.

Some representations of poses plastiques that were exhibited about this time found no favour, and were cried down, but the enterprising manager of them, who was really a clever fellow, shifted his ground from the study of the human frame to that of the human head, and gave phrenological disquisitions on the sculls of Jenkins, Stewart, and others, who had been executed by the Vigilance Committee. As the bump of acquisitiveness had probably been the cause of the execution of these men, the lecturer had some difficulty in avoiding personalities, for this bump was largely developed in the craniums of his audience. However, he had an advantage over most lecturers on the same subject, for he could prove two distinct facts: first, that the subjects of his dissertation had been hung, and secondly, that many of his audience had helped to hang them.

Since that date, a famous Mexican robber, Joaquin Carrillo by name, has with much trouble and loss of life been caught and decapitated. When I left San Francisco his head was to be seen by the curious preserved in spirits of wine; and however revolting such a spectacle may be, it is a punishment that one would think would deter the reflective from crime. Fancy one's features distorted by the convulsive throes of a violent death, staring whitened and ghastly from a glass bottle, turned from with horror by the gaping crowd, and then deposited for all ages, growing more hideous with each year on the shelves of a surgical museum !

To take one's head as in olden times, and place it on a pole until it became a whitened scull, is a benevolent act as compared with the glass bottle and aqua fortis that hand distorted features down to posterity. For my own part I can contemplate with calmness my bones bleaching, as they may do, perhaps, in a desert, but the mere thought that a diseased liver or brain of mine should ever be labelled and ticketted in the museum of the College of Surgeons, excites a disgust that makes me think burning or drowning preferable to a quiet death-bed and a *post mortem* examination ; for your operative surgeons always find something in their subjects worth pocketing, and if robbing the dead of their valuables is sacrilegious, robbing the dead of their liver and lights is equally so.

But still every scruple must fall before the necessities of science ; and I remember exhuming a Malay rajah who had been buried about a week without the slightest compulsion, simply because science required the skeleton of a Malay rajah. I felt it was the duty of every man to aid science, and the only remorse I felt was when I found no jewels in the coffin—not even a ring : it was a shabby burial the rajah had !

The practice of carrying fire-arms in San Francisco was still popular among a large proportion of the citizens ; but the arguments by which I have sought to justify this habit in a mountain population are not applicable to the inhabitants of the city, for life and property were safe, and a proper police force had been instituted. Cases of shooting therefore were still very common, and duelling in particular became quite the rage. Taking up the newspaper one day, I observed a conspicuous advertisement, in which one gentleman gave notice to the public that another gentleman "was a scoundrel, liar, villain, and poltroon," and signed his name to the announcement. The next day it was understood that the gentleman with the unenviable titles intended to shoot his traducer "on sight,"—that is to say, as soon as he could see him, without any of the preliminary formula of a hostile meeting. When I reached the Plaza, I found a large concourse of people already assembled to see the sport ; and it was such a novel and delicious excitement to stand in a circle and see two men inside of you exchange six shots a-piece, that had the matter been more generally known, I do not think there would have been room for them to fight! I declined waiting to stand and be shot at; but it appeared afterwards that the two gentlemen, attended by their friends, soon made their appearance on opposite sides of the square, and that then they commenced walking about the square as if they did not know each other, and when within shot, one said to the other, "Draw and defend yourself!" which the latter did by sending a bullet through the assailant's arm. The fire then became warm; six shots were exchanged in rapid succession, and both combatants were taken wounded from the field—not mortally, however, for they recovered, and arranged a regular meeting, where after exchanging half-a-dozen shots one was seriously wounded; since when, I believe, no more powder has been burnt in the cause.

CHAPTER XX.

—◆—

January, 1852.

RATS are very numerous in San Francisco, as also are ratting-dogs. The roughest Skyes and most ferocious bull-dogs seem to have congregated in that city; and so much interest do the people take in the destruction of the common enemy, that a crowd is instantly collected if by chance a Scotch terrier, arrested by the flavour of a rat, wags his tail over a heap of shavings. You will one day see a crowd in the street, dense and excited; you try in vain to obtain a glimpse of what is going on in the centre; from expressions that reach you, you feel certain that a horrid murder is being perpetrated, and this opinion is confirmed as you hear re-echoed the cry, " He is dead!—all over ! " As the crowd disperses, there issues from it the rejoicing owner of two young prize-fighting quadrupeds, and in his hand is a large rat, now all tail and teeth, " the balance," as the owner remarks, having been " considerably chawed up."

Great risk and expense attend the shipment of these little dogs to California; and I was so unfortunate as not to land one of four very useful brutes that I shipped from the London Docks for that country. A good horse or dog is a treasure to a Californian; and he will look upon one or the other as his friend, and treat it with great kindness.

An immense quantity of drays are required in the city for the transport of goods, and the stranger will be at once struck with the superiority of breed of the horses, and the high condition in which they are kept. It has not been worth while of late to send anything commonplace to San Francisco; the horses therefore that are driven across the plains are generally strong and showy animals. " Draying " has paid very well here, and many of the proprietors of these vehicles, although they drive for themselves, are well to do. The dray harness is often mounted in German silver; and you may see any day a respectable-looking quiet man in spectacles carting a load of hay or lumber, with a handsome four-in-hand team, well groomed, and ornamented with bear-skin trappings.

The new machinery being completed, I again

started for the mines, and arrived at Tuttle-town without accident.

We had tolerable hunting ground in our vicinity, but the game was wild from having been too much shot at. The deer lived in the mountains, and to reach them required much walking, as the reader will understand if he glances at the background of the sketch that forms my frontispiece. The earth on the side of the red-wood hills is generally friable, and as it gives way to the pressure of the foot, the toil of ascending is very great, when the glass is at ninety.

There was, however, ample employment for the shot-gun, as the crested partridge abounded in our neighbourhood. I have not yet mentioned this bird; it is smaller than our partridge, and has all its habits, with this exception, that it will fly to trees when disturbed. This I imagine arises from an instinctive fear of vermin, with which the country abounds, the silver grey fox being very destructive,—not to speak of coyotes, snakes, and birds of prey. There is also little cover on the ground, with the exception of stones, and when the partridge is undisturbed, it will busk among these. The call of the male is similar to that of the English bird. The crested partridge is hard to put up, being a great runner;

harder still to shoot flying, for it is particularly strong on the wing, and flies low on a ground of much its own colour. When shot and cooked it is white, dry, and insipid; still it is a partridge, and as such is much relished.

I will mention a circumstance here in connection with shooting, which has so much of the marvellous in it that I had determined to omit it.

Whilst encamped at Santa Rosa Valley, after leaving Carrillo's house, we were visited one morning by some Sonorians (probably those who afterwards stole our cattle). As they requested us to fire a few shots with our rifles at a mark, we consented willingly enough, and being in good practice and in good luck, we fired with success at dollars and other small targets.

An hour or two afterwards, the three of us proceeded in search of venison; it was about mid-day, the sun was very powerful and the sky cloudless. Making for a shady thicket where we hoped to find, we unexpectedly started a doe from the long grass; she was out of shot before we could raise a gun, but there still remained a fawn. Pretty innocent! there it stood gazing at us wondrously, and I warrant had there been meat in our larder at home not one of us would have touched a trigger; but lamb is innocent, and yet you eat it, Madam, and the only difference between us is that you have a butcher to take life, and I had not.

The fawn stood motionless as I advanced a few paces and took, as I imagined, deadly aim. I missed, and still it did not move : the others fired, and missed also. From the same distance (about seventy-five yards), we fired each four bullets without success ; still the fawn moved but a pace or two, and our rifle ammunition was exhausted. I then crept up to the fawn, and within twenty paces I fired twice at it with my pistol ; it then, unharmed, quietly walked away in search of its mother. We looked at each other in some doubt after this, and for a long time I was puzzled to conjecture how to account for this apparently charmed life.

At last I solved the problem in this way, as I thought. The sun was intensely powerful, and had been reflected back to us from the yellow grass on which we had kept our eyes throughout a long walk ; either this glare or the rarefaction of the air had, probably, caused an optical delusion, and the fawn appearing nearer to us than in reality it was, we fired under it. Had this struck me at the time, I would have searched in the long grass for the place where the bullets struck, and I have no doubt, considering the practice we were in, that they would all have been found in the same range, and short; but on account of the height of the grass, we were unable to see whilst firing where our balls fell. And this is the sole way I can account for this curious adventure.

This is the sole marvellous story I have to tell, and is a fact; but so capricious is reading man, that I dare say many a one who would have believed me had I related the destruction in one long shot of three buffaloes, two coyotes, and a digger Indian, will smile incredulously at my party firing fourteen barrels within seventy paces of a motionless deer! So be it —and annotators of circulating library books will write "Gammon!" in black-lead pencil on the margin, and I must grin whilst I writhe under this infliction.

About three miles from our camp was the Stanislaus River; and crossing this in a ferry-boat, we would be at once in the vicinity of a famous digging, " Carson's Hill," by name. All that we read of that is bright and fairy-like, in connection with reported gold discoveries, has been presented as a Gradgrind fact at Carson's Hill.

The rivers produced, the hills produced, and even the quartz * produced, having previously been rotted

---

* Rich deposits were discovered, but I am not aware of the value of the quartz generally at Carson's Creek.

by nature, that man might pick the gold out with his penknife. "Rich nests," "tall pockets," "big strikes," lumps and chunks, were the reward of labour at Carson's Hill; whilst the miserable population elsewhere were content with ounces of gold, or, at the best, pounds.

No one knows how many fortunes have been made at Carson's Hill, nor how many bloody battles have been fought there for the rich earth—but a great many. Two small armies met once on the brow of the hill, and parleyed, weapons in hand and with savage looks, for as much quartz as you might carry away in a fish-cart.

Mr. James Carson, the discoverer of these diggings, asserts that in 1848 the man who would work could make from fifty to one hundred pounds sterling a day, and I have no doubt of the truth of this.

At the time when this digging was first yielding such immense profits, strict honesty was the characteristic of the miners; and a man need have no fear then, as he has now, relative to keeping his dust after he had found it, for all had enough, and it is astonishing how virtuous we become under such circumstances. A sailor once asked his chum if a bishop was a good man? "He ought for to be," replies the other, "for he has nothing to do but to eat, drink, and sleep, and altogether he has a deuced fine berth of it!" and Jack hit the truth in his own way.

And sailors are, perhaps, after their manner, tolerable Christians themselves; certainly they swear a little, and are said to devour in a sandwich the bank-note that would serve to enrich a hospital, as from Bill Bobstay, Esq.; but whenever there is sickness or poverty among sailors, there Jack is found at the bedside the tenderest of nurses, and sharing—honest heart!—his last copper with a comrade. A sailor in the mines is at best a rough and uncomely fellow to the sight; but will you show me anything more pleasing to contemplate than that sturdy fellow there who plies his pickaxe to the tune of "Oh, Sally Brown!" that he may take at night to his sick friend in the tent hard by the luxuries he needs? The sailors in the mines have been ever distinguished for self-denial; and whenever I see "prim goodness" frown at the rough, careless sailor's oath that will mingle now and then with his "ye-ho!" I think to myself, "Take out your heart, 'prim goodness,' and lay it by the side of Jack's and offer me the choice of the two, and maybe it won't be yours I'll take, for all that you are faultless to the world's eye."

Liberality was so great in those days, that if a stranger came to the mines and had but the

appearance of one who would work, he had no difficulty in borrowing from any one all that was required
for starting him, his muscles and sinews being
the sole guarantee for repayment.

It was near Carson's Hill that poor Boyd worked
with a gang of men, though with what success I do
not know. Boyd was an English gentleman of
independence; and in his yacht, the "Wanderer,"
he had visited nearly every place on the globe.
He was fitted in every respect for the roving life
he had chosen, and was equally at home whether he
roughed it in the mountains or played the host on
board the "Wanderer." Shortly after he left San
Francisco, he landed at Solomon's Island to shoot
wild fowl, and there was cruelly murdered by the
natives. None who knew him heard of his fate without regret; and as a finale to the life of this adventurous man, the "Wanderer" soon after went ashore
and was lost.

A gulch which branches off from Carson's, and
which proved very rich, was discovered under circumstances of great solemnity, and I am indebted
to Mr. Carson for the anecdote.

One of the miners died, and having been much
respected, it was determined to give him a regular
funeral. A digger in the vicinity, who, report said,

had once been a powerful preacher in the United States, was called upon to officiate; and after "drinks all round," the party proceeded, with becoming gravity, to the grave, which had been dug at a distance of a hundred yards from the camp. When this spot was reached, the officiating minister commenced with an extempore prayer, during which all knelt round the grave. So far was well; but the prayer was unnecessarily long, and at last some of those who knelt, began, in an abstracted way, to finger the loose earth that had been thrown up from the grave. It was thick with gold; and an excitement was immediately apparent in the kneeling crowd. Upon this, the preacher stopped, and inquiringly said,

"Boys, what's that? Gold!" he continued, "and the richest kind of diggings,—the congregation are dismissed!" The poor miner was taken from his auriferous grave and was buried elsewhere, whilst the funeral party, with the parson at their head, lost no time in prospecting the new digging.

The population of the diggings, in 1848, was as varied as can be well imagined; every nation and calling was represented there, from an ex-governor to a digger Indian. But amongst this motley crew lawyers predominated; and if we may judge by the fees they received, and the quality of the law they exchanged for them, they had brought their forensic knowledge to a fine market. As magistrates and other officers were required in the different mining districts, they were elected by a majority of the miners, and formed a court of law.

All mining disputes were submitted to these courts, and whatever might be the decision given, *that* was considered the law, which saved all trouble of appeal. The following incident will convey some idea of law in the diggings at this time.

Two Spaniards, who had amassed a large quantity of gold dust by successful digging, quarrelled over the possession of an old mule that was scarcely worth her keep, and applied to the alcalde or magistrate to

settle the dispute. Before a word was said, however,
each "greaser" had to pay three ounces of dust for
expenses of the court; and then, both speaking at
once, each related his own tale in Spanish, which was
a language unintelligible to the court. After this,
they were informed by his Honour, through an interpreter, that they had better leave the case to the
decision of a jury. To this they agreed, and having
paid two ounces more in advance to the sheriff, that
officer summoned a jury from the adjacent diggings.
After hearing their statements, which were very

contradictory, the jury retired, and returned with a verdict that the costs should be shared by the plaintiff and defendant; and as there was not evidence to show who the mule really belonged to, they were to *draw straws* for her!

The bill of costs amounted to twenty ounces,—the *liquor bill* to three ounces more. This sum the Spaniards paid, and then they went out to cut for the animal; but some other Spaniard had already settled the dispute, for whilst all were inside he had mounted the mule and rode off with it, nor did it ever, to my knowledge, turn up again. But for the comparative insignificance of the fees, this trial might have taken place, judging by the result, in our own Court of Chancery.

A few digger Indians worked occasionally in our vicinity, having discovered that gold would purchase fine clothes and rum, which was all they cared for. The outfits they procured with their dust varied according to taste. One would prefer half a-dozen shirts, and wear them all at once; another would be content with a gaudy Mexican hat and a pair of jack boots; so that their partial adoption of civilised costume only served to render the uncovered parts of their bodies ridiculously conspicuous.

The Indians of California have a tradition among

them which points to the days when volcanic eruptions devastated the country, and destroyed all living things but Indians. No traces of an earlier race are to be found, however, as yet, in Upper California ; nor have the Indians the faintest knowledge of pictorial signs or symbols. I am inclined, therefore, to think that the present tribes have been migratory.

It is a peculiarity of California, that although it is so rich in flowers, the wild bee is never found there, nor did I ever hear a singing-bird. Digging in the mines is suspended by general accord on the Sabbath, and that day is usually spent very quietly in camp, particularly as the more boisterous characters go to the nearest town to amuse themselves. A walk over the mountains, rifle in hand, with an eye to business in the shape of "prospecting," is often the employment of the more sedate ; and if the miner sometimes finds on a Sunday what serves him for an honest livelihood on week days, he is, mayhap, no worse, sir, than you whose thoughts, even in a church, are not always separate from the pounds shillings and pence you require for the engagements of the coming week.

During this time the work at the mines progressed steadily ; and the new machinery being ready, we started it, fully confident of success.* Again

* Our object was still only to experimentalise.

was our engine placed under contribution for four horses' more power than it was built for, and again did our machinery turn out a signal failure: in fact we had iron only where we should have had the hardest of steel, and in consequence, instead of our mill grinding the quartz, the quartz had the best of it and ground the mill; and as it was gold I wanted, and not iron filings, I determined for the present to abandon my third profitless speculation.

Agriculturally, architecturally, and mineralogically, I had been sported with by fate,—and the plough in the north, the steam-engine in the south, and the hotel in the middle, had each been accompanied by pecuniary loss. Yet the days I had passed had been very happy, and Philosophy said: "You have had health, and contentment, and warm friendship; and if these were purchasable, many would buy them of you for twenty times what you have lost in money!" To which I replied, "Very true, oh Philosophy! but had I taken my steam-engine to Russian River, and there applied its power to sawing red-woods, and had I with my plough turned up the fertile hills and valleys at Vallejo, and further, had I erected my hotel at Sonora, where it was much wanted, I might have still had the unpurchasable articles you allude to, and the money too." Upon which Philosophy, seeing me thus unreasonable, retired from the contest.

Close upon this disaster there arrived a batch of letters for me. My friend in San Francisco had died, and letters from home rendered my return to England necessary. To return again, though—and to Tuttletown—on that point I was determined, " wind and weather permitting," as we say afloat.

I sold my steam-engine to some wretched favourites of fortune, who took it to a gulch and made money there and then. I sold Mainspring, and Tiger, and Bevis, with grief. I might have given them away, but I know that a man will often give more care and kindness to the animal he has paid for, than to that he gets for nothing ! and many a one who cares little for the comfort of a horse, is mightily particular in respect of the hundred guineas the animal is worth !

The tools and houses I left with Rowe, Barnes, and Thomas. The Mexicans I discharged, and presented them with the bullock hides, and frying-pan, so that they were not altogether homeless ; then I bade farewell to my mining village, but not yet to the Virginia men, the carpenter Judge or constable Rowe, for these good fellows accompanied me for the first thirty miles of my journey. Then we parted, and I firmly believe with equal regret on either side—why not ? there had never been an unkind word between us in a year of mountain life, and as I reiterated at the last, " I'll soon be back, boys ! " they knew full well that my resolution would be upheld by the memory of kindnesses received from them.

Again I plod down on the " Old Soldier," who has seen the last of Choctaw, although he does not know it.   Is it a wonder that I was sorrowful when I left behind me so much that had contributed to render my life happy?   But I should have been more so had I known then that I had seen the last of Tuttle Town and its inhabitants !

CHAPTER XXI.

———◆———

ADVICE TO EMIGRANTS—GOLD COUNTRIES—SELF-DOCTORING—ADVICE CON-TINUED—I ARRIVE AT STOCKTON.

January, 1852.

WE know that the militia of the United States is very numerous, inasmuch as it consists of every man capable of bearing arms; but it certainly would appear that all the officers have emigrated to California, so universal are the military titles there. Now as I proceed to Stockton I meet here and there old mining acquaintances working at the gulches that I have to cross. I am startled by a voice from a deep hole with, "How are you, Captain?" (I rank as Captain in California, being *nothing;* if I was a real Captain I should of course be a General there). I turn then and at once recognise a familiar face, spite of the mud with which it is plastered. "Ah, Colonel," I reply, "what luck? How does the gulch pay?" "Pison bad," replies the soldier, and as I depart he shouts, "You'll see the judge at Cock-a-doodle Creek, and the

373

Major with him, working on shares, and they're the two meanest,"—the rest is lost to me, as the Colonel again disappears in his subterranean coyote digging.

Further on I encounter the Judge and Major at work at a " long tom " and " How are you, Captain ? " I am asked again. " Did you see the Colonel? " says the Judge, I answer in the affirmative. " He's considerable of a snake," says the Major. " He's nothing shorter," adds the Judge. " He's small potatoes * any how," remarks the Major. I back these opinions being out of shot of the Colonel's revolver. " Will you trade that horse? " asks the Judge. " He's not for sale," I answer, and ride off. He was for sale though, but not to carry gravel from the hill side for Judges and Majors to make money from, whilst the " Old Soldier " picked a scanty subsistence from the brushwood on the mountains. When I leave these worthies behind me, I have seen the last of the diggings.

I have written favourably, it will be perceived, as regards the reward held out by the gold-fields of California, to those who *having arrived there* have seized properly the advantages that surrounded them, and I have no hesitation in saying, that to the industrious, healthy, and temperate man, a comfort-

---

* The reader will perceive the bitter irony conveyed in this expression as contrasted with the complimentary one of " some pumpkins."

able livelihood is certain ; beyond this much will depend upon his energy and ability, and as regards grand results, I may add *speculative feeling*. I find it impossible to place in proper shape any remarks that could be adapted to the intending emigrant, but I will attempt to lay down a few broad facts that will apply equally to all gold countries.

It has appeared to me that a great number of those who fail, must attribute their ill success to not having previous to starting laid down the course they intended to pursue.

The emigrant, of whatever class, should have something definite in view; for, like a ship of discovery, he has before him, as it were, an unnavigated sea, and unknown rocks and shoals will cause him often to deviate from his track, but it should be only to return by a circuitous route to the prosecution of his journey. But if he leaves home on the broad principle of " trying his luck," he will not only be the easier cast down by adverse circumstances, but he will stand the least chance of any of becoming eventually successful. The truth of this was exemplified in the case of the English officers whom I found watering cabbages at Napa; they had not even decided then what they should do, or how they should turn their ability to account.

It is a great drawback to the labouring emigrant to a gold country that he generally lands without capital and is obliged at once to work, where and how he may. This, however, may be said to him—that Californian experience shows that, in the long run, the man does best who, having prudently amassed some money at the diggings, turns his capital and abilities to the channel into which they were originally directed at home : thus, if he has been an agricultural labourer, let him farm so soon as he has saved something ; if a tailor, let him turn back to the mining city, with his nuggets in his pockets, and there set up in trade : for the diggings will be replenished by new comers, and high prices, whether for potatoes or trowsers, will still (unless peculiarly affected by over-shipment) be maintained in a fair proportion to the yield of gold ; and it stands to reason that, if all labour in the diggings is compensated proportionately with that of the digger, it is better for a working man to labour at the trade he understands. The uncertainty of the miner's life is thus avoided, and if the profits are sometimes smaller, that is more than compensated for by regularity ; for it is an extraordinary fact that, let the diggings fall off as they will, the miners will still require *bread* and *breeches*, and will find the money to pay for them.

When gold-fields are first discovered the profits of professional labour are proportionately great with the rate of wages, and it would appear, at the first glance, that a fine field was opened at these times for the emigration of professional young men; but I find that those occupations which combine at first large profits with comparatively easy labour, have soon so many aspirants that the markets become glutted, and the large profits are short-lived. Thus, in California the proportion of lawyers is very great, and it would be a sad thing for that country if every legal man there could live by his profession. Therefore it would seem that a man of education should more than all shape his course before he starts; and I think it would be wise for every emigrant, let his ability be what it may, to consider what he is fit for, to *fall back upon* in event of his finding his profession profitless.

It is requisite for an emigrant of superior class that he should possess at least three qualifications independent of his abilities; viz., a small amount of capital, a good constitution, and an absence of all pride but that which nerves a man to accomplish all that he undertakes honestly, be it what it may! Such a man is an acquisition to a colony, and if his fortunes are adverse he is an exception to the rule.

The reader may observe that my own failures

scarcely bear out this remark, and this is true ; but my efforts were of an experimental nature, and, as I observed elsewhere, Fortune has ever snubbed me, but the jade does it so gently that I forgive her.

The emigrating reader may try farming, house-building, or quartz-mining with perfect security for all that bears upon the case in my experience, unless indeed my narrative serves to point out to him the folly of embarking in what one does not understand ; and I would rather, if he pleases, attribute my failures to that cause, for I thereby bring to his notice a golden rule he can never keep too much in view.   But this much is borne out by the histories of California and Australia, that gold countries increase permanently in wealth and prosperity ; therefore the emigrant need not be downcast by present misfortune, he has but still to strive, and, in common with all, he will reap eventually the fruits of the great blessings which the Creator has been pleased to shower on these lands.   He needs no better assurance than that he carries health, industry, and patience to a colony that is in a state of rapidly progressing improvement ; and if, in those countries he may visit, as much care has been taken as in California to provide hospitals for the sick, and asylums for the destitute, *free of charge*, why he may land, if it so happens, shattered in mind and body, and be yet turned out a good man and true, to aid by his pickaxe or his plough the general prosperity of the state that provides with so much forethought for the casualties that may beset him.

Something has been said already, and with good purpose, to aid the emigrant in preserving his health under the influence of a new climate, and I will introduce a few remarks that have resulted from my own experience, which has not been confined entirely to the adventures herein related.

I would strongly advise every man to wear flannel or woven stuff next his skin, and let him never remove that which encases the upper part of the body but of a morning, when he bathes himself from head to foot; flannel on the chest and abdomen is more requisite perhaps by night than by day to those who are subjected to exposures.

Dispense with what is termed a medicine-chest, but which is, generally speaking, a box of rubbish, and even if well fitted is a dangerous thing to have by you.

Certain merchant vessels, which do not carry "an experienced surgeon," are supplied with medicine-chests and an accompanying book of reference. It is related that one tarry fellow once applied to his captain for relief; his complaint was " that he had something on his stomach." Under these circumstances the skipper turned over his pharmacopœia, and at once prescribed two teaspoonfuls of No. 15 (the drugs being numerically arranged) ; on an inspection of the " chest " it was found that No. 15 had " given out," and for the moment it seemed that Jack was likely to die from want of medical assistance ; but the skipper had a forethought. There was plenty of No. 8— plenty of No. 7 ; seven and eight make fifteen, says the captain, and Jack, to whom this calculation seemed quite natural, took two teaspoonfuls of the joint mixture, and with so much benefit as this, that whatever *was* " on his stomach " came up with a rapidity that would have astonished the Royal College of Surgeons. Although the intelligent emigrant would not make so great a blunder as this, he might make a greater, and kill himself, even whilst strictly following out his medicine book. For self-doctoring becomes a mania, and, as with some men, you must keep the bottle away if you would have them sober, so with others, you must deprive them of calomel and opium if you would have them healthy. I have met many infatuated fellows, who, on the first symptom of fever, have salivated themselves, from an inherent faith in the efficacy of mercury ; and to see a man in the rainy season in a canvass tent, lying on a damp floor and in damp blankets, bolting calomel pills, is a sight that soon becomes very sad, and yet is very common. American emigrants are very prone to carry with them a preparation of mercury, called "blue mass;" fortunately for them there is more clay and rubbish than anything else in the composition. I shall carry with me, when I next start for a region where doctors are not, half a gallon of castor-oil in a tin bottle, a few trifles for the cure of wounds, mustard, and *quinine;* if the emigrant can afford it, this latter should always form part of his stock.

As regards castor-oil, I can only say that it was the sole medicine I took when attacked by malignant yellow fever, and that I was the only survivor of the passengers of the steamer "Dee" that were attacked.

When first arrived at his new home the emigrant should avoid exposure to the mid-day sun, or night air; but if he be a digger in the gold-fields, let him make this rule, that so soon as he feels the first symptom of illness, he will *lay by* for twenty-four hours. Premonitory fever can be arrested very easily by rest and quiet, but in nearly every instance it is aggravated to a dangerous pitch, by a feeling of pride that will not allow a man to surrender; and the fear of the jeers of his healthier companions will often cause a man to continue work, when prudence would dictate an opposite course. When headache and sickness attack you, *then* you may give in. A dose of medicine and a little rest will restore you, and shortly you will become acclimated; but if you fight against feverish symptoms, you may recover, but will probably be a wreck for life. There is an inclination to bathe when fever first appears; avoid that. I became very ill from bathing in the Chagres river one evening, to relieve, as I thought, the headache consequent on exposure to the heat, and Barnes nearly succumbed to a fever produced by the same cause; and although they are not mentioned in this narrative in their proper places, several cases of intermittent fever have from time to time appeared among my party, otherwise I should not presume to lay down any rule for the guidance of others; nor would I now, but that I have seen so many lose their lives from a want of the most ordinary precaution. I would advise the emigrant to the gold-fields to encumber himself as little as possible with what is called an "outfit." Flannel clothing, thick socks, and the best highlows that can be made for money, he should select with care. Let him take also good blankets. There is no better protection for a man in wet seasons than a blanket with a hole cut in the middle for his head to come

through : the body is free, the perspiration is uncon-
fined, and you can't wear the blanket out.   India-
rubber I cannot recommend; it is, I believe, more productive of ague than anything else, for it confines the
perspiration, and subjects the wearer to a sudden
check, when it is removed.   An India-rubber counter-
pane is useful, but should be placed over, not under,
for it absorbs the moisture at all seasons, and makes
a point of sending the rheumatism into your back if
you lie on it.*   An India-rubber cap, with a curtain
to protect the neck, is very useful in rainy weather,
but should be lined with flannel or felt.   (See sketch
on page 95.)   If you intend to dig, have one or two
pickaxes and crowbars made under your own super-
vision ; exported tools are too often made of very
inferior iron, and it is money well spent to pay something over the market price for a pickaxe that won't
turn its nose up at you the instant you drive it into
the hill-side.

After one of the San Francisco fires an intelligent
blacksmith bought up a quantity of " burnt-out "
gun-barrels ; these were filled up to give weight, and
the breach of each was fashioned to the shape of a
crowbar.   These instruments sold very well, but if

---

* The best use to which an India-rubber sheet can be put, is to protect
during the day that part of the ground on which you sleep at night.

ever there is a calendar of saints in California, that enterprising blacksmith will not be one of them! or if he is, he will have been sworn at more than a saint by right should be.

I have said all that occurs to me would be of service to the emigrant : it is little enough, and may have been said before ; but if it only corroborates the experience of others, it answers fully the end I have in view. And I have no hesitation in submitting these remarks, for the great advantage of one man falling into a pit is that he can show thousands how to avoid it. I have plunged headlong into many such holes, and as I would myself avoid them for the future, so I would that others should. And although in the form that this is published it will not probably meet the eye of the poor man, still if those who through the journals they conduct so bravely cheer and assist the emigrant, see anything in these remarks that may save him from unnecessary expense or sickness, they will, I know, too gladly in their own way extend the aid which I intend. Above all, I would that the emigrant who has a little money should be impressed with the necessity of carrying as much of his fund out with him as he can. The best ten pounds a poor man can spend is that which enables him on his arrival in a new country to look about him for a day or two before he begins his work.

When I arrived at Stockton, I found the streets of that city so cut up by the traffic of the winter, that in many parts of the public thoroughfare there were mud holes that it was necessary to avoid. The spectators on the pathway became quite interested as I plunged through the main street on the Old Soldier, and one would have thought that I was a steamboat on the point of explosion by the crowd that followed my movements. I was already deep over my saddle-girths, but the Old Soldier, maddened by the jeers of the inhabitants, made short work of it, and landed at last, "blown," on comparatively dry ground. It appeared afterwards that I had entered Stockton by a street that had for the last month been considered impassable, and was so to any but a high-couraged animal; but as the Old Soldier's feet were nearly as large as soup-plates, he had an advantage over most beasts in getting through dirt.

I slept that night in a Stockton Hotel, and waking at dawn, I started out of bed and raised a shout; it was but the force of habit; but although the Tuttle-tonian pigs were nearly a degree of longitude away, I had mechanically armed myself with the water-jug before I remembered the fact.

The next morning I started for San Francisco in a very small steamboat, and seeing the San Joaquin river for the first time by daylight, I observed that it was very ugly ; it only required alligators to make it perfect in this respect.   There was but one wheel to our boat, and that was astern, and as the accommodation part of the vessel was built to a great height, it was something like a small wheelbarrow with a large trunk on it, going the wrong way.   We passed Benicia with a fair tide, and after stemming a stiff breeze, of which the Old Soldier got the full benefit, as he was in the stem of the boat, and formed a temporary figure-head, we arrived at San Francisco about dusk.   I was fortunate in getting a kind master for the old horse, and I have seen him since, fatter than ever he was with me, carrying vegetables about the town with no more pride than if he was a common animal.

CHAPTER XXII.

March, 1852.

WHEN I arrived at San Francisco, I found the authorities very busy altering the grades of the streets, and covering them with planks.

As the rear of the town had been built on sand, at an elevation of some twenty feet above the new grade, the houses there had soon the appearance of being built on the edge of a dry ravine, into which most of them tumbled one by one. These house-slips would generally take place by night, but as the buildings were of the band-box style of architecture no harm was done when one of them rolled down the hill, further than an awful smashing of the domestic crockery. Those tenements that outlived this trying season, were seized with a panic, and changed their quarters.

Some were raised bodily by means of lever screws,

and being placed on rollers, were pushed and hauled into a position of safety, whilst the very small ones were removed down the ravine by the help of half-a-dozen yoke of oxen, and were planted somewhere else; but the appearance of these was so far marred by this operation, that they presented ever afterwards a crushed appearance, and the two front windows seemed to squint.

The Americans are very clever at raising houses and removing them; I have often seen one prised from one side of the street to the other without injury, and a house that I have since inhabited in San Francisco, was raised bodily four feet, to correspond with the new grade, without in any way interfering with our internal arrangements. Brick houses have thus been raised and a new basement built under them; but one peculiarity is apparent after all is completed, that the doors and windows that have been left open cannot be afterwards shut, and those that have been shut cannot, by the same rule, be opened.

I was present at more than one of the general elections at San Francisco, and in connection with this ceremony lies one of the greatest drawbacks of the country.

Setting aside the means by which governors and

legislators are brought into office by a majority of votes, I will take the case alone of the elected judges of the state of California. Many who have barely a knowledge of common law, here come forward for the office of judge, and are elected—how, it matters not —but such men have been elevated to the bench, and once there, have detracted as much from its dignity as men well could. Murderers passed and re-passed before them unpunished, and this in part gave rise to the actions of the Vigilance Committee.

It has been unfortunate for California that the elections have been long controlled by a dishonest class, the least likely to support such candidates as would place a check upon crime ; however, the press of the country and the people, are fully alive to the existence of this evil,* and it is possible that before long, the Judiciary will be appointed by the governor and senate, when good men, of whom there are plenty, will come forward for office.

It has been very difficult to get a jury to convict a murderer in this country; I am puzzled to say why, for self-interest would dictate an unusual degree of severity—still the fact stands, that in twelve hundred murders, but two men have been publicly executed.

* Since this was written, an election has taken place, calculated to give satisfaction to the Reform Party.

One man acting under jealousy, ill-founded as it appeared on trial, walked up behind his victim in the street, and then and there blew his brains out; yet the jury would not convict this man, and he was sentenced to a year's imprisonment only.

The judge should not have been bound by such a verdict, for either the man was guilty of cold-blooded murder, or was altogether innocent.

The press,* which has vastly improved in California, has taken a firm stand in opposition to this evil, and before long I have no doubt that the criminal law will be wholesomely administered there. We must not expect perfection in a self-regulated colony of six years' growth, particularly when we remember that law reform and integrity of election occupy attention in older countries.

When once the seed of reform is implanted in California, it grows with great rapidity. It may be that the greatest sinners make the greatest saints, but certainly, the most carelessly dissipated community that ever was brought together, have already, in their new position, enacted laws for the complete overthrow of many of those so called " necessary evils " that are borne with in cities of older growth,

---

* A little paper called the " Sun " deserves great credit for the courage with which it has attacked existing abuses !

and more self-assumed wisdom, and infinitely greater professions of sanctity.

It is said that one surfeit of raspberry-tarts will produce, in the pastrycook's boy, a permanent nausea for these luscious things; thus with Californians, they have seen vice and debauchery in so awful a shape, that in the reaction of feeling more good is being done to the country as regards sweeping reform, than would have happened in twenty times the time had the early colonists been at the first but ordinarily virtuous. The thorn is extracted at once, and there is an end of temporising and preaching, which lead to nothing at times, as any one may see who will visit some of our cathedral cities, and learn something of the statistics of the immorality which exists within them, and the number of divines who are there to raise their voices against it.

One of the Irish convicts who had escaped by breaking his parole, arrived in San Francisco about this time, and was feasted and made much of by a certain class who are to be found in many parts of the United States, and are monomaniacs on the subject of America opening her arms and welcoming to her soil the political exiles of other countries.

The free hospitality which America extends to

exiles of all classes, is to be admired ; what a pity, then, to detract from its dignity by a vulgar " émeute," which, after all, is extended as much to a singer or fiddler, as to a (so-called) champion of liberty.   But the exiles generally do not seem to improve on acquaintance, and the days of triumphal entry are passed for them, and no wonder ; for they are not always grateful.

Take the case of one who, being welcomed to the United States, at once devotes his energies to the production of a journal which will not only arouse political bitterness on the spot, but carefully keeps alive what remnant of bigotted hostility to England yet slumbers in the country.   Now, as the man who sows discord between this country and America, is an enemy as much of the latter as of the former, is it not inconsistent that such a one should be be-speeched and be-dinnered on his arrival?   However, a man may be bowed obsequiously into a house, only to be kicked on acquaintance ignominiously out of it, and I imagine that more than one political refugee in America will live to experience a similar reverse of fortune.

The "Know Nothings" it would appear have set their faces against foreigners holding office in the United States.   If this political sect would exert their influence to prevent rabid runaway rebels, who land among them, from revenging themselves by exciting animosity against the country that has cast them off, they would do a great deal of good to the United States.

And indeed, as regards the exclusion of naturalised subjects from office, the "Know Nothings" are, in my opinion, right to a certain extent; for if we divide those who swear allegiance to the United States into two classes, we have firstly the poor emigrants who leave an over-populated country to spread themselves, in obedience as it were to a law of nature, over the vast unpeopled forests and plains of a new continent, and secondly the educated class who can do well at home but can *do better* by forsaking one flag to cling (as long as it suits them) to another. This class are known as "Whitewashed Yankees," a term that may be complimentary, but does not sound like it. It is from this educated class of naturalised subjects that the aspirants for office step forward, and under all the circumstances, I am not surprised that a large sect of Americans now oppose them. For it appears to me, that a man who has felt so little patriotism for his native land as to abjure it formally from interested motives, is not likely to remain faithful to the new country he adopts, any longer than suits his purpose.

His motives are at the best, based on self, and he is consequently not the best qualified either to hold office or to conduct the public press.*

There is a disproportionate number of jewellers and goldsmiths in San Francisco, yet all drive a flourishing business. Two articles are in great demand, viz., gold watches, and silver speaking-trumpets. Nearly every one in California has a gold watch—every nigger has, I am sure, and very much dignity does a " coloured person " exhibit whenever he draws out his ponderous gold turnip, the chain of which is nearly as large as the cable of a ten-gun brig.

The speaking-trumpets, of which so many may be seen in the jewellers' shop fronts, are accounted for by the habit the San Franciscans have of presenting a testimonial to the Captain of any ship who may have brought them safely into port. This testimonial is almost invariably a speaking-trumpet, which is tendered to the skipper, with a request that he will blow it, from the undersigned, &c., &c. This mania became so strong at one time, that if the captain of any Oregon schooner with a cargo of lumber arrived in safety with two passengers and a dog, there was no knowing what honours awaited him ; at least a letter

* I beg to forestall the remark that may here be applied to me, that I am myself a *know nothing*, and defend the sect from fellow-feeling.

of thanks from the passengers and dog, but probably a speaking-trumpet; so that soon there was more ridicule than honour attached to these testimonials.

When nearing San Francisco one day in a noble steam-ship, whereof the captain had done his duty by piloting the ship in safety and attending to the comforts of his passengers, a gentleman arose towards the close of our last dinner on board, and amidst profound silence, commenced eulogising our skipper. I sat next to this latter, and when the orator continued, " therefore gentlemen it has been moved and carried by a committee of the passengers, that to mark the high sense they entertain," the poor skipper turned to me with anguish in his eyes, and whispered, " By G—d, they're going to give me a speaking-trumpet." He was right, too, and got a tremendous one; however, I whispered comfort to him, and showed him how, by putting a bottom to the large end of the trumpet, and a handle at the top, it would make a splendid claret jug, capable of holding a gallon at least, and then suggested I, "you might erase the inscription, and say you won it at a steeple-chase." Whether he followed this wholesome advice or not I never heard.

I secured my passage on board the " Northerner," and started on my way to England, in company with about two hundred and fifty passengers. The weather was delightful, and the wharf was crowded with friends who had come down to see us off: the partings were not very heart-rending; in fact, the great joke seemed to consist in those who were on the wharf pelting us with oranges and cheap novels as we cast off.

As we steamed out of the bay and lost sight of the busy city at last, we could not but think of the changes and reverses that all of us had been witness to, and most of us had shared. I for my part, as I recalled the noble courage with which misfortune had been borne with by the people, echoed the remark that Smith and Jones had made conjointly on the ruins of the first fire.

SMITH. It's a great country!

JONES. It's nothing shorter!

We were very comfortable on board, and arrived at Panama, so much pleased with the ship and the voyage, that it was lucky for the captain that there were no speaking-trumpets to be purchased at Panama; as it was, we did not let him off without a letter of thanks—and our thanks in one form or the other he certainly deserved; his name was Isham. Captains of ocean steamers do not always perform their duty, many are apt to forget that more devolves upon them than mere seamanship, some forget even this.

In the great points, of cleanliness as regards the ship, attention to the real wants of the passengers, and a judicious arbitration of such little outbreaks as will occur in crowded vessels, the commanders of the Pacific Mail Steam Ship Line (to which the " Northerner " belonged) deservedly enjoy a reputation. The ocean steamers on this line, as also on the opposition, which takes the Nicaragua route, are magnificent vessels. Many of them are over three thousand tons burden, and are very fast and beautifully found. Ventilated with open ports two feet square between each state-room, they are comfortable and wholesome even when carrying eight hundred passengers ; and it is the want of ventilation that makes a crowded ship unbearable anywhere, and in the tropics unhealthy.

A large proportion of ocean steamers are wretchedly off in this respect, and travellers in the East or West Indies are often limited when under hatches to such air as can penetrate through a scuttle hole about the size of a saucer.

One American steam ship, the " George Law," possesses what I have never met with in any other boat ; she has not only life-boats * suspended from her davits on all sides, but she has two metal air-boats elevated on deck, that can be launched *imme-*

---

* Air-boats with life lines and floats suspended from their gunwales.

diately under any circumstances.   Besides these boats there are on board several hundred life-buoys, one of these being suspended to each bunk throughout the ship.   These life-buoys are formed of cork and painted canvas, and have straps to fasten them under the arms.   As I recall the fearful and unnecessary loss of life that has been recorded in the last two years, I have scarcely patience when I reflect how much of it might have been avoided had each passenger, as on board the " George Law," been provided with ten shillings worth of cork and canvas. I was ten days on board the " George Law," and each night as I went to bed, my eyes were arrested by my life-buoy.   It said plainly to me, did this life-buoy, (not knowing that I was a sailor by profession) " Collisions will take place, spontaneous combustion will break out, and sunken wrecks and rocks and sand-banks will be run upon ; should any of these occur, will you not quietly buckle me on, being *prepared by your daily contemplation of me for any such emergency*, and will you not then calmly assist wherever you are wanted, in the full confidence that even if the ship sinks under you, you can float without exertion until you are picked up by the life-boats ? "   Certainly the contemplation of a life-buoy by one's bed-side, will bring such thoughts to mind, and by keeping the danger before each man night and day, prepares him when the hour comes, to act coolly and reflectively.   But we may look farther even than this; if the presence of life-buoys accustoms passengers to contemplate danger, and to meet it calmly when it comes, does it not stand to reason that the captain and crew of a sinking vessel are better able to exert themselves for the safety of the vessel, or otherwise the lowering and *provisioning* of boats, when the passengers, confident in their cork and canvas, are calmly awaiting the *order* to jump overboard, instead of at once plunging into the waves, only to struggle and call piteously for help, thus unmanning some and rendering others unable to assist them.   How many boats have been successfully lowered from a sinking ship, but being overloaded too suddenly, have turned over and drowned all that could not swim : would this be so if all had life-buoys ?   How many boats have left a ship in the dark night but half full, fearing the impetuous rush which a panic-struck crowd would make at it if again it touched the ship's sides ?   Yet the cost of such a buoy is but ten shillings, and that of a life-boat thirty pounds.

It may be said that every passenger can carry his own life-preserver, and that most do so : this is nothing ;

it gives me no increased confidence to know that Muggins who sleeps next to me has an India-rubber bag that he can blow out each night before turning in. The advantage of disposing life-buoys throughout the ship, as in the " George Law," is in the general confidence which their presence gives to all, and when the moment of danger comes, that ten shillings' worth of cork and canvas will enable those who cannot swim to keep above water, and those who can swim to double their exertions to form a raft and save the helpless. There is not, to my knowledge, an ocean steamer that leaves England that is properly found in this respect, nor will there be until government inspectors are appointed to see that they are supplied with life-boats that can be lowered in all weather, and do not necessarily swamp if a " fall " gives way, or bilge as they surge against the vessel's side. And captains of vessels should be made to keep their boats clear, so far as this, that falls should be kept clear for running, and lashings and gripes so secured as *easily to be cast off*, precautions which are seldom taken.

Judging not only by the details we receive from the survivors of lost ships, but from what actually comes before our notice as we travel to and fro, it appears as a fact indisputable, that not only are steamboats ill supplied with the requisites for saving life in case of shipwreck, but that what they have are seldom of use when wanted. With long boats on board that can only be hoisted out under favourable circumstances, cutters and gigs at the davits lashed and secured, and covered with tarpaulin, filled with hay perhaps, or vegetables, containing neither oars, compass, or tow-rope, is it a wonder that in nearly every case of shipwreck we find the loss of life aggravated by the confusion and mismanagement which accompanies the lowering of boats, or the attempted construction of a raft? A few hundred pounds would amply supply every ship with the requisites for preservation of life in addition to those they already possess, and of what account is this sum in the grand total of the cost of a steam-ship? Air-boats, or life-buoys, are by no means perishable or costly articles, but how much less sad would have been the history of sinking and burning troop-ships, had they been supplied with them? *

* As this goes to press I add a few extracts from a report in the "Times" of December 8, 1854, of the loss of the troop ship "Charlotte" and 117 lives in Algoa Bay, September 20th :—

" * * * On the life-boat coming alongside it was found that every one on board was completely *paralysed*, or overcome by the calamity. * * * Three separate times the life-boat pulled alongside, but there was no one in a position even to cast a line to it. * * * A great number *threw themselves overboard*. Some were fortunate enough to reach the shore, but the majority were drowned."

This ship was apparently in a position favourable for the preservation of life, had *confidence* existed.

Of what avail is the splendid discipline and admirable courage that is displayed by soldiers in burning and sinking ships, when each man has but to wait the hour when he must go overboard and drown helplessly. I would not only have each soldier in a troop-ship provided with a life-buoy, but I would also that each man, previous to sailing, should be made to go once into deep water with the life-buoy on, so that he might be convinced in smooth water that the cork would uphold his weight—a fact more difficult to believe when the trial has to take place in a hurricane, and from a sinking ship.

Each vessel carries (or rather should carry) a sufficient number of spare spars to replace those that may be carried away; there is seldom a call for the largest of these in a well-managed ship, yet they form part of her furniture, and are generally lashed on deck or under the chains.

By a little management these spare topmasts and yards might be so fitted, without impairing their utility, as to form a raft, in conjunction with casks, in a very short time. The crew might be practised shortly after leaving port at launching these spars and connecting them; the passengers would be instructed equally with the crew; and in emigrant and troop ships those who could swim might at once be sent

overboard (with their life-buoys) to assist in the construction of the raft.*

To make this more plain, let us suppose a ship,
whether carrying troops, emigrants or passengers, to
be twenty-four hours out of port; an order is posted
up that all hands are to muster on deck with their
life-buoys at a given hour, when the fire-bell will be
sounded. The ship or steamer is hove to, the spars
are unlashed, launched, and the raft is put together,
the boats are lowered, and the passengers then see at
least that the means of safety are provided for them.
Those that can swim can go overboard if they please
and lend a hand. Hoist everything on board, and
you have lost perhaps three hours of your passage
time, but a vast deal has been accomplished towards
saving life, if the ship that night should run upon
a rock and perish. Everything would be in its place,
and all that could be done would be done.

I fear that there would be much opposition to such
a plan on board passenger ships, for when danger is
far off there is little disposition to submit to any
arbitrary regulations, even though adopted for their
own safety; but in emigrant and troop ships the
practice might be enforced. I would have troops and
emigrants mustered regularly with their life-buoys on,

---

* These remarks were written previous to the loss of the "Arctic."

and the swimmers formed into a squad with a certain duty appointed for them. Each man should know his station in the hour of danger, and the fire-bell be sounded once a week for practice. A little ingenuity in the formation of buoys, adapted to the peculiarities of the frame of the raft, would so secure a large body of men in the frame that, even if they perished from exposure or starvation, they would still be found there floating, and although suspense might have made death more terrible to them, this would be preferable to their being washed off one by one, after vain attempts to cling to rolling casks, and spars, and hencoops, lashed together, with no more system than the urgency of the moment suggested to the few who, under ordinary circumstances, are prepared, in case of shipwreck, to make a rational effort for the preservation of their lives ; for the want of a lashing, or an axe, or a tow-rope for a boat at such times will peril the lives of all ; but, when all is provided, confidence and courage are there also, and life may be saved.

They say drowning men will catch at a straw ; let us give our brave soldiers something to catch at, in the hour of emergency, that will serve to keep them at least a short time above water ; and let our " Royal Mail lines " take some precautions of this nature for their passengers, and charge for it extra, if they like, in the passage money.

Shortly after the loss of the "Amazon" I was taking a passage in one of the West India boats, and I observed that, in the ship's fire bill, which was exposed, the crew and officers only had been stationed. I ventured to suggest to the captain that an extra clause might be inserted, to the effect that those passengers who chose to render assistance in case of fire should assemble with their blankets in some part of the ship specified, there to be placed under the charge of one of the ship's officers; for it seemed to me that, daily perusing such a regulation, a hundred able-bodied passengers would be found, at the sound of the fire-bell, ready with their blankets, which, under the direction of an officer, they would proceed to wet if necessary. This plan, I thought, would not only render the passengers useful, but would keep them away from the boats, and, being prepared to act as a disciplined body in case of danger, the silence so necessary in these cases would be observed among them. The captain did not agree with me; but, as he did not inform me how I was in error, I was led to believe that captains of large boats get testy sometimes from serving in the Tropics, and object to passengers having any opinion in matters connected with their own safety.

CHAPTER XXIII.

—◆—

May, 1852.

THE weather being fine, the roads were in tolerable order when we arrived at Panama ; we made light, therefore, of the journey, and, having arrived at Gorgona, we dismounted from our mules, and, taking boats, went swiftly down the rapid river, landing at the village of Barbacoes, to which point the railway was now completed.

The station-house consisted of a large shed, in which hundreds of fowls and thousands of eggs were being cooked, eaten, and paid for with astonishing rapidity. I observed, among other things, that the coffee was just as weak and scalding hot at Barbacoes, as at Wolverhampton, or any other refreshment station.

There was no time-table here at this period; but the line had this advantage over most others, that the

406

train started at the time specified by the authorities; for they waited until it suited them, and then gave the order to "let her slide."

On this eventful day, however, we had not "slid" above two miles when the train stopped. Returning Californians are of a vivacious temperament generally, and are seldom at their ease when sitting down inactive; therefore, the instant the train stopped, every man jumped out to see what was the matter. The cause was soon apparent; we were ascending an inclined plane, and the little engine—which, Hercules by name, was not Hercules by nature—had declined to proceed any further. In vain the sooty stoker emptied his oil-can into the fire to induce if possible more steam; the little engine, as it ineffectually tried a fresh start, looked piteous, and seemed to say, " How can you expect a little chap like me to pull nine hundred of these big fellows up a hill like this? Let 'em get out and shove me over." This argument seemed to strike the conductor, for, without further preface, he said, " Now, lads, heave together," and at once we all set our shoulders to the concern, and got more speed out of it than " Hercules " had done from the start. There was but one line of rails laid down, and, although the authorities were not particular with regard to the time of starting, we had the comfort of knowing that a collision with the other train could not be very serious. I wonder what we should have done had we been met by an up-train ; one of us would have had to retire, for " Hercules " could not have taken us back, and it was not likely we were going to shove ourselves back to Barbacoes.

The scene would have been splendid, for like the two goats that met on the narrow bridge, one train would have tried to force the other back, and in this contest of personal strength I think the nine hundred returning Californians would most probably have won the day, and entered Aspinwall in triumph.

Having reached the top of the hill, we all got in, and Hercules making the most of the descent ran away with us for three miles, when we got out again, and so on. The road lay through a thick jungle of splendid teaks, and palms, and ferns of every variety ; the rich epiphytes brushed against our carriage windows, and the air was suffused with that sweet fragrance which is alone known in a tropical forest after rain has fallen. Myriads of little land-crabs of a turquoise colour lined the banks, and as the time had now arrived when we might discharge our revolvers and put them away, the blue land-crabs had the advantage of several hundred bullets, and whilst Hercules rushed impetuously through the jungle, pop, pop, pop, went the "six-shooters," and as the land crabs turned over on their blue backs to die, they presented to the astonished beholder yellow bellies and green eyes.

In a pouring rain we arrived at Aspinwall, and this being the terminus, we proceeded at once on board the steamers that were waiting to convey us to New York. There happened to be an unusual number of opposition boats in the bay, so that fares were so reduced that the roughest fellow there could take a first-class berth. This was very unfair to those of us who had booked our places through at the office of the Mail Line in San Francisco, for we had paid a certain price for a certain degree of comfort and room, and this was denied to us so soon as the price of the saloon fare rendered it so overcrowded that the tables had to be laid *twelve times* each day to accommodate the first-class passengers with first-class fare.

Thus the saloon was continually occupied, and each moment it was, "Sound the gong"—"Hurry up the soup," and down rushed the "next lot," as an auctioneer would say, leaving a hecatomb of Californian hats at the foot of the companion ladder. We had on board the junior partner of some English house, who was returning from a business visit he had made to some part of South America. He gave himself great airs, and being dressed with the extreme taste which characterises your fast city man, he threw us all into the shade, for we as yet were not fashionably attired, nor had we put razors to our chins.

One day at dinner this fellow, being affronted at some negligence on the part of the waiter, said, " Aw ! do you take me for a returned Californian ? "

This remark being audible above the din of knives and forks produced a sudden silence, and, for a moment I thought that Mr. Bobbins's ears would have been taken off with a carving knife. Fortunately, for him, however, each one was in high spirits at the thought of reaching home, and being very hungry continued his dinner without waiting to resent the impertinence.

There was a man on board who had brought with him from the mines two young grizzly bear cubs, who were just getting large enough to be dangerous, and that evening, as Mr. Bobbins was dreamily enjoying a cigar on deck, he was aroused from the contemplation of his patent leather boots by moonlight with, " Sir, allow me to introduce to you two returned Californians." Ursa major, thereupon, being held up, scratched Bobbins's face, whilst ursa minor attacked the patent leathers, which he forcibly removed, together with a toe-nail or so, with his teeth.

Whilst one miner held a screeching, biting, ring-tailed monkey over Mr. Bobbins's head, another produced a savage bull-terrier, who, having done his duty at the mines dogfully, seemed very anxious indeed to make the acquaintance of Mr. Bobbins's throat.

It was some time before the "returned Californians" could tear themselves away from their new acquaintance, and when they did, they tore away more of his cross-barred trousers and cut-away coat than any tailor could repair.

The next day we arrived at Havannah, and Mr.

Bobbins was wise enough to leave the ship and await a passage in another vessel, and I only wish that every travelling " gent " who, puffed out with conceit, causes his countrymen to blush for his ignorance and vulgarity, may get as durable a lesson as that which Mr. Bobbins received from the four-footed " returned Californians."

At Havannah we found that Americans were in bad odour, on account of the fillibustering expeditions which had but lately been repulsed. As we steamed out of the harbour, an intelligent miner observed to me, " I guess that place will soon belong to our people."

" Do you think Spain will sell it ? " I asked.

" Our people will take it," he replied.

" But," said I, " suppose England and France should interfere."

" Whip them," was the laconic reply, and he turned on his heel.

I mention this, because a large portion of the people of the United States, remembering only the successful frigate actions in which, during the last war, they reaped laurels, are ignorant respecting the real strength of their navy at this moment.

As our captain wished to arrive at New York before the opposition boats, all steam was carried that the boilers could bear, and a little more, I suspect. In fact we were to "rush the ship," and she so trembled fore and aft with the work, that it was almost impossible to read a book in any part of her. The bearings of the engines became so hot that they were pumped upon day and night.

She was a beautiful boat, built for the most part of pine, I believe, and there was no difficulty in placing, under favourable circumstances, three hundred and fifty miles a day on her log board, independent of any favourable current.

Soon, however, we were in the Gulf stream, and were met by signs of a south-easter; first it "clouded up," as a miner remarked, and then it "breezed up considerable," after which night came on and with it the gale. These south-easters have a way of chopping round when at their height, and by this eccentric conduct many vessels are lost. One of the officers informed me that a short time previously a brig called the John Hill, was taken aback in this way, and her cargo of molasses shifted and burst the decks, upon which, "John Hill" became water-logged. Two days after the mate was taken off the wreck with two legs and an arm broken; and, concluded my informant, the captain was found two miles off "in good shape" floating on a hen-coop—the rest of the crew were lost. Fine weather succeeded the gale,

doubly fine by contrast, and as we passed Sandy
Hook, and steamed up New York Bay, the shores on
either side, white with snow, shone brilliantly in the
winter's sun ; and the leafless trees that grew in
copses here and there in naked desolation, had more
charm for us, being nearer home, than ever had the
vivid green of the palms and ferns that ten days
back we had seen at Panama.

Thus is our appreciation of the beautiful ever
dependant on association ; and to me the white cliffs
of my own country, whether I am casting the last
glance on leaving them, or straining my eyes as I
first catch a glimpse of them as I return, these ugly
chalky cliffs have more actual charm for my eye
than all that I have ever seen elsewhere of nature's
rarest gifts.

*   *   *   *

There is nothing left for me to say of New York,
others having recorded more than I could learn of it
in a week's sojourn there. Having visited many places
of note, that have been already accurately described,
I turned into Barnum's Museum to see the woolly
horse, but I could not find it ; being disappointed in
the natural history department, I stopped to witness
the theatrical performance, and this so impressed me
that I subjoin for the benefit of the reader a bill of

performance, which I extracted from an American journal :—

Just opened, with 100,000 Curiosities, and performance in Lecter-Room; among witch may be found
TWO LIVE BOAR CONSTRICTERS,
Mail and Femail.
ALSO ! !
A STRIPED ALGEBRA, STUFT.
BESIDES ! !
A PAIR OF SHUTTLE COCKS AND ONE SHUTTLE HEN—alive !
THE !
SWORD WITCH GEN. WELLINGTON FIT WITH AT THE BATTEL OF WATERLOO ! whom is six feet long and broad in proportion.
WITH ! ! !
A ENORMOUS RATTLETAIL SNAKE—a regular wopper !
AND !
THE TUSHES OF A HIPPOTENUSE !
Together with !
A BENGALL TIGER : SPOTTED LEPROSY !

GREAT MORAL SPECTACLE OF 'MOUNT VESUVIUS!'

PART ONE.

Seen opens. Distant Moon. View of Bey of Napels. A thin smoke rises. *It is the Beginning of the Eruction!* The Napels folks begin to travel. Yaller fire, follered by silent thunder. Awful consternation. *Suthin rumbles!* It is the Mounting preparin' to Vomic! They call upon the Fire Department. *It's no use!* Flight of stool-pidgeons. A cloud of impenetrable smoke hang over the fated city, through witch the Naplers are seen makin' tracks. Awful explosion of bulbs, kurbs, forniquets, pin weels, serpentiles, and fourbillon spirals! The Moulting Laver begins to squash out !

End of Part One.

COMIC SONG.
The Parochial Beedle . . . . . . Mr. Mullet.
LIVE INJUN ON THE SLACK WIRE.
Live Injun . . . . Mr. Mullet.
OBLIGATIONS ON THE CORNUCOPIA, BY SIGNOR VERMICELLI.
Signor Vermicelli . . . . . . Mr. Mullet.

In the course of the evening will be an exhibishun of Exileratin' Gas !
upon a Laffin Highena !

Laffin Highena . . . . Mr. Mullet.

PART TWO

Bey of Napels 'luminated by Bendola Lites. The lava gushes down.
Through the smoke is seen the city in a state of conflagration. The last
family ! *"Whar is our parents?"* A red hot stone of eleving tuns weight
falls onto 'em. The bearheaded father falls scentless before the statoo of
the Virgin ! *Denumong !!*

The hole to conclude with a

GRAND SHAKSPEARING PYROLIGNEOUS DISPLAY OF
FIREWURX ! !

Maroon Bulbs, changing to a spiral weel, witch changes to the Star of our
Union : after, to butiful p'ints of red lites ; to finish with busting into a
Brilliant Perspiration !

During the performance a No. of Popular Airs will be performed on the
Scotch Fiddle and Bag-pipes, by a real Highlander.

Real Highlander . . . . Mr. Mullet.

Any boy making a muss, will be injected to once't.

As the Museum is Temperance, no drinkin' aloud, but anyone will find
the best of lickers in the Sloon below.

Could I have witnessed such an entertainment as
this, together with the woolly horse, my chapter on
New York would have been swelled both in size
and importance.

CHAPTER XXIV.

———◆———

Christmas, 1852.

" I'LL soon be back, boys," was my last remark, it will be remembered, as I parted from the Tuttletonians on the road; consequently, in the winter of 1852 I found myself at the Island of St. Thomas, on my way back to the scrofulous pigs, the Carpenter Judge, and Constable Rowe. I had made up my mind that for the time being I would have no more to do with quartz mining. I saw that there was much respecting it that would remain enigmatical until the application of capital and science had produced results; so as the English Mining Companies appeared to possess both capital and science in abundance, I determined to wait and learn something from their operations, and for that matter I am waiting still. As my wife accompanied me I had

417

made up my mind to jog on by easy stages to San Francisco, and when arrived there, visit either Southern California or the Great Salt Desert. Having had a rough passage out we were resting for a few days at St. Thomas, when the yellow fever broke out with great violence; soon the ships in harbour lost all their crews, and the population ashore became panic-struck with the virulence and suddenness of the disease. I was glad when the Company's steamer, Dee, arrived to take us on to Aspinwall; and as this ship was considered healthy, we congratulated our-selves as we left the anchorage on having left Yellow Jack behind us; but, unfortunately, we had embarked on board the very ship that was doomed to suffer the most of all the steamers of the mail line. We had scarcely been forty-eight hours out, when the funeral service was read over nine of the ship's crew; arriving next day at Carthagena, we landed there about a dozen hopeless cases. The day after, my servant died in great agony.

The features of the yellow fever, as then exemplified, were very horrible. I shall not, therefore, describe them, but merely mention that the disease com-menced with a bleeding from the nose and gums, and this hemorrhage in many cases could not be checked whilst life remained.

We had about twelve passengers on board, all
English but one ; five of them were sturdy Cornish
miners proceeding to California. The first passenger
attacked was Mr. Adams, an American, and as we
were then in sight of Aspinwall, we hoped to land in
an hour or two, and fly from the epidemic, which had
not as yet appeared on the Isthmus. We left Mr.
Adams bleeding profusely from the nose, and we
afterwards heard of his death. There was a vague
fear among us that we were not quite safe, so we
hurried on to Gorgona, which village we reached that
night. The rain descended without cessation, and
we had arrived at the close of one of the heaviest wet
seasons that had been known for years. The roads
were described as being in many places impassable,
and such mules as we could hire were so worn out by
the winter's work that they could scarcely bear our
weight when we mounted. The luggage was charged
at the rate of a shilling a pound, and the muleteers
would not engage to take it through in safety. Much
trouble there was, I believe, in starting from Gorgona
in the early morning ; much falling of mules and
immersion of riders in thick ponds of mud, ere our
party had proceeded a mile on the road. The rain,
I believe, fell as if it would blind one, and as the
thunder reverberated through the dark forest of palm

trees, the lightning made the darkness of the black covered road before us more horrible.

Had not the yellow fever been behind us, our party would, I believe, have turned back to spare the women such a fearful trial. I say, believe, for the night before I had been attacked by yellow fever, and now as we stumbled and slid, and scrambled and swam through the red fat mud, I knew nothing.

My head was of wood, as it were, or lead, and if any one had chopped it off I should not have known it, but have gone on quite as comfortably. I had but one fixed idea, and that was that I wanted water; sometimes I got it, oftener it was not to be had, and I have no doubt that I pondered dreamily over this circumstance as something remarkable.

Of course I tumbled off a great many times, but not so often as was expected; a habit of riding enabled me to keep a certain kind of seat even under such trying circumstances. I cared little for tumbling off, but was roused to anger at being lifted on again; however, my wife did the best she could for me, and by night-fall we arrived at a hut on the side of the road to sleep. There was no Californian traffic on the road at this period, and our party consisted but of three men and two women, the Cornish miners having proceeded on foot the day previously. They placed us in a small loft, through the chinks of which could be perceived some half dozen ruffian-looking armed natives, who had congregated below. I suppose they did not murder us because they thought we had no money, otherwise they would have done so, unless they made an exception in our favour over other unarmed passengers who got benighted at these seasons. It rained still as we plodded on next day, and we passed a slough where, a day or two before, a woman had fallen off her mule and was suffocated before assistance reached her. My head was, if possible, more wooden than ever, and I became much distressed at one place where I lost my boots in the mud; for the moment I argued quite reasonably on this subject, but soon becoming unmanned, I burst into tears, and proceeded on my way, stolid, stupid, and bootless. Our party arrived at Panama half dead with fatigue, draggled with mud, and shivering in the torn clothes that for nearly sixty hours had been drenched in rain. I was placed in bed; the other male passengers—all of whom had arrived in good health—made themselves comfortable, and thought no more of the Dee, or the rain, or the mud. In less than ten days *they all died of yellow fever but one*, and I alone of those attacked recovered.

Of the whole party a Mr. Mears alone, who was travelling with his wife, escaped unharmed.

The hotel we had selected was undergoing a complete restoration, and was very merry with the noise of whistling carpenters, who kept time with their hammers.

The best accommodation we could procure was a small whitewashed room at the furthest end of the courtyard; in this room were two small stretcher beds, without mattresses or covering of any kind, and as times went, we were fortunate in procuring these, for Panama was very full. There were no servants in the hotel; there was seldom anything to eat, and when there was, the cooks were drunk and mutinous and refused to cook. After six o'clock the fires were put out, and the cooks went away altogether until the next morning, when they would stroll in early or late, just as suited them.

I was laid on a stretcher bed, and fortunately for me the doctor who attended me was clever in his profession, and gave me no medicine. After a day or two I commenced bleeding at the mouth as the others had done, and a sad time my wife must have had, as she sat by my bedside and wiped away the hot blood as drop by drop it trickled from my lips, watching me die, as all thought then I should do.

During this time I felt no pain, and although I never lost my consciousness, I was in that dreamy state in which I could embrace no fixed idea; my reflective faculties were lost to me, I never thought whether I was to get up again or die. I wished to be left alone in that undisturbed enjoyment which one can fancy a dog feels as he lies in the sun winking and blinking at humanity.

When at last I recovered and could sit up, I found that all my companions of the Dee had died. I soon got ravenously hungry, and then came the worst part, for I was restricted to a very small allowance of food. I was so yellow that I became quite vain on the subject, and my chief delight for a long time was to contemplate myself in the glass. It is customary to say of a man with the jaundice, that he is as yellow as an orange; an orange paled by my side, and my skin was of so bright a hue, that to have given me a coat of gamboge would have been to paint the lily.*

It seemed that we had brought the yellow fever with us to Panama, or rather it appeared at the time of our arrival, and it was now spreading with great rapidity. Cholera also broke out, and deaths from one or the other of these causes became very numerous.

---

* I trust the reader will understand that if I omit to write seriously of my feelings on recovery from a death-bed, it is because I consider a work like this no place for them.

The people being panic-struck, a great rush was made for the Californian boats, of which there happened, at this time, to be very few.

So soon as I was able to move, there was but one small screw steamer in port, and as the place was daily becoming more unhealthy, I secured, by great favour, a cabin in her.

Nothing could excuse the state in which this ship put to sea, not even the panic; for she was not only ill-found in every respect, but was so crowded with passengers, that it was not until it was ascertained that there was scarcely standing-room for those on board that she tripped her anchor.

I had secured a dog-hole of a cabin, and was no sooner on board than my wife, worn out by fatigue and anxiety, was attacked by violent fever. There were two young doctors on board, but both were attacked shortly after we started. Then the epidemic (an aggravated intermittent fever) broke out among the passengers, who—crowded in the hold as thick as blacks in a slaver—gave way to fear, and could not be moved from the lower deck, and so lay weltering in their filth.

During this time, I could get no medicine or attendance, and my wife was in the last stage of prostration.

The epidemic raged, and from the scuttle-hole of our small cabin we could hear the splash of the bodies as they were tossed overboard with very little ceremony. There was little to eat on board but ham and biscuit, and it was hard work to get enough of that. On the fifth day out, there sprang up a gale, a heavy one too, for all it was the Pacific Ocean. Our overladen screw steamer could make but five or six knots at the best of times, but now she could make no headway against the storm, and she pitched so heavily in the long seas with which we were met, that she sprung a leak and made water fast.

When we commenced to work the pumps they were found to be useless, for the coal had started and the pumps became choked. This new danger drove the epidemic out of the passengers' heads, and they at once proceeded to throw overboard the cargo (and with it my luggage), and then they baled by means of tubs and buckets.

For two days and nights we were in suspense as gang relieved gang at the buckets, and the old " screw " pitched heavily in the trough of the sea. All were black and filthy with the coal dust, which now mixed with the water in the hold, and as they howled and shouted over the work, these fellows looked like devils. They worked bravely though and coolly, and when the carpenter hallooed from the hold, " Hurrah, lads, it's gaining on us; " there was no wincing on the part of those who worked, but a more steady application to the bucket ropes and falls. Then the gale broke, and as the ship became easier, the leak gave way before the exertions of the coal-begrimed passengers; we steamed into Acapulco, still baling out the black water from the hold, and felt ourselves safe, at least, from shipwreck. A favourable change had taken place in my wife's health, and I determined on remaining at Acapulco, until I could procure a passage in some safer and more commodious vessel.

I forbear to mention the name of this steamer, as the captain of her was a good sailor, and behaved nobly, and it was no fault of his that the agents at Panama had so cruelly risked the lives of so many people.

The British consul at Acapulco was kind enough to interest himself in our behalf, and through his influence we procured a large room in the house of a Mexican family of note. With the exception of a few chairs there was no furniture in this room, but it was clean and well ventilated, and " looked out " upon a court-yard of fragrant orange trees which were now heavily laden with fruit.

Nor have the natives of Acapulco much need of furniture, for they seldom live in their houses, preferring to hang their hammocks in the porch, where they swing lazily to and fro, and enjoy the cool breeze. The principal apartment is used occasionally as a reception room, but it is not considered requisite to employ more decoration on this than other parts of the house, which is a lamentable proof of the ignorance which exists here of the usages of polite society in those countries of which the inhabitants do not consider what is good enough for themselves good enough for their visitors.

The Custom-house officers of Acapulco were very suspicious, and such of my baggage as had not been thrown overboard was subjected to a very severe scrutiny. There is a heavy duty on the exportation of specie and playing cards in this part of Mexico, and the manufacture of the latter is monopolised by the Government, and gives rise to a great deal of smuggling. As many invalids had been landed at Acapulco from the Californian steamers, and had there died, it was not unnatural that an occasional victim should be enclosed in a shell, and be reshipped for interment in another country. During a season in which Acapulco air rather accelerated death than aided recovery, so large a quantity of " remains " were hermetically sealed and addressed to distant friends, that the commandant became suspicious, and insisted one day on opening a coffin. No corpse was there, but in its place was the devil; that is to say, as far as a good cargo of playing cards and doubloons can represent that functionary! Since then the dead man who goes out is searched equally with the live one who comes in.

There had been an earthquake at Acapulco immediately before our arrival, and the best proof of the severity of the shock was in the fact that numerous adobe buildings were lying crest-fallen on all sides. A Spanish mud-built house has a strong constitution, and is built with a view to earthquakes, but, like us poor mortals, it is built of dirt, and must crumble to dirt again, as the Fates direct.

The mosquitos at Acapulco were as numerous as any I remember to have seen, and, in certain constitutions, every bite produced a sore, which was aggravated by the climate. We are accustomed to look jocularly on the attacks of these, or any other hungry insects, but to an invalid their bites are often productive of most serious consequences.

I was enabled at last to secure a passage in a large steamer, which touched at Acapulco on her voyage to San Francisco. She was a magnificent boat, but,

having eight hundred passengers on board, it was
with difficulty we could procure accommodation. We
secured, however, a couple of sofas in the main
saloon, and, two bags of bones as we were, we
managed to find either sofa much too big for us.

Asiatic cholera broke out on the day we left
Acapulco, and I began to think that we brought ill luck
with our presence. It was sad to hear the groans of
the dying passengers in the cabins right and left, but
perhaps less so to us than to others, for we had seen
so much sickness on our voyage that we had come to
look upon it in a stolid sort of way, and were free
from those fears and anxieties which the more robust
about us experienced. We arrived at San Francisco
with a loss in one week of fifty passengers, and if we
did not thank God for his mercy in preserving us we
were surely the most ungrateful of his creatures.

I would gladly have been spared this record of a
very miserable voyage, and yet without it my narrative would have been incomplete, as presenting but
one side of the picture. At the same time I can
assure the reader that I have not described one half
its horrors.

As we glide swiftly down the stream one day
without a care, so, on the next perhaps, with the
pole to our breast, we must sturdily stem the rushing

current to arrive at our goal with a fainting frame and panting heart, if God so wills ; or otherwise, with broken oar and shattered bark, meet our destruction in the cruel eddies of the swollen river.

*   *   *   *

During my absence the State of California had progressed in the seven-leagued-boots manner which had characterised it from the first.

The vast blocks of brick houses that had risen on every side in San Francisco looked so very new and red that, the streets being filled with empty packing-cases, it seemed as if the city had been sent out piece-meal, packed in shavings, and put together like a box of toys.

Let us take one final glimpse at this colony of six years' growth.

The wharves of the city still grow, and the clipper ships appear to grow proportionately ; each " Flying Dragon," " Flying Fish," or " Flying Cloud," that arrives requires more room for her pinions than those that have come before her.

Theatres have sprung up like mushrooms, and actors are so plentiful and good that I think of the days of the little " Dramatic " and Mr. Warren's " last appearance but one " in fear and trembling, lest any one should recognise that individual in me.—

Concerts and Balls, Fancy fairs and Picnics!—A planked road that leads to a sweet nook in the country, where, in spring time, the hills are bright with wild flowers, and the air fragrant with their odour.—A planked road that leads to the wild and rugged cliffs outside the bay, where the rollers break in one continued foam, as they lash themselves angrily against the massive wall that dares to check their course; and where, in the midst of fog and mist and the spray of struggling waters, sea lions live on lonely rocks, barking joyfully as the heavy surge sweeps over their oily backs.—A pleasant road that leads to a quiet lake, where you may dine at the hotel and enjoy, as it may suit you, the fragrance of the flowers, or the invigorating salt sea-air.— Horses and carriages; country villas and country inns; libraries and debating societies; ladies in plenty, children in plenty, and pleasant society, are here.—Steamers running to the Sandwich Islands, steamers running to China, steamers running to Panama and Australia, are here.—There are electric telegraphs throughout the country, and soon they say there will be a railroad that will connect San Francisco with the Atlantic States of America.

There is grain enough sown for the consumption of the country; there are brick-fields, stone quarries, lime works, and saw mills enough to supply fifty cities.

There are foundries, and steam flour-mills, ship-yards, and docks.

And in the mines:—where shall I stop if I begin to tell of the towns and villages that have sprung up there, of the bridges and roads, the aqueducts and tunnels, that meet one on every side?

And not least, the Press has taken a firm tone, and devotes itself to the eradication of existing evils.

*   *   *   *

Again I am leaving San Francisco on a bright Sunday morning. As we glide past the hills, the sound of bells from twenty churches is borne to us over the calm bay; we can see artisans strolling in groups with their families, and schools of children on their way to church, who merrily wave us an adieu.

Soon the bells are heard no more, and now having passed the Heads, we meet the fat fog which the sun has turned out of the bay.

As we plunge boldly into this, we say farewell to California.

APPENDIX.

———◆———

EXTRACTS from a work by Dr. J. B. TRASK, (U. S.) on the Geology of California.

SOILS OF THE VALLEY SANTA CLARA AND SHORES OF SAN FRANCISCO BAY.

The soils on the Bay San Francisco differ much on its eastern and western sides ; both borders of the bay present the tertiary series, but both do not present the trapean rocks to the same degree of development ; this, then, of course, will cause a distinctive and marked difference in the productive capabilities of either shore. It will be found in all the soils which have been derived in whole, or in part, from rocks more recent than the tertiary group, that a more extensive and varied adaptation to agricultural purposes will be present; this will be particularly manifest in those sections where the tertiaries, containing organic remains, enter somewhat largely into the components of the soil produced from such sources.

Under a proper course of treatment these lands will be made available for the purposes of the agriculturist, and our already large domain of arable lands thus much increased. The situation of these lands in the interior is such that they may be easily reclaimed should they ever fall within the jurisdiction of the State, which undoubtedly they will, under the law regulating " saline lands." In the counties of San Francisco, Santa Clara, and Alameda, the wet land that

433

may be made available by drainage is about seventy square miles, exclusive of the "saline lands" at the southern part of the county of Santa Clara.

Most of the valley sections of this range of country is arable land, and that which is not can easily be made so when required; the agents for bringing this about being found in the adjoining hills to the east. The character of the soil and climate adapts it to all the productions of temperate climates, and where local position modifies the climate of any section, it is found capable of producing plants of the tropical latitudes.

The extreme south-eastern part of this valley would be adapted to the growth of foreign fruits and other products, but it must be beyond the influence of the cold sea-wind that passes inland across the range of lower hills which divides the Salinas, Pajaro, and Santa Clara valleys, the effect of which would be to blight the fruit, though the plant or tree might continue to thrive.

The low hills that flank the east side of the valley contain all the elements required for the culture of tropical plants and fruits; the climate and soil will be found adapted, and the only agent that appears in the least to be wanting is water sufficient to supply the demands of those plants. From the appearance of small lagoons and rivulets at different elevations it is presumable that a sufficient quantity of this agent may be found a short distance below the surface.

As a general rule the mountains lying upon the east border of the valley Santa Clara are covered with a soil superior to that of the plains, and of much greater depth. I have measured the depths of these soils in many places, and where it is well developed have found it varying from four to eleven feet for miles continuous : its extreme fertility produces heavy crops of the native grains and grasses, which annually contribute to its increase by their decomposition.

Although these lands are situated within the reach of the sea breeze from the Bay of San Francisco, they are protected from its cold by the slope of the hills and the modifications of its temperature acquired in its passage down the bay before reaching the northern portion of the valley. So much is the temperature increased that an addition of ten degrees is often acquired in its transit from San Francisco to the head of the valley, a distance little rising fifty miles. This increase of temperature in the air is accompanied with an increase in its capacity for moisture, hence it is usual to find a slight aqueous haze, which results from the condensation of its moisture, hanging about this entire range of hills during the summer months, and is usually seen early in the morning.

* * * * *

THE STRUCTURE OF THE VALLEYS OF SACRAMENTO AND SAN JOAQUIN.

These valleys form a "single geographical formation," stretching from the terminal spurs of the Cascade Mountains at the north to the junction of the Sierra Nevada with the southern terminus of the Monte Diablo range with the thirty-fourth parallel of north latitude. The length of the valley is is about three hundred and eighty miles in length on an air line, with a breadth of fifty miles at its widest point.

The general appearance of the valley is that of an extended plain composed of alluvium, and this opinion would obtain in the mind of any person whose line of travel would lead him over the lower terraces of the plain, or what is denominated its bottom lands. It is only by making a transverse section of this plain that we should be able to arrive at any correct conclusions of its structure and peculiarities of its formation; by pursuing this course, very distinctive and marked features are observable of different periods of elevation to which this portion of the country has been subjected subsequent to its emergence above the level of the sea.

The character of the soil in many parts of this valley will

render it of little importance as an agricultural district, unless water in ample quantities for irrigation can be obtained. (These remarks apply particularly to the upper terrace of the valley on each side of the river.)   And we hope that attention may be called to this very important subject of making the extensive areas of the arid districts of the basin available for market and agricultural purposes.

Experience has demonstrated the almost certainty of obtaining water, and in sufficient quantities, for agricultural and other purposes, in all valleys resting upon sedimentary formations, and having a basin-shaped structure, and where the different beds have a degree of uniformity or regularity in their position, and are of a texture that will admit the free percolation of water through the superior beds, and sufficiently firm to prevent its escape in those below.

These conditions are all fulfilled in the basin of the Sacramento, and from the united testimony of different observers, we have ample evidence that the sedimentary formations of one side are the same as those upon the other, with the exception, perhaps, of the conglomerate.

The report, after classifying the rocks of the coast, mountains, &c., goes on to describe their order and more recent volcanic rocks.   In relation to the discovery of coal, the author says :—

From a careful examination of this part of the country, with this object in view, I feel no hesitation in saying that coal will not be found in any part of the coast mountains south of the thirty-fifth parallel of north latitude ; what there may be north of this point, I know nothing, having never visited it.

It is not unfrequent, in passing over the country, to hear of beds of mineral coal; during the past season I have visited four such localities, and, as was anticipated, each of them proved to be merely small beds of lignite, and two of them hardly deserving that name.   One of these deposits proved to be but a bed of leaves, having a thickness of about three inches, resting upon a tertiary sandstone containing marine shells, and covered with twelve feet of a sandy alluvium. This is one of those coal beds which has figured so largely in the public prints of the State during the past year, and has induced several gentlemen to pay the locality a visit, and to return as deeply disappointed as their previous anticipations were elevated.

The report of coal veins in the Coast Mountains must be received with many grains of allowance, and, at the best, none but tertiary deposits will be found, and these, even should they exist, would be capable of supplying but a limited demand, and that usually of an inferior quality.*

*   *   *   *   *

MINERAL RESOURCES OF THE COAST MOUNTAINS.

The minerals of these mountains are widely dispersed throughout their entire extent; they consist principally of copper, iron, lead, silver, gold, nickel, and antimony, with agates, chalcedony, and many others, too numerous to mention here.

SILVER.—In the county of Monterey this metal occurs in the form of argentiferous galena (or lead and silver), and this mineral is found in the primitive and transition lime-stone abounding in this section; it is found in small veins and disseminated; the range in which it occurs extends from the Gabilan peak to the Chapedero on the south, a distance of twelve miles inclusive.

IRON.—This metal is found in almost every variety of form, from one end of the Coast Mountains to the other; the prevailing mineral, however, is the peroxide and protoxide of this metal; the latter is often found in the form of hydrate, and when occurring in proximity to serpentine rocks, often found

---

* Extensive fields of good serviceable coal have been discovered in Southern Oregon.—AUTHOR.

to be more or less auriferous. This mineral is largely developed in some parts of the auriferous district of Mariposa
County, and forms one of the most valuable receptacles of gold
among the gold-bearing rocks of that section.

SULPHATE OF IRON.—This article, known in commerce
under the name of "copperas," is found native in large
quantities near the town of Santa Cruz. Its principle had
occurred a short distance west of the house of Mr. Medor, in a
gulch running from the mountains through the low hills to
the coast. I followed the course of the ravine from where it
enters the high hill near the crossing of the road north-west
of the town to near the sea. The average depth of its banks
varies from fifteen to thirty feet, its length from the hill to the
coast being about two miles.

MAGNETIC IRON.—At the distance of two miles north-west
of the above locality, an extensive bed of magnetic iron occurs,
running down to the coast, at which point it crops out and
exhibits a depth of several feet.

GYPSUM.—Sulphate of lime is reported to abound in the
northern part of Santa Cruz, and in the vicinity of the Palo de
los Yeska, some six miles from the mission. It was frequently
spoken of by the inhabitants of this place, but I was unable to
learn its precise locality.

CINNABAR is also reported to exist in this locality.

NICKEL.—The ores of this metal are found from Contra
Costa on the north, to the utmost southern limit reached in
the Coast Mountains. It occurs in the primitive rocks, associated with chronic iron in almost every case where the latter
may be obtained. It appears as a bright green mineral on the
fractured surface of the other ores, and is known in technical
language as "nickel green." The scarcity of this metal
renders the discovery of its ores in this country an object of
some importance, and its wide distribution leads to the belief
that it exists in sufficient quantities to warrant investment
for its extraction from other ores, at no distant day. It is

extensively used in the manufacture of German silver for wares and household utensils.

GOLD.—This metal has been found in the Coast Mountains, from the county San Francisco on the north to Luis Obispo on the south. The slates and serpentine formations which have been previously noticed in this report, are found to be receptacles of gold here as in the Sierra Nevada; the rocks are extensive in the Coast Mountains, often comprising an entire ridge for miles; they are usually flanked by the granite. During the past summer, the placers in the county Santa Cruz were much worked; the gold found there was principally on the San Lorenzo and its tributaries; it was fine, and much resembled that found in the Coyote Hill, near Nevada; under the glass it had all the appearance of having suffered but little from attrition by water, the surface of the grains being rough, as though just detached from their original matrix. The slates and serpentine rocks occur on both sides of this creek, with small veins of quartz running through them; and, from what we know of auriferous districts of this and other countries, the presumption is that gold in *situ* exists here almost to a certainty.

On the upper portions of the Carmello, in the county of Monterey, gold is also found, in the immediate vicinity of the rancho Tulecita. Farther to the south-east, near the head waters of the creek, it is also found on the tributaries of the main stream that flow from the western ridge of these mountains. On the Francisquito, a tributary of the Carmello, coming from the south-west, and twelve miles from the coast, it is also found near the house of Barondo. Three or four Mexicans were working with the battea at the time I passed that ranche. The serpentine rocks are largely developed on the east flanks of the granite ridges, and from their course they may be considered as forming the northern part of a series which occurs at the Mission San Antonio, fifty miles south.

The district of country in the Coast Mountains in which the

auriferous deposits are now known to occur, is about eighty miles in length, and thus far is confined to the counties of Santa Clara, Monterey, and the north part of Luis Obispo. This is a material addition to the already known area in which this metal is found, and its location in what has heretofore been considered the agricultural districts of the State, will in time exert a beneficial influence in the permanent settlement of those sections.

ANTIMONY.—The common sulphuret of this metal is very abundant in the Monte Diablo range; at Mount Oso it is found in large masses, also at various other points throughout these mountains; it occurs in considerable quantities in some parts of the county of Santa Barbara. This mineral is deserving of attention, as it often contains a notable quantity of silver, though as yet no specimens which have been found in this country contain a large per centage of this metal.

BITUMEN.—Bituminous springs abound through the Coast Mountains, and in some places is much used in the construction of buildings and walks in front of buildings; for the latter purpose it is admirably adapted in situations where the sun will not have too powerful an effect upon it, as in such cases it is apt to become soft. In the counties of Santa Clara, Santa Cruz, and Monterey, several of these springs occur, and further south, are found more abundant. Information has been received of an extensive deposit of bitumen in Contra Costa, some six miles from the shores of the bay, but at what point I have as yet been unable to learn. This article has been used of late in the manufacture of gas, for illumination, and it possesses some advantages over the common oil or resin gas in general use; a sufficient quantity for the illumination of the country may be easily obtained, and at low rates, when required for this purpose.

*   *   *   *   *

PLACER MINING.

The writer enters into a long treatise on this branch of mining, and represents its progress as being very extensive during the last two years.

It is now ascertained to a certainty that the placer ranges extend to the east, within ten or fifteen miles of the " summit ridge," so called, of the Sierra Nevada; and the condition in which it is found at these points is similar in all respects to that in the older or more western sections, with, perhaps, one exception, and that the relative age of both. There are evidences which clearly indicate a deposit of gold older than the diluvial drift of the lower or western diggings, (which latter is often confounded with the drift deposits of the tertiary periods in this country,) the character of which differs in almost every respect from any other deposit yet observed in this country, except in this particular range.

Its direction has been traced for about seventy miles, and is found to extend through the counties of Butte, the eastern part of Yuba, Sierra Nevada, Placer and El Dorado; it appears to have an average breadth of about four miles, with an elevation of four thousand feet above the sea for the greatest part of its length.

*   *   *   *   *

QUARTZ MINING.

After a few preliminary remarks upon the permanency of the gold mines of this State, the author proceeds to an elaborate consideration of the geological position which the quartz veins hold to the rocks with which they are connected. Under the head of " Character and positions of the older veins below the surface," he concludes thus :—

From what testimony we have in our possession relative to these veins, it seems but reasonable to conclude that their integrity is perfect, or as nearly so as can be reasonably expected

G G

considering the short period which has been employed in developing their true character, and that the confidence which they formerly possessed was well grounded ; all subsequent examinations have only tended to confirm this belief in the minds of those who have carefully and diligently studied this subject. The present condition of our gold mines, their flourishing state and prospective value, based on facts as now developed, most clearly indicate their importance as an industrial pursuit, and one destined ere long to form one of the leading interests in the economy of the State ; and as such it would seem that all prudent measures to develop farther their extent and value, and place them upon that footing before the world which that value and importance demand, should be used ; either through the State or general government, and through them promote such measures as will prove an inducement to more extensive and permanent operations than has yet been done.

In concluding this part of the report, and in connection with the magnitude and importance of perhaps a somewhat exciting principle in relation to it, I would beg leave to call your attention to a point on which there has heretofore existed much diversity of opinion, which not unfrequently has engendered angry discussion and belligerent feeling in a large proportion of our mining population. The experience of the last three years has elucidated the fact most clearly that the two mining interests of this State cannot be governed by the same rule of law in all cases, and prove alike advantageous to both ; it is therefore suggested whether some method more congenial to this interest may not be adopted, that will favour the occupancy and improvement of the metallic veins of this State, giving at the same time the widest scope and protection to all at present engaged, and those who may wish hereafter to enter upon those pursuits.

*　　　*　　　*　　　*　　　*

The mines of this State are of a character and value which,

if placed in a proper position, will invite investment from abroad to an amount little less than twenty millions of dollars within the next eight years. This presumption is founded on the fact that more than one-sixth of that amount is at the present time in active operation in this country, and its largest proportion has been derived from American sources during a portion of that period when public confidence had been shaken in regard to their value. Negotiations are now pending which involve nearly one million more of capital investment in this branch of mining, nearly one half of which is in the cities of Boston and New York.

Considering the disadvantages that now surround them, as shown from the facts relating thereto, they can but be regarded as the prolific sources of wealth in this country; and every inducement consistent with the liberal policy adopted in the government of the placers, is equally applicable, and should be extended to them.

Dr. Trask concludes his very able report by briefly reviewing the operations of the following mines, viz. : Lafayette and Helvetia, Gold Hill, Osborne Hill, Wyoming, Gold Tunnel, Illinois, Jones and Davis Mine, Calaveras county; Spring Hill, Amadore Company, Ranchoree, Keystone, and Eureka Mine, Calaveras County, all of which he represents in a prosperous condition.

THE END.

BRADBURY AND EVANS, PRINTERS, WHITEFRIARS.